**MEDICAL INNOVATION AT THE CROSSROADS**

VOLUME II

# The Changing Economics *of* Medical Technology

Annetine C. Gelijns and Ethan A. Halm, Editors

Committee on Technological Innovation in Medicine
INSTITUTE OF MEDICINE

NATIONAL ACADEMY PRESS
Washington, D.C. 1991

**NATIONAL ACADEMY PRESS** • 2101 Constitution Avenue, N.W. • Washington, D.C. 20418

The Institute of Medicine was chartered in 1970 by the National Academy of Sciences to enlist distinguished members of the appropriate professions in the examination of policy matters pertaining to the health of the public. In this the Institute acts under both the Academy's 1863 congressional charter responsibility to be an advisor to the federal government and its own initiative in identifying issues of medical care, research, and education.

The Committee on Technological Innovation in Medicine was established in 1988 by the Institute of Medicine to design a series of workshops that would (a) provide a more fundamental knowledge of the process by which biomedical research findings are translated into clinical practice and (b) address opportunities for improving the rationality and efficiency of this process. This volume consists of the proceedings of the second workshop in the series "Improving the Translation of Research Findings into Clinical Practice: The Changing Economics of Technological Innovation in Medicine," held December 20–21, 1989. This workshop and its proceedings were supported by the Howard Hughes Medical Institute and the Agency for Health Care Policy and Research of the Department of Health and Human Services (grant 5 RO9 HS055 26 02). The opinions and conclusions expressed here are those of the authors and do not necessarily represent the views of the Howard Hughes Medical Institute, the Department of Health and Human Services, the National Academy of Sciences, or any of their constituent parts.

**Library of Congress Cataloging-in-Publication Data**

The Changing economics of medical technology / Annetine C. Gelijns and
Ethan A. Halm, editors ; Committee on Technological Innovation in
Medicine, Institute of Medicine.
p. cm. — (Medical innovation at the crossroads ; v. 2)
Proceedings of a workshop held Dec. 20–21, 1989, supported by the
Howard Hughes Medical Institute and the Agency for Health Care
Policy and Research of the Dept. of Health and Human Services (grant
5 R09 HS055 26 02).
Includes bibliographical references and index.
ISBN 0-309-04491-X
1. Medical innovations—Economic aspects—Congresses.
2. Pharmaceutical industry—Technological innovations—Economic
aspects—Congresses. I. Gelijns, Annetine. II. Halm, Ethan.
III. Institute of Medicine (U.S.). Committee on Technological
Innovation in Medicine. IV. Howard Hughes Medical Institute.
V. United States. Agency for Health Care Policy and Research.
VI. Series.
[DNLM: 1. Economics, Medical—congresses. 2. Public Policy—
congresses. 3. Technology, High-Cost—economics—congresses.
4. Technology, Medical—economics—congresses. W1 ME342F v. 2 / W
74 C456 1989]
R855.2.C48 1991
338.43'61'028—dc20
DNLM/DLC
for Library of Congress 91-14157
CIP



Printed in the United States of America

The serpent has been a symbol of long life, healing, and knowledge among almost all cultures and religions since the beginning of recorded history. The image adopted as a logotype by the Institute of Medicine is based on a relief carving from ancient Greece, now held at the Staatlichemuseen in Berlin.

# Committee on Technological Innovation in Medicine

GERALD D. LAUBACH, *Chair*, Former President, Pfizer, Inc.
SUSAN BARTLETT FOOTE, Associate Professor, School of Business Administration, University of California, Berkeley
BEN L. HOLMES, Vice President and General Manager, Medical Products Group, Hewlett-Packard Company
WILLIAM N. HUBBARD, JR., Former President, the Upjohn Company
ROBERT I. LEVY, President, Sandoz Research Institute
KENNETH L. MELMON, Arthur L. Bloomfield Professor of Medicine and Pharmacology, Department of Medicine, Stanford University School of Medicine
PAUL D. PARKMAN, Former Director, Center for Biologics Evaluation and Research, Food and Drug Administration
JOHN E. WENNBERG, Professor of Epidemiology, Department of Community and Family Medicine, Dartmouth Medical School

*Project Staff*

Division of Health Care Services

KARL D. YORDY, Director
KATHLEEN N. LOHR, Deputy Director
CLIFFORD GOODMAN, Senior Staff Officer
ANNETINE C. GELIJNS, Study Director
ETHAN A. HALM, Research Associate
HOLLY DAWKINS, Research Assistant

EVANSON JOSEPH, Project Assistant
THELMA COX, Project Assistant
DONALD TILLER, Administrative Assistant

Division of Health Sciences Policy

RUTH BULGER, Director
STEVEN J. BONGARD, Director, Forum on Drug Development

# Acknowledgments

The Committee on Technological Innovation in Medicine thanks the authors for presenting their papers at the Institute of Medicine workshop "Improving the Translation of Research Findings into Clinical Practice: The Changing Economics of Technological Innovation in Medicine," and for preparing their subsequent chapters. The committee also recognizes the substantial contributions of the moderators, panel discussants, and workshop participants, who provided valuable insights into the issues discussed in this volume. Special thanks are due to Fredrick W. Telling, Jane Newman, and Cathy Barr for their input to the planning of the workshop. The committee also values the skillful and expeditious editing of the papers by Edward Edelson.

The committee would like to express its gratitude to Samuel O. Thier, President of the Institute of Medicine, and Enriqueta Bond, Executive Officer, for inspired leadership and support of committee activities. The committee is equally grateful for the substantive and organizational support of Ruth Bulger, Steven Bongard, Kathleen Lohr, Holly Dawkins, Sharon Baratz, and Wallace Waterfall. The workshop and the publication of this volume would not have been possible without the dedicated efforts of Evanson Joseph and Thelma Cox, who devoted long hours to the logistics of the meeting as well as to the preparation of several drafts of this manuscript. Finally, the committee acknowledges a considerable debt to Clifford Goodman, Annetine Gelijns, and Ethan Halm for their organization of the workshop and for the editing of this volume.

The Committee on Technological Innovation in Medicine greatly appreciates the opportunity provided by the Howard Hughes Medical Institute and the Agency for Health Care Policy and Research (grant 5 RO9 HS055 26 02) to investigate the process of medical innovation.

GERALD D. LAUBACH
*Chair*
IOM Committee on Technological Innovation in Medicine

# Preface

GERALD D. LAUBACH

This volume summarizes the second in a series of Institute of Medicine workshops whose intent is to examine critically the process by which biomedical research is translated into actual benefits in medical practice. Contemporary biomedical research has given us a rich harvest of innovation—new pharmaceuticals, biotechnology products, medical devices, and clinical procedures—which in the aggregate essentially define modern medicine. As always, such success is accompanied by challenges and problems.

Not least among these challenges and problems is the fact that the economics of medical innovation itself has changed substantially. The cost of research and development (R&D)—particularly for the regulated medical technologies such as pharmaceuticals and devices—has escalated dramatically over the past two decades. Significant factors associated with higher R&D costs include the shift in research emphasis toward more complex chronic conditions and, more importantly, demands for more extensive demonstration of safety, efficacy, and cost-effectiveness. Simultaneously, the economic returns to the innovator have become increasingly constrained by a host of policies intended to contain health care expenditures. These policies take varied forms, but not infrequently they raise barriers to technology adoption, restrict reimbursement, and force price concessions among technology suppliers. In addition, we see the emergence of models of "managed care," defined for our purposes to include various entities ranging from health maintenance organizations to modified fee-for-service programs that attempt to create incentives for physicians and hospitals to provide more cost-effective care. These policies will have implications for technology diffusion as well as for its development.

In view of these trends, the Committee on Technological Innovation in Medicine chose to devote its second workshop to an examination of the economics of medical innovation, drawing on experience in the United States, Europe, and Japan. The papers presented in this volume provide a rich array of insights into how the economic incentives for technology development and diffusion are changing, and what their likely impact will be on the provision of cost-effective care and future innovation. One of the important conclusions, however, is that the need is clear for additional research on the economics of innovation in medicine. As a result, this volume tends to pose more questions than it answers. For example, important questions remain about the impact of recent policy changes on the small and often highly entrepreneurial parts of the innovation enterprise: the new biotechnology company, the small device company, and the individual physician innovator.

The committee has decided to have its third workshop examine in more detail some of the issues raised in this volume about the impact of managed health care systems on medical innovation. In addition, a workshop is being organized that intends to explore actual case studies of medical innovation to provide more empirical data on the nature and dynamics of the innovation process itself. Together, this series of workshops will offer a coherent body of study and analysis for improving our understanding of medical innovation. It is our hope that this work will encourage a more rational and efficient transfer of biomedical research findings into direct patient care.

# Contents

LIST OF TABLES AND FIGURES ............................ xi

LIST OF ABBREVIATIONS ............................ xiii

1. AN INTRODUCTION TO THE CHANGING ECONOMICS OF TECHNOLOGICAL INNOVATION IN MEDICINE
   Ethan A. Halm and Annetine C. Gelijns ............................ 1

2. THE DIFFUSION OF NEW TECHNOLOGY: COSTS AND BENEFITS TO HEALTH CARE
   Peter J. Neumann and Milton C. Weinstein ............................ 21

3. THE CHANGING ECONOMICS OF PHARMACEUTICAL RESEARCH AND DEVELOPMENT
   Henry Grabowski ............................ 35

4. PUBLIC POLICY AND ACCESS TO NEW DRUGS: THE CASE OF CANCER CHEMOTHERAPY
   Lee Mortenson ............................ 53

5. THE IMPACT OF PUBLIC POLICY ON MEDICAL DEVICE INNOVATION: A CASE OF POLYINTERVENTION
   Susan Bartlett Foote ............................ 69

6. THE DYNAMICS OF MEDICAL DEVICE INNOVATION: AN INNOVATOR'S PERSPECTIVE
Alan Kahn ........................................ 89

7. REIMBURSEMENT AND THE DYNAMICS OF SURGICAL PROCEDURE INNOVATION
Sophia W. Chang and Harold S. Luft ........................ 96

8. EUROPEAN POLICIES INFLUENCING PHARMACEUTICAL INNOVATION
Michael L. Burstall ................................. 123

9. MEDICAL DEVICE INNOVATION AND PUBLIC POLICY IN THE EUROPEAN ECONOMIC COMMUNITY
John Hutton ...................................... 141

10. JAPAN'S PHARMACEUTICAL INDUSTRY POSTWAR EVOLUTION
Robert Neimeth ................................... 155

APPENDIXES

A. THE IMPACT OF REGULATION AND REIMBURSEMENT ON PHARMACEUTICAL INNOVATION
Commentary by Peter Barton Hutt ........................ 169

B. THE ECONOMICS OF PHARMACEUTICAL RESEARCH AND DEVELOPMENT: AN INDUSTRY PERSPECTIVE
Commentary by Francis H. Spiegel, Jr. ..................... 181

C. CONTRIBUTORS ..................................... 192

INDEX .............................................. 199

# List of Tables and Figures

TABLES

3.1 New drug products achieving $100 million sales in the U.S. market within the first 6 years of market life, 36
4.1 Out-of-package insert use for eight common chemotherapy agents, 60
7.1 Aspects of innovation in drugs, devices, and surgical procedures, 101
8.1 Pharmaceutical production and consumption in the European Community, 1987, 125
8.2 Measures of the innovatory strength in pharmaceuticals of various countries, 126
8.3 Trends in pure scientific spending and output, 127
8.4 General methods of controlling pharmaceutical expenditure in the European Community, 1989, 130
8.5 Price control systems in the European Community, 1989, 131
10.1 Pharmaceutical R&D spending, 1985, 163
10.2 Number of patents related to drugs, 1984, 163
10.3 Leading countries by new product launch, 166
10.4 Leading countries by new product originator: number of NCEs, 166

FIGURES

1.1 A linear model of the innovation chain, 3
1.2 A dynamic representation of the innovation chain, 4
3.1 Consensus new drug approvals by nationality of originating firm, 1970-1985, 38

3.2 Duration of IND and NDA phases, self-originated NCEs of U.S. firms, 38
3.3 FDA approvals versus R&D spending, 39
3.4 Effective U.S. patent life, 41
3.5 Waxman-Hatch Act: generic impact on sole-source product sales, 42
3.6 GNP versus PPPI, 43
3.7 Sales profile of 1970-1979 compounds, 44
3.8 Present value of cash flow versus R&D investment, 45
3.9 Present values by decile, 46
3.10 Medicaid formulary delays, 48
3.11 R&D expenditures: NIH versus PMA members, 48
4.1 Percentage and total annual sales of approved versus unlabeled usage of eight common chemotherapy drugs, 1986, 59
5.1 The stages of innovation, 71
5.2 The stages of innovation: impact of federal and state institutions and activities, 72
5.3 Public policies that promote or inhibit innovation, 74
5.4 Interaction of public policies that affect innovation, 84
8.1 How government actions may affect pharmaceutical innovation, 124
9.1 Social objectives, 144
9.2 Transfers of benefit, 144
9.3 Technology assessment model, 145
9.4 Diffusion model, 146

# List of Abbreviations

| | |
|---|---|
| ACCC | Association of Community Cancer Centers |
| AIDS | Acquired Immune Deficiency Syndrome |
| AMA | American Medical Association |
| ANDA | Abbreviated New Drug Application |
| BERC | Bureau of Eligibility, Reimbursement and Coverage |
| CABG | Coronary Artery Bypass Graft |
| CON | Certificate of Need |
| CPT | Current Procedural Terminology |
| DRGs | Diagnosis-Related Groups |
| EEC | European Economic Community |
| ESWL | Extracorporeal Shock Wave Lithotripsy |
| FDA | Food and Drug Administration |
| FD&CA | Food, Drug, and Cosmetic Act |
| GAO | General Accounting Office |
| GMP | Good Manufacturing Practices |
| GNP | Gross National Product |
| HCFA | Health Care Financing Administration |
| HMOs | Health Maintenance Organizations |
| IDE | Investigational Device Exemption |
| IND | Investigational New Drug |
| IOL | Intraocular Lenses |
| IOM | Institute of Medicine |
| IRB | Institutional Review Board |
| MRI | Magnetic Resonance Imaging |
| NCE | New Chemical Entity |

| | |
|---|---|
| NCI | National Cancer Institute |
| NDA | New Drug Application |
| NHLBI | National Heart, Lung, and Blood Institute |
| NIH | National Institutes of Health |
| NSAIDs | Non-steroidal Anti-inflammatory Drugs |
| PLA | Product License Application |
| PMA | Pre-marketing Application for Devices |
| PMS | Post-marketing Surveillance |
| PPOs | Preferred Provider Organizations |
| PPPI | Pharmaceutical Producer Price Index |
| PPRC | Physician Payment Review Commission |
| PPS | Prospective Payment System |
| ProPAC | Prospective Payment Assessment Commission |
| PTCA | Percutaneous Transluminal Coronary Angioplasty |
| R&D | Research and Development |
| RBRVS | Resource-based Relative Value Scale |
| RCT | Randomized Controlled Clinical Trial |
| SBIR | Small Business Innovation Research Program |
| TURP | Transurethral Resection of the Prostate |

# 1

# An Introduction to the Changing Economics of Technological Innovation in Medicine

ETHAN A. HALM and ANNETINE C. GELIJNS

The rapidly rising costs of health care became an increasingly urgent issue of policy concern during the 1980s, and they can be expected to remain so in the 1990s. Technological change generally is believed to be an important factor driving costs up, although, as Neumann and Weinstein argue in this volume (Chapter 2), significant conceptual and practical problems defy measurement of technology's precise contribution (1). In the 1970s "big-ticket" devices and procedures were singled out as the major culprit (2). Some states established certificate-of-need regulations to control their diffusion, but limitations of this approach soon emerged (3). It became apparent that the critical issue was not medical technology per se but a combination of economic, professional, and social incentives in our health care system that tend to diminish the importance of costs in decisions about patient care. For example, the establishment of Medicare and Medicaid in 1965 greatly increased the demand for medical services, thus increasing indirectly the demand for medical technology. At the same time, traditional systems of physician fee-for-service and hospital reimbursement according to retrospective charges insulated providers and patients from the immediate financial consequences of their decisions. These incentives applied to the acquisition of large expensive devices as well as to routine clinical choices to order a test, prescribe a drug, or perform a procedure. Payment policies in these years could be generally characterized as encouraging innovation.[1]

Today the pendulum has started to swing the other way. Attention has shifted toward coverage and reimbursement as major instruments for promoting cost containment. This is illustrated by the adoption of the Prospective

Payment System (PPS) for Medicare based on diagnosis-related groups (DRGs), the rapid growth in health maintenance organizations (HMOs) and preferred provider organizations (PPOs), and the creation of a resource-based relative value scale (RBRVS) for physician services. These policy changes create very different incentives for providers to adopt and use medical technology. Less apparent, but also very important, they exert a strong indirect influence on investment in research and development (R&D).

In addition to payment, a wide range of public policies has evolved that foster or inhibit innovation. These policies attempt to accomplish a variety of different public goals (4). For example, policies to encourage a high level of public and private R&D include the federal support of biomedical research, tax credits, and legislation to protect intellectual property. Premarketing approval regulation of new health care products and liability statutes aim to prevent the diffusion of unsafe or inefficacious technologies. Trade policies attempt to encourage health-related exports, whereas antitrust legislation intends to encourage competition.

Recently, concerns have been raised that various combinations of these policies may have unanticipated—and perhaps unwanted—effects on technological innovation in medicine. The main objective of this volume is to address these concerns and consider the complex interplay between innovation and public policy. The term "innovation," in this context, refers to the development and introduction of new drugs, devices, and surgical procedures into clinical practice. Surgical procedures are included as an example of clinical procedures whose development does not necessarily depend on new health care products and may not involve the pharmaceutical or device industry. Within the broad range of policies that affect innovation, this volume focuses on the impact of United States regulatory and payment policies. In the final chapters, the policy environment for industrial innovation in the United States is compared with that in Europe and Japan.

## A DYNAMIC MODEL OF TECHNOLOGICAL INNOVATION IN MEDICINE

Before we address the main theme of this volume, it seems useful to examine briefly the nature and dynamics of technological innovation. The increasing reliance of technology upon science during the twentieth century has given rise to a "linear model" of technological innovation, in which results were perceived to flow from basic research to applied research, product development, manufacturing and marketing, adoption, and use (see Figure 1.1). This is a supply-oriented model in which the critical need is assumed to be the provision of adequate funding for biomedical research. This model, however, has a number of theoretical and practical limitations. One of the more important limitations, from the perspective of this book, is

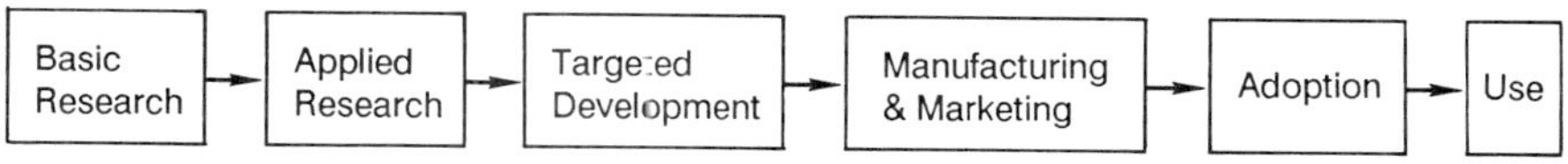


**FIGURE 1.1** A linear model of the innovation chain

that it emphasizes advances in research as the main impetus to development and disregards the influence of demand considerations.

Empirical studies, undertaken primarily in the 1970s, began to question the primacy of research advances in stimulating technological change. These studies asserted instead that market demand was the major impetus to innovation. Following years of debate whether "science-push" or "demand-pull" factors were the governing influence on the innovation process, Mowery and Rosenberg decisively maintained that development is an iterative process in which an evolving scientific and engineering knowledge base and market demand interact to achieve a particular technology (5).

Nelson and Winter further defined the influence of market demand on R&D project selection (6). They observed that theories of innovation often have tried to make a neat distinction between R&D on the one hand and adoption on the other, with all uncertainty piled on the former. However, they acknowledged that not all uncertainty associated with a new technology can be resolved before its use in practice and that development does not end with the adoption of an innovation but continues for an extended period. Their premise is that the behavior of users in adopting or rejecting certain technologies over time provides important feedback signals as to the kind of development projects that firms subsequently will find profitable to undertake.

Most studies of innovation have focused on areas where preferences of users are expressed and mediated through market mechanisms. However, the "market" in medicine differs from markets in other sectors of the economy, where, in principle, consumer preferences determine what products are purchased (versus other products and their prices). Empirically, the following important differences can be discerned:

- Market demand generally implies autonomous choice and realistic information of available alternatives by consumers. However, both autonomous choice and knowledge of the alternatives are often severely limited for patients, and health care professionals usually determine the kind and level of medical interventions needed. Although patients are the ultimate users, providers are the primary users for those that develop new medical technology.
- In other sectors of the economy, the separation between developers on the one hand and users on the other is relatively clear. This is not the case

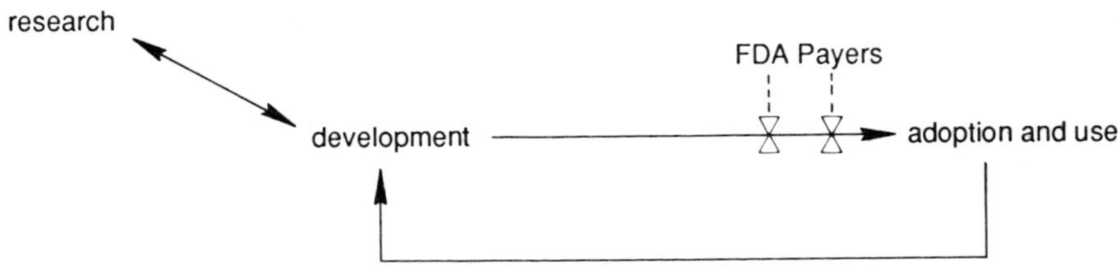


**FIGURE 1.2** A dynamic representation of the innovation chain

in medicine. Clinicians, for example, have a dual role; they not only are the users of new technology, but also play an active role in its development. This duality is most visible in surgical innovation, especially when one considers the minor modifications in technique that occur in everyday surgical practice. It also exists in device and drug innovation, where the introduction of new products in clinical practice often leads to the unexpected discovery of new indications of use. For instance, after beta blockers were introduced for the treatment of cardiac arrhythmias and angina pectoris, physicians discovered their potential therapeutic value for more than 20 other conditions, not all of them cardiac (7).

- New technologies—in addition to their benefits—may often entail a certain element of risk. However, the beneficial or adverse effects of medical technology are considered to be quintessentially different from those of many other technologies because, as Renee Fox observes, they affect "basic and transcendent axes of the human condition: life, conception and birth, body and mind, . . . and ultimately mortality and death" (8).
- Finally, in other sectors of the economy new technologies generally are purchased by users. However, in medicine, technologies usually are paid for by public and private third-party payers and not by health care professionals or patients.

These idiosyncrasies of the health care market have prompted considerable government intervention in the development process. In view of their potential serious risks and because individual physicians cannot be expected to evaluate all emerging products, the Food and Drug Administration (FDA) exists to ensure the safety and efficacy of new drugs and certain classes of devices before they are marketed. Furthermore, with health care costs continuing to rise faster than the rate of inflation, public and private payers have emerged as important parties at interest in the innovation process. They have become increasingly critical as to what new technologies will be covered in their benefit package. Moreover, with the rapid growth in prepaid health plans and fee-for-service insurance programs with active utilization review and case management, incentives to use new technologies have changed. Thus, in addition to users, regulators and payers now influence the demand for new technology, and hence the incentives for R&D investment (see

Figure 1.2). In the following sections we more closely consider the impact of regulatory and payer policy and related decision making on drug, device, and surgical innovation.

## THE DYNAMICS OF PHARMACEUTICAL INNOVATION

The papers in this volume on pharmaceuticals describe the ways in which the government affects the rate and direction of innovation. The economics of pharmaceutical innovation, however, need to be understood in terms of the interactive public policies that have evolved over time. A case in point is the strong interdependence that exists among pre-marketing approval, patent, and payment policies.

Regulatory policies for pre-marketing approval of drugs traditionally have exerted a strong influence on the dynamics of pharmaceutical innovation. Hutt (Appendix A) makes explicit that two sources are responsible for current regulatory policies statutes and administrative practices (9). The relevant statute (the Food, Drug, and Cosmetic Act) requires "substantial evidence . . . of safety and effectiveness . . . consisting of adequate and well-controlled investigations." This broad mandate gives the FDA considerable discretion in determining the acceptable risk-benefit ratio for a marketing approval decision. Since the thalidomide tragedy of the early 1960s, there have been strong social and political pressures to reduce pharmaceutical risks to essentially zero. Under these pressures and because of the growing sophistication of animal toxicology and clinical research techniques, pre-marketing requirements have become increasingly detailed over time. The resulting system has provided important information on the safety and efficacy of new drugs, but it also has considerably lengthened the pre-marketing development process.

The tension between increasingly thorough pre-marketing evaluations and early product availability becomes urgent in the case of life-threatening disease. In the early 1980s this tension led the FDA to create a category of regulatory exceptions for cancer drugs (so-called group C drugs) to allow desperately ill patients to use promising but still experimental drugs before they are officially approved. However, it is only with the advent of the human immunodeficiency virus (HIV) epidemic and the activism of patient advocacy groups for acquired immune deficiency syndrome (AIDS) that the need to streamline the drug approval process for life-threatening diseases has come into the national spotlight and has further transformed regulatory practice. In 1987 the FDA created the "treatment IND" (investigational new drug) procedure for life-threatening and serious disorders. This procedure shortens the pre-marketing evaluation stage by merging Phase II and Phase III trials into more definitive Phase II trials, and it emphasizes more strongly the post-marketing evaluation stage (Phase IV) for providing safety and effectiveness information. More recently, the FDA has created the "parallel track system" that may allow clinical use of an investigational drug prior to its release under a treatment IND, at least for those patients who cannot participate in clinical trials (10).

There are medical and economic reasons to expect that some of these changes will be extended to other disease categories. First, despite increasingly detailed pre-marketing trials, there are no zero-risk drug approval decisions. For example, the detection of delayed or rare adverse effects (less than 1 in 10,000) would require extremely long periods of testing or the exposure of many thousands of patients. Furthermore, valuable therapeutic information on the risks and benefits of a drug may emerge only after its diffusion into the often uncontrolled environment of general use; for example, side effects may be influenced by differing pharmacogenetic profiles of patients, comorbidities, environmental influences, and other factors. These side effects may go unnoticed in carefully controlled and selected pre-marketing studies; their detection requires post-marketing evaluation. Second, there is an economic argument that favors more emphasis on post-marketing research, especially if the pre-marketing evaluation period can be shortened. The increasing duration of pre-marketing development has made the process more costly and has reduced the effective patent life of new pharmaceuticals. Grabowski (Chapter 3) estimates that it takes an average of $231 million (in pre-tax 1987 dollars) to discover and develop a drug (11), and that by 1985 the effective patent life of new compounds had decreased to roughly 9 years[2] (12).

In view of the high-cost, high-risk nature of R&D and the relative ease with which new drugs can be copied by non-innovative firms, patents are crucial to R&D investment. The need to halt the continuing erosion of patent protection was recognized in the Drug Price Competition and Patent Term Restoration Act of 1984. Under its terms, manufacturers can have their patent term extended for up to 5 years to compensate for time that passes while waiting for approval.[3] At the same time, however, the 1984 act makes it less time consuming and costly for generic drugs to get to market by making them eligible for an abbreviated new drug application (ANDA). Instead of the extensive animal and clinical data for a full NDA, this simplified application merely requires demonstrating that the active ingredient is bioequivalent to an already-approved drug whose patent is about to expire.[4] Thus, the law has not lengthened the product life of innovative drugs, because when their patents expire, they lose their market share to generic drugs much more rapidly.

The loss of market share to much-lower-priced generic drugs has been exacerbated by the more stringent payment policies of the 1980s. Historically, drugs have been the least expensive of all medical technologies; with higher patient coinsurance rates and out-of-pocket fees, they were not main targets for cost savings. Except in the Medicare program (a major exception), prescriptions were generally reimbursed liberally. In the 1980s payers came under increased pressures to contain costs, and with improvements in computerized insurance claims systems and utilization review, they began to scrutinize claims for medications more critically. As Mortenson indicates (Chapter 4), three issues permeate recent policy debates: (a) payment for experimental drugs and the care of patients in clinical trials, as well as payment for experimental drugs used outside of clinical trials (compassionate use); (b) payment for the use of approved drugs for non-approved purposes (off-label use); and (c) the coverage of new drugs under formularies and the passage of generic substitution laws (13).

Medical benefit contracts for nearly all payers, public and private, have standard provisions that specifically exclude coverage for "investigational or experimental" therapy. Until recently, this clause, especially with respect to medications, was not strictly enforced. Medications in Phase I, II, or III trials now are categorically denied reimbursement, however, and payers are starting to deny the associated costs of hospital care. The hesitancy to pay for the (often higher) costs of care associated with experimental drugs is understandable. One can question, however, whether, instead of refusing payment for all costs of care, payers should accede to the principle of "opportunity cost" (i.e., the cost insurers would otherwise have paid for patient care) when patients are involved in clinical research (14). Mortenson argues that this approach would be especially attractive to the treatment of solid tumors, where standard medical regimens are not very effective and experimental therapies offer the best chance for a clinical response (13).[5]

The second issue concerns reimbursement for drugs used for conditions that have not been specified on their label. As mentioned, drug development occurs not only before a drug is introduced into practice but also continues afterwards as additional indications emerge during its use in clinical practice. As Mortenson indicates, roughly 50 percent of chemotherapy regimens, which represent state-of-the-art oncological practice, are officially off-label (13). Reimbursement of off-label use has become controversial, for many payers interpreting their contracts restrictively have designated off-label drugs as investigational and excluded them from coverage. This would be less of a problem if FDA approval could be obtained rapidly for additional indications via so-called supplemental NDAs, but the FDA tends to give supplemental NDAs low priority for review. In addition, many new indications are found late in the life cycle of a drug, often near the time of generic competition, at which time manufacturers have little financial or marketing incentive to invest in further clinical trials. The use of such medical compendia as the U.S. Pharmacopeia *Drug Information* or the American Medical Association *Drug Evaluations* may provide a more valid basis for reimbursement than FDA approval.[6] Some payers, such as members of the Health Insurance Association of America, have begun to revise their policies in this direction.

Finally, coverage policy for new FDA-approved drugs is undergoing profound change. A case in point is the rapid growth of formularies in both the public and private sectors.[7] One way that formularies can influence the economics of innovation is by introducing delays beyond those for FDA approval; for example, state Medicaid programs (which reimburse 15 percent of prescription drugs) may take 1 to 3 years to reach a formulary decision (15). At the same time payers have started to enforce generic and therapeutic substitution more stringently.

These changes in the regulatory and payment environment pose appreciable stresses for pharmaceutical R&D. According to Grabowski (11), the main strategic response of the industry to increasing R&D costs and shorter product life cycles has been to increase the prices of drugs sharply. The recent introduction of biotechnology drugs with thousand-dollar price tags has galvanized the HCFA and the U.S. Congress to look more closely into how manufacturers make pricing decisions. Grabowski presents new data on the private returns on pharmaceutical R&D (11). He finds that the average compound earns a real annual return of 9 percent. However, if prices had not increased during the 1980s, then an average drug would not have broken even within its expected market life.

Close scrutiny of drug pricing policies by government and an increase in the number of large, sophisticated institutional buyers will make it difficult for the drug industry to continue its price increases (16). Current trends will place a heavier burden on the industry to develop breakthrough drugs or second- and third-generation drugs that lead to important improvements in clinical outcomes and efficiency. For example, many innovators are focusing on drugs that require less frequent dosing and have less expensive costs of administration. Furthermore, because economic arguments have become central to the case for formulary acceptance, the development of new pharmaceuticals is increasingly supported by cost-effectiveness studies. Finally, as Spiegel states (Appendix B), there is a strong trend toward industry mergers and consolidation to create economies of scale in research and marketing. Although the pharmaceutical industry generally has been very profitable and recent advances in research seem to present exciting opportunities for the development of new drugs, the papers in this volume underscore that the risks for pharmaceutical R&D have recently increased and may constitute impediments to drug development in the long run.

## THE DYNAMICS OF DEVICE INNOVATION

The policy environments differ considerably for drugs and for devices, as can be expected given differences in the two industries and the nature of innovation. The device industry is younger, less concentrated, and comprises mostly smaller firms. There is much greater heterogeneity of medical devices in terms of design, purpose, and use and in the firms that manufacture them. Foote (Chapter 5) estimates the industry—7,000 manufacturers—to produce roughly 1,700 different types of medical devices (17).

In addition, as Kahn explains (Chapter 6), the nature of the R&D process is different (18). Because a device for a specific application often can be designed in a number of different ways, patents are less significant for device than for drug innovation. For example, the first lithotripter—invented and developed by Dornier—used shock waves generated by spark gap technology. However, Dornier's patent was not a significant entry barrier for competitors, who could easily design around the patent by generating shock waves electromagnetically, piezoelectrically, and by microexplosive technology (19). Except for complex and costly devices, such as lithotripters or imaging devices, medical device innovation does not require the large R&D investment required for drug development.

Furthermore, a high level of incremental innovation characterizes the development of new medical devices. As Kahn contends, "from the time the first preclinical testing is done to the time the product is introduced, and then for the first 6 months, a device is in state of flux" (18). Also, the product life of a device usually is much shorter than that for drugs; competitors may rapidly introduce a slightly modified version. Finally, the ultimate effectiveness and benefit of the device is often crucially dependent on the skills of the practitioner using or implanting the device. These elements of device heterogeneity, incremental innovation, and dependence on users can help explain some of the differences in the way medical devices are regulated.

The history of medical device regulation is shorter and less complicated than that of drugs. Although the FDA had some jurisdiction over medical devices as early as 1938, not until the 1976 Medical Device Amendments to the Food, Drug and Cosmetic Act were all medical devices required to be reviewed by the FDA before marketing. The law classifies devices in two ways: by level of risk (Class I, II, or III) and by descriptive category (pre-amendment, post-amendment, substantially equivalent, implant, custom, investigational, and transitional). The underlying principle is that the more potentially dangerous the device, the more stringent the regulatory scrutiny.[8]

Device manufacturers obtain FDA approval for marketing their products in two basic ways. The simplest, quickest, and most popular route is by designating that a device is the "substantial equivalent" to a pre-amendment device.[9] In this case, under the 510(k) provision of the law, only pre-marketing notification is required. Since device innovation is predominantly incremental, this provision was intended to reduce the regulatory burden for technologies that were not significantly different from those already marketed. The other main route is more comparable to drug regulation and involves full pre-market testing and approval.

The differences between these two FDA approval routes are significant.

Because a 510(k) application requires much less time and effort on the part of a manufacturer, the average FDA response time to pre-marketing notification in one study took one-fifth the time taken to approve a pre-marketing application (PMA). This dramatic difference has not been overlooked by the industry—approximately 55 substantially equivalent 510(k)s are filed for each PMA filed (20).[10]

Foote reviews the trade-offs and conflicts among the various policies that affect device innovation (17). She refers to recent concerns about the implementation of the device amendments. For example, studies by the General Accounting Office (GAO) found weaknesses in pre-marketing review (broad use of 510(k) applications) as well as failures of post-marketing surveillance[11] (21-23). In response to these concerns, Congress enacted legislation in 1990 that "streamlines the device classification process, and expands FDA authority to track devices, recall defective products, and impose civil penalties on the industry. It also extends reporting requirements to hospitals and other facilities" (17). These reforms will address some of the weaknesses in current device evaluation. However, lessons from the pharmaceutical experience warn against creating a "device lag." Foote recommends that Congress provide adequate resources to the FDA so that the agency can evaluate devices in a timely manner and make better use of post-marketing controls, as they are less restrictive for innovation than pre-marketing requirements. This recommendation is especially relevant, because the vast majority of device companies are small and do not have the resources (manpower, money, or time) to deal with an elaborate regulatory process.

Liability law also intends to deter the diffusion of unsafe products, as well as to permit compensation for injured users. Devices (like drugs) are caught up in an increasingly litigious society. The legal environment is complex and relatively unpredictable, and it can have serious negative effects on innovation. For example, a surge of liability suits, and the subsequent unavailability of insurance for manufacturers, was one of the major reasons that American industry virtually withdrew from contraceptive R&D (24). Consequently, there is a growing recognition that reform of the liability system is in order and that unnecessary overlap between regulation and liability in their pursuit of device safety should be eliminated (17).

Expensive medical devices were seen as the personification of rising costs in the 1970s; as a result, they have been the focus of cost-containment efforts for a longer time than have drugs.[12] Implementation of Medicare's DRG-based PPS especially has affected expensive medical equipment. For a new device the increasingly restrictive payment circumstances often became manifest first in the form of the HCFA coverage decision for the Medicare program. Coverage decisions usually are made locally by HCFA fiscal intermediaries. Coverage issues of national importance are referred to HCFA's Office of Coverage Policy, which may request a formal technology assessment by the Office of Health Technology Assessment (OHTA) of the

Agency for Health Care Policy and Research in the U.S. Public Health Service. The statutory provision indicates that the coverage decision should be based on whether a device is considered "reasonable and necessary," which has been translated to mean "accepted by the medical community as a safe and efficacious treatment for a particular condition." Although it is reasonable for the HCFA to be wary of granting automatic coverage for all devices, given the leniency with which many get approved via simple 510(k) applications to the FDA, some observers have raised the question whether OHTA's review of the safety and effectiveness of FDA-approved devices is redundant given the FDA's mandate to ensure that new devices are safe and efficacious (25).

Following a Medicare coverage decision, a technology must be assigned to a certain DRG category. Although the price system is intended to be neutral under PPS, this is not always the case. For example, percutaneous transluminal coronary angioplasty (PTCA) was first assigned to a surgical DRG; this DRG provided a much higher level of reimbursement than the procedure cost, thus stimulating the adoption of PTCA. By contrast, cochlear implants were placed in a DRG that covered only a fraction of the cost of the device. This not only led to underdiffusion but also had adverse effects on subsequent R&D investment. For example, innovators developing second- and third-generation implants were unable to attract venture capital or to interest larger manufacturers to further pursue development.

In general, hospitals have a strong financial incentive to provide the least resource-intensive treatment under PPS (although competition, patient demand, and malpractice concerns may provide countervailing forces). The system promotes a significantly lower level of growth in service intensity than traditionally has been the case. Recalibration of DRGs could mitigate disincentives to use costly new technologies, but readjustments often considerably lag changes in medical practice (26). Furthermore, as Neumann and Weinstein point out (1), because PPS applies only to inpatient hospital services (Medicare Part A), hospitals have an incentive to provide more services in the outpatient setting (even if they could be provided more efficiently in inpatient care) and to use only those technologies that are cost effective over the short term of hospitalization. Hospitals may have little financial incentive to use technologies with long-term benefits, even though those technologies may ultimately have a greater impact on the efficiency of the system as a whole.

The incentives for capitated plans, such as HMOs and PPOs, to restrict utilization are somewhat different from those for hospitals under PPS. Because HMOs receive a fixed amount per enrollee and also deliver outpatient care, they have less incentive to (inappropriately) shift to outpatient care, and decision making is more likely to reflect concern with long-term cost effectiveness. This long-term perspective, however, may be tempered by the fact that HMOs may not pay for all patient services (such as long-term nursing home care) as well as by the significant number of HMO enrollees who leave the system (1).

The change toward a more stringent payment policy seems to have exerted a strong effect on medical device innovation. For example, incentives to avoid restrictive Medicare Part A reimbursement controls have done more than change the locus of care; they have also stimulated the development of a whole range of new devices to be used exclusively in the outpatient setting. These include everything from smaller, lighter, and less expensive versions of hospital machines (which are more amenable to office use) to new, user-friendly, computerized infusion devices for the growing number of home health care applications. Moreover, the development of cost-effective technology has become an explicit R&D target, and device manufacturers are increasingly under pressure to demonstrate the cost utility of their innovations. A proposed HCFA rule change would require that device manufacturers have not only FDA approval attesting to safety and efficacy but also data showing that their technology improves outcomes or lowers resource use relative to existing alternatives. Yet the very essence of a new device is that its costs and benefits are uncertain until applied more widely and subject to considerable change thereafter. Foote discusses interim coverage as a more appropriate payment alternative—that is, covering costly devices for a designated period of time during which providers can gather information on costs and effectiveness.

## THE DYNAMICS OF SURGICAL INNOVATION

Although surgical procedures typically involve the use of drugs and devices, their defining characteristics may be the special combination of surgical skills and abilities they entail. The dynamics for those procedures that do not center on a new product (e.g., the laser) are very different from those described above. According to Chang and Luft (Chapter 7), incremental innovation often occurs in everyday practice, but major surgical procedures generally are developed by specialists in academic centers (27). Whereas profit considerations play a role in the selection of drug and device R&D projects, in the case of surgical procedures return on investment must be defined broadly. Surgical procedures cannot be patented; although surgical innovators may gain higher fees and more patients, they receive no licensing fees for procedures performed by others. Motivating factors may include the need to offer patients improved surgical technology, the thrill of being first, and the attainment of national reputation and academic prestige. In comparison with drugs and devices, the costs of R&D are generally lower and less dependent on external funding.

Finally, if a new procedure is not centered on the use of a new product, no formal government regulatory system exists to evaluate it prior to diffusion. The realm of surgical procedure evaluation has been left to the medical profession in the spirit of clinical autonomy. This takes place largely through peer review, the activities of medical societies, and Institutional Review Boards (IRBs). Although IRBS are responsible for reviewing university-based research, they are interested primarily in protecting the rights of human subjects and not in issues of evaluation. As a result, new surgical procedures generally are not systematically evaluated for safety and efficacy, and controlled clinical trials are often undertaken only after their diffusion.

In this context payment policies take on a quasi-regulatory rigor. Coverage and reimbursement decisions represent crucial determinations that limit or expedite the adoption and use of new procedures. Some commentators argue that they have become the rate-limiting step in diffusion—the true technological gatekeeper (28). The proliferation of managed care policies, such as surgical second opinion, pre-certification, concurrent review, and case management, signals a new level of scrutiny of surgery by payers. However, as mentioned, other factors affect the adoption of new technology as well. For example, Chang and Luft (27) call attention to the powerful influence that competitive forces can have on the adoption of new technologies. Sometimes, the presence of a new technology or a surgical team capable of performing an experimental operation has such cachet that it helps an institution portray itself as a modern facility that uses breakthrough technology to provide high-quality care. This technology/quality "halo" helps hospitals attract physicians and patients, and provides them a competitive advantage in their local and regional markets.

Changes occurring in the payment situation appear to affect surgical development and diffusion considerably, although empirical research is scarce. Chang and Luft point out that new procedures are identified chiefly through the coding system for insurance claims or hospital discharge summaries. In most cases an innovator seeks payment for an innovation by pursuing a new billing code or an additional code descriptor. Physicians must use the Current Procedural Terminology (CPT) system to describe their interventions to payers. Hospitals, under PPS, must categorize the world of care into specific DRGs. Payment systems are very sensitive to the experimental versus accepted status of a procedure just as they are for drugs and devices. Weaknesses in data and methods for assessing the value of new operations often are at the center of disputes about whether payers should reimburse practitioners or hospitals for a given procedure. More rigorous coverage criteria are forcing clinicians to improve their evaluation of the safety and efficacy of new procedures; however, the very nature of surgical innovation poses several challenges to traditional modes of evaluation that need to be addressed.

Chang and Luft describe how PPS has—and the implementation of the new RBRVS for physician payment will—affect the diffusion and development of surgical interventions (27).[13] They extensively discuss the growth of selective contracting as an attempt to both control costs and maintain quality. The underlying principle is that a good outcome from a complex, risky operation is highly dependent on the talents of a stable, experienced, well-run surgery team. As a prerequisite for bidding on a selective contract, an institution must demonstrate experience with the procedure, good success rates, and institutional commitment to maintaining the program in question. More recently, the nature of selective contracting has changed. It is more common to select only a few institutions among those that have met certain minimum standards. This has resulted in price competition among large institutions; for example, institutions have started to offer a package rate for coronary artery bypass grafting. Thus, selective contracting has become a way for large insurers to bargain for certain high-cost procedures with a center that has high-quality outcomes.

These payment changes are creating incentives to encourage the efficient use of resources, and they may limit the premature diffusion of costly surgical procedures. One drawback is that the mortality and morbidity data used to evaluate outcomes are relatively limited; insofar as this is true, selective contracting may focus on price because it has no adequate measure of quality. Changes in payment schemes also provide greater incentives for surgeons to develop more efficient variations of operations. Reducing operating room time is the most direct way of reducing the costs of surgery itself and of complications and their associated costs. Furthermore, interest is growing in developing less invasive operative procedures, such as laparoscopic gynecological surgery, cholecystectomy, and herniorrhaphy (31). The downside of payment reforms, however, may be to reduce the financial ability of hospitals to fund developmental activity and to evaluate and document the utility and costs of new procedures. Proposals that might remedy this situation include interim coverage and modifiable selective reimbursement; they require serious consideration if we want to continue incentives for innovation.

## INTERNATIONAL COMPARISONS: EUROPE AND JAPAN

The United States, Europe, and Japan provide large-scale natural experiments as to the impact of public policies on medical innovation. In general, European governments are more heavily involved in the delivery, financing, and regulation of health care than is the United States, although considerable differences among European countries exist. Burstall (Chapter 8) provides an in-depth discussion of the European environment for pharmaceutical innovation (32). In comparison with American firms, European companies face several distinct disadvantages. First, Burstall argues that Europe cannot compete with the United States in basic science, partly because of Europe's smaller government support for academic and related research. Second, legislation to restore effective patent life has not yet been enacted in Europe.

Third, the majority of nations in the European Economic Community (EEC) regulate prices, and in some European countries' price levels are too low to provide adequate support for R&D. On the other hand, European firms enjoy certain advantages (32). In contrast to the United States, for example, generics are not as actively promoted; they account for no more than 5 percent of the market. Furthermore, the procedures to bring a drug through regulatory review seem to be more flexible and less time consuming in Europe. Finally, structural differences in the liability system contribute to making Europe significantly less litigious.

This situation will change with the creation of a truly common European market in 1992. EEC proposals to lengthen effective patent life will, if implemented, put Europe in an advantageous position relative to the United States. The harmonization of product-licensing procedures could either reduce or lengthen approval times, depending on the policies followed, and pricing issues still need to be resolved. Burstall surmises that American companies (as they are large and innovative) stand to benefit from the unification of the European market, but that it is difficult to be as optimistic about the European drug companies.

Hutton (Chapter 9) reviews the European policy environment for device innovation. In 1985 Europe was estimated to represent 25 percent of the world market for devices (33). Pre-marketing regulatory policies are less stringent in Europe; most nations tend to confine themselves to safety and technical performance criteria and do not include efficacy. Hutton contends that changes in payment policies, such as a growth in hospital budgeting systems, have had a greater impact on device innovation than regulatory policies. In addition to national policies, the EEC is expected increasingly to affect device innovation through its active anti-trust policy, support for R&D, and attempts to harmonize regulatory requirements among its member states.

Neimeth (Chapter 10) describes how the Japanese government used a combination of policies to rebuild a pharmaceutical industry whose manufacturing facilities were virtually destroyed during World War II (34). The government first enacted protectionist rules, established a patent law only for pharmaceutical processes and not for products, rewarded "me-too" products similar to breakthrough products, and gave physicians financial incentives to prescribe and to dispense drugs. Furthermore, in 1967 a system of pre-marketing approval was enacted that had pre-clinical and clinical requirements different from those in other industrialized nations and that required clinical research to be undertaken in Japan.

In response to these patent and payment policies, Japanese firms focused on the development and manufacturing of me-too products. At the same time, the 1967 act established an entry barrier to foreign firms. Furthermore, the financial incentives embodied in the payment system formidably increased demand; by 1981, 40 percent of the overall health bill in Japan was spent on drugs (by contrast, in the United States the share of national health care expenditures for drugs was 6 to 8 percent) (35). By that time, as Neimeth mentions, Japanese firms had acquired the basic technology, R&D capability, and financial strength to generate major new drugs, and the government then enacted a product patent law to protect these products. In the 1980s significant downward adjustment of prices occurred, and pre-marketing approval requirements were harmonized with international standards, allowing international competition. As a result of increased competition and decreased profitability, Japanese companies increased their investment in research and their globalization efforts.

Neimeth thus shows how patent, regulatory, and payment policies have combined to create a strong industry. This growth, however, has come at a price. First of all is the likely inappropriate use of drugs reflected in the immense share of total health care expenditures. Moreover, some observers believe that Japan's innovative capacity might have developed sooner if policies had allowed more foreign competition and if patent protection had been in place earlier.

## CONCLUDING OBSERVATIONS

This society generally values technological innovation in medicine. Over time, a set of public policies has evolved to encourage the development of new medical technology. At the same time, in our pursuit of other policy objectives—such as enhancing safety, access, or cost-effective care—we may inhibit innovation. This volume discusses the complex interdependencies and trade-offs in public policy that affect the nature and rate of technological change.

In contrast to other sectors of the economy, research on the economics of innovation in medicine is just emerging, and this volume tends to pose more questions than it answers. This is especially true when one takes into account the influences that motivate innovation in the small device firm, the new biotechnology firm, or the surgeon innovator. Obviously, improved understanding of the basic mechanisms that underlie technological change is necessary if government interventions are to be successful in encouraging not only the diffusion, but also the development, of cost-effective technology. We hope that this volume stimulates much-needed empirical research on the economics of medical innovation and contributes to a better understanding of the critical issues in public policy during the 1990s.

## NOTES

1. The term "payment policy" encompasses both coverage and reimbursement strategies and practices. Coverage refers to the decision to pay or not pay for a technology and under what circumstances. The reimbursement decision involves how much to pay for the technological intervention and how.

2. Patents provide a restricted period of monopoly power to an inventor to make, use, and sell an innovation. Effective patent life refers to the period between approval of the product and the patent expiration date. Officially, a U.S. patent entitles the holder to 17 years of legal protection, and it commences at the date of receiving the grant. In most European countries patent terms are 20 years, and they commence at time of filing.
3. According to the FDA, the mean approval time for new drugs in 1989 was 31.5 months or 2.7 years. Under patent term restoration, on average, 1.5 years will be added back to the patent "clock" (11).
4. Bioequivalence means that the generic compound must contain the same active ingredients as the brand-name counterpart and must be identical in strength, dosage form, and route of administration. A manufacturer demonstrates bioequivalence by showing in a small number of subjects (20 to 30) that the pharmacological absorption, availability, and excretion profile is within a 20 percent margin of variability to the brand-name product.
5. A related issue concerns experimental drugs that are unapproved for treatment of life-threatening diseases but are nonetheless used outside of the context of a clinical trial. Payers have been reluctant to pay for the use of these so-called compassionate use drugs The Health Care Financing Administration (HCFA), in a ruling seemingly in conflict with its policy toward other investigational drugs, permits coverage for certain experimental cancer drugs (group C drugs). These inconsistencies need to be clarified.
6. These compendia provide a means by which physicians can ascertain the appropriate and effective indication of a drug referenced with up-to-date scientific literature the FDA may not have at the time of labeling. For example, the U.S. Pharmacopeia's drug information volume includes 25 percent more indications for drugs than are listed on the FDA label (K. Johnson, Director of Research, U.S. Pharmacopeia Drug Information, personal communication, September 1989).
7. A formulary is a list of drugs carried by a given institutional provider. Large organizations use formularies to buy drugs in bulk, as well as to limit the number of different drugs that are covered and/or that must be kept in stock. Choices about which drugs are carried usually are made by a hospital, HMO, or Medicaid pharmacy and therapeutics advisory committee. Decisions often are based upon assessments by committees of the relative safety, effectiveness, and cost-effectiveness compared to other formulary pharmaceuticals.
8. Class III devices, those that pose the most risk, are regulated the most restrictively. A manufacturer must demonstrate safety and effectiveness before receiving premarket approval. Class II devices must meet performance standards, and Class I devices, the least risky and regulated of the group, are subject only to general controls. In addition, all devices must meet these general control requirements, which include pre-market notification, reporting of adverse events, record keeping, labeling, and good manufacturing practices (17).
9. "Substantial equivalence" is not defined by the law, but it has been interpreted to mean modification of a previously approved or marketed pre-amendment device in a way that does not negatively affect its safety or effectiveness.

10. More recently, the FDA has sought to better ensure the safety and effectiveness of substantially equivalent devices, sometimes by requiring sponsors to submit performance and clinical data with their 510(k) application. This has been called a "mini-PMA" or "hybrid 510(k)."
11. One GAO survey found that 99 percent of the problems associated with the studied medical devices, including those that could or did cause injury, had not been reported to FDA (21). The study found failures of communication at every level, from device users to manufacturers and independent distributors.
12. An exception to this observation is that, unlike pharmaceutical firms, device manufacturers are allowed to charge investigators for the use of investigational devices, and they, in turn, can charge patients. The rationale behind this asymmetry is that device innovators usually are small firms that could not afford to run clinical studies unless they were able to recover costs during the development period. Devices also tend to cost much more than most experimental drugs. However, some observers have expressed concern about the commercialization of investigational studies for devices such as intraocular lenses, contact lenses, and the YAG laser (25).
13. Under a RBRVS system, payment is based on the estimated cost of resources, including amount of physician time and work effort; the costs of nonphysician personnel, office space, equipment, and supplies; and the cost of malpractice insurance. The fee schedule will also be adjusted for geographical variations in practice costs that partially reflect differences in cost of living (29,30).

## REFERENCES


1. Neumann PJ, Weinstein MC. The diffusion of new technology: costs and benefits to health care. In this volume. Washington, D.C.: National Academy Press, 1991.
2. Altman SH, Blendon RJ (eds). Medical Technology: The Culprit Behind Health Care Costs? Washington, D.C.: DHEW Publication 79-3216, 1979.
3. Hillman BJ. Government health policy and the diffusion of new medical devices. Health Services Research 1986;21:681-711.
4. Maynard A, Hartley K. The regulation of the pharmaceutical industry. In Lindgren B (ed). Pharmaceutical Economics. Stockholm: Liber Forlag, 1984.
5. Mowery DC, Rosenberg N. The influence of market demand upon innovation: a critical review of some recent empirical studies. In Rosenberg N (ed). Inside the Black Box: Technology and Economics. Cambridge: Cambridge University Press, 1982.
6. Nelson RR, Winter SG. In search of useful theory of innovation. Research Policy 1977;6:36-76.
7. Frishman WH. Clinical differences between beta-adrenergic agents: implications for therapeutic substitution. American Heart Journal 1987;113:1190-1198.
8. Fox RC. The cultural shaping of biomedical science and technology. A preface. International Journal on Technology Assessment in Health Care 1986;2:189-194.
9. Hutt PB. The impact of regulation and reimbursement on pharmaceutical innovation. In this volume. Washington, D.C.: National Academy Press, 1991.

10. Rothman DJ, Edgar H. Drug approval and AIDS: benefits for the elderly. Health Affairs 1990;Fall:123-131.
11. Grabowski H. The changing economics of pharmaceutical research and development. In this volume. Washington, D.C.: National Academy Press, 1991.
12. Grabowski H. Health Care Cost Containment and Pharmaceutical Innovation. Boston: Center for the Study of Drug Development, 1986, Reprint RS S707.
13. Mortenson L. Public policy and access to new drugs: the case of cancer chemotherapy. In this volume. Washington, D.C.: National Academy Press, 1991.
14. Laubach GD. Clinical research and managed care: who should fund the cost of care in clinical investigation? In Institute of Medicine. Resources for Clinical Investigation. Washington, D.C.: National Academy Press, 1988.
15. Wagner JL. Strategies for containing Medicaid prescription drug costs. Testimony for Senate Finance Committee. Washington, D.C.: September 1990.
16. Pollard MR. Managed care and a changing pharmaceutical industry. Health Affairs 1990;Fall:55-65.
17. Foote SB. The impact of public policy on medical device innovation: a target of polyintervention. In this volume. Washington, D.C.: National Academy Press, 1991.
18. Kahn A. The dynamics of medical device innovation: an innovator's perspective. In this volume. Washington, D.C.: National Academy Press, 1991.
19. Gelijns AC. Innovation in Clinical Practice: The Dynamics of Technology Development. Washington, D.C.: National Academy Press, in press.
20. Food and Drug Administration, Office of Device Evaluation, Center for Devices and Radiological Health. Annual Report, FY 1985. Rockville, MD: Food and Drug Administration, 1985.
21. General Accounting Office. Medical Devices: The FDA's Implementation of the Medical Device Reporting Regulation. Washington, D.C.: Government Printing Office, 1989 (GAO/PEMD 89-10).
22. General Accounting Office. Medical Device Recalls: An Overview and Analysis 1983-1988. Washington, D.C.: Government Printing Office, August 1989 (GAO/PEMD 89-15BR).
23. General Accounting Office. Medical Devices: Early Warning of Problems Is Hampered by Severe Underreporting. Washington, D.C.: Government Printing Office, 1986 (GAO/PEMD-87-1).
24. Mastroianni L, Donaldson DJ, Kane TT (eds). Developing New Contraceptives. National Research Council and Institute of Medicine. Washington, D.C.: National Academy Press, 1990.
25. Kessler DA, Pape S, Sundwall DN. The federal regulation of medical devices. New England Journal of Medicine 1987;317:357-365.
26. Anderson GF, Steinberg E. To buy or not to buy technology: acquisition under prospective payment. New England Journal of Medicine 1984;311:182-185.
27. Chang SW, Luft HS. Reimbursement and the dynamics of surgical procedure innovation. In this volume. Washington, D.C.: National Academy Press, 1991.
28. Halm EA. The payer as technological gatekeeper: methodological issues in technology assessment and payment policy. Paper presented at the Sixth Annual International Society of Technology Assessment in Health Care Meeting, Houston, Texas, May 21, 1990.

29. Hsiao WC, Braun P, Yntema D, Becker ER. Estimating physicians' work for a resource-based relative-value scale. New England Journal of Medicine 1988;319:835-841.
30. Physicians Payment Review Commission. Report to Congress. Washington, D.C.: Physician Payment Review Commission, 1990.
31. Goldsmith, MF. Some new twists to one of the most common procedures in U.S. general surgery. The Journal of the American Medical Association 1989;262:3248-3249.
32. Burstall ML. European policies influencing pharmaceutical innovation. In this volume. Washington, D.C.: National Academy Press, 1991.
33. Hutton J. Medical device innovation and public policy in the European Economic Community. In this volume. Washington, D.C.: National Academy Press, 1991.
34. Neimeth R. Japan's pharmaceutical industry postwar evolution. In this volume. Washington, D.C.: National Academy Press, 1991.
35. Spilker B, Cuatrecasas P. Inside the Drug Industry. Barcelona: Prous Science Publishers, 1990.

# 2

# The Diffusion of New Technology: Costs and Benefits to Health Care

PETER J. NEUMANN and MILTON C. WEINSTEIN

The American public has a love-hate relationship with medical technology. Technologies are extolled for saving lives, improving health status, and improving the quality of care. At the same time technology is vilified as one dominant factor responsible for the continuing escalation of medical costs. Highly visible "big-ticket" items, such as organ transplantation, diagnostic imaging systems, and new biotechnology products attract a major share of both praise and blame.

Five facts about new medical technology underlie this paper. First, new technologies do, on average, improve the quality of medical care by improving health outcomes. This is not true of every technology in every clinical use, but it is true on average. Second, many new technologies are ineffective or redundant and do not improve health outcomes. The trouble is that it is not always easy to discriminate between effective and ineffective technologies at the time they are introduced. Third, new technologies do, on balance, add to health care costs. Some technologies may actually reduce costs by replacing more expensive alternatives or preventing expensive health consequences, but the overall effect is to increase costs. Fourth, the incentives and regulations built into the American health care sector lead to inappropriate diffusion of technologies, both underdiffusion of effective and cost-effective technologies, and overdiffusion of ineffective and cost-ineffective technologies. Reimbursement systems, professional reward structures, legal considerations, and patient demands all contribute to the problem. The fifth inescapable fact about new medical technology is that the American public cannot get enough of it. We demand the best and newest from our providers, and they are, in general, happy to oblige.

The problem is that costs continue to rise, and the ability of the public and private sectors to finance health care is being strained. American society is approaching, or may have reached, the point at which it is not possible to provide the best available health care to every American, regardless of cost. The de facto solution has been to restrict access to health care for a growing segment of the population—the uninsured—while preserving the myth of best available care for those fortunate enough to have coverage.

Upward pressures on health care costs will only increase in the 1990s. A growing array of new technologies will claim an increasingly large share of national resources. The birth cohort of 1945 to 1965, the "baby-boomers," will move into the age range associated with increasing prevalence of chronic disease. Universal health insurance, in some form, may well be adopted. Any of these three forces will force hard choices, challenging the myth of "best available technology for all." Medical technologies, especially new ones, will have to justify their costs in a climate of competing claims on resources.

This paper addresses four aspects of the relationship between new medical technology and costs. First, we review the evidence regarding the contribution of new technology to the aggregate cost of health care. Second, we review a normative model of optimal diffusion of technologies, based on evaluation of their cost effectiveness—that is, the ability of a technology to improve health outcomes. Third, we examine the influence of economic incentives that affect adoption of new technology in the U.S. health care system and contrast the resulting priorities with those derived from the normative cost-effectiveness model. We examine incentives for hospitals, fee-for-service physicians, and managed care organizations. We cite examples of incentives for underdiffusion of cost-effective technologies and overdiffusion of cost-ineffective ones. Finally, we comment on future policy options for achieving a more cost-effective pattern of technology diffusion.

## HOW MUCH DOES NEW TECHNOLOGY ADD TO HEALTH CARE COSTS?

Researchers generally agree that medical technology has contributed to rising health care costs (1-3). Health insurance removes financial barriers to consumers, thus raising demand for technology and inducing providers to offer a more expensive mix of services. But researchers have struggled to measure how much technology has contributed to increasing costs. Part of the difficulty lies in defining medical technology. The term is commonly defined broadly to include drugs, devices, surgical procedures, and organizational support systems within which medical care is delivered (4). Identifying the changes in cost attributable to these items in any given period is virtually impossible. Even if the more important innovations could be listed, it would be extremely difficult to trace their overall economic impact.

Another caveat is that the economic impact of a technology is often confused with the purchase price of a piece of equipment or a drug, or the fee paid to a surgeon. The total impact of a technology on health care costs is much broader than that and may include offsetting savings as well as induced costs. The direct cost of a capital-embodied technology includes not only the capital cost itself but also the operating costs required to implement it. The operating costs of even the most capital-intensive technologies may be greater than anticipated because of the need for operating and supervisory personnel, training, insurance, supplies, and space. A new drug or device, on the other hand, may be more expensive to purchase but less expensive to administer than its alternatives (5). Furthermore, a new technology may affect the utilization of other health services. These effects constitute the "induced" costs and savings of a technology. A new imaging device may lead to increased utilization of other tests for confirming a diagnostic hypothesis that would not otherwise have arisen, or the new technology may make other diagnostic procedures unnecessary. Treatments that would not have been considered may be induced by a new diagnostic test (6), or treatments may be avoided because the new technology offers an alternative course of action. Technologies and their induced procedures may lead to side effects and complications requiring further tests and treatments, or side effects and complications may be avoided if the new technology leads to a safer clinical strategy than was possible in its absence. Technology that extends life may require more extended periods of care, often at great expense and in institutional settings. Technology that prevents disease may save resources that would otherwise be required for diagnosis and treatment, although few preventive technologies are cost saving on balance (7,8).

Some researchers have tried to estimate the effect of technology on U.S. health care expenditures by first estimating the impact of other, more easily identifiable sources including price inflation and age-specific population growth (9,10). The portion of the increase in health expenditures not accounted for by these explanatory variables is attributed to technology. Such research does not draw distinctions between expanded applications of existing technologies and introduction of new technologies. Other researchers have sought to measure changes in the cost of treating certain illnesses over time (2,12-14). Still others have used case studies to analyze the impact of important technologies such as intensive care units and computed tomography (15,16).

All three approaches suffer from a variety of problems. For our discussion of the economics of new technology, these approaches are problematic because they do not distinguish between the impacts of new and existing technologies. In general, residual approaches do not pinpoint the precise cause of increases. Many studies attribute cost increases to an increase in "intensity per hospital admission," which could be explained by non-technological factors, such as changes in the severity or nature of disease. In addition, these studies do not easily identify indirect costs of using new technologies, such as the need for more skilled hospital nurses and technicians, nor do they identify induced costs. Although the specific illness and case study approaches do analyze the impacts of particular technologies, it is difficult to generalize from them. Unlike cost-effectiveness research, to which we will return, this body of research does not attempt to relate cost increases to improvements in health outcome.

Empirical evidence from these types of studies suggests that medical technology accounts for about 10 to 40 percent of the increase in health care expenditures over time (1). Fuchs (3) concluded that technology contributed 0.6 percentage points of the 8.0 percent annual rate of increase in health expenditures from 1947 to 1967. Davis (9) found that technology accounted for about 25 percent of the increase in hospital expenses per admission between 1962 and 1968. More recently, Freeland and Schendler (10) reported that 21 percent of the rise in hospital costs between 1971 and 1981 was due to "intensity per admission." The Health Care Financing Administration (HCFA) estimated that from 1985 to 1986, 35 percent of changes in personal health expenditures were accounted for by "consumption per capita" and the intensity of consumption because of such factors as demographic changes and changes in income level (11). Employing a specific illness approach, Scitovsky and McCall (2) found that, from 1951 to 1971, cost-increasing changes in treatments generally outweighed cost-saving changes. The main cost-increasing factor was the rise in the use of ancillary services, such as laboratory tests and X-rays. Fineberg (12) and others have also noted the high cost of clinical chemistry tests and other little-ticket technologies. Scitovsky (13) found that from 1971 to 1981 increases in the cost of ancillary services slowed, but several new and expensive technologies raised costs substantially. Showstack et al. (14) also found evidence that big-ticket items, such as intensive care unit management of the critically ill, caused large increases in the 1970s.

Researchers have shown that any individual technology makes a relatively small contribution to health expenditures. For example, a 1979 study found that a 50 percent reduction in the annual operating costs of four expensive technologies—computed tomography, electronic fetal monitoring, coronary bypass surgery, and renal dialysis—would yield savings of 1 or 2 percent of the nation's health expenditures (15). One exception is the use of intensive care units, which Russell found to account for about 10 percent of hospital expenditures in 1974 (16).

## OPTIMAL DIFFUSION OF TECHNOLOGY: THE COST-EFFECTIVENESS PRINCIPLE

If new technologies increase health care costs, how much technology is appropriate? To judge whether the degree of diffusion of particular technologies or of technologies in general is appropriate, we need some standard or criterion. One such criterion is based on the proposition that the objective of medical technology is to improve health outcomes. Each clinical use of a technology utilizes some of society's limited health care resources and, ideally, improves health outcomes. The more the society spends on health care, the more health is improved. Moreover, there are diminishing returns to health care: the first billion dollars yields more health improvement than the six hundredth billion dollars. The more we expand the resources applied to health care, the more health can be improved but the higher the incremental cost per additional unit of health improvement.

The criterion for resource allocation that follows from this formulation of society's objectives is cost effectiveness: if a new technology produces health outcomes at a lower cost per unit than existing technologies, it should be adopted; otherwise, it should not. The principle is that clinical practices having low cost per unit of health benefit should have priority over practices having a higher cost per unit (17,18). Cost-effectiveness analysis has been used widely to assist policy formation and is gaining acceptance in the medical community as an appropriate criterion for resource allocation (18,19). Cost-effectiveness analyses of new medical technologies often are useful guides to their potential role in health care; one of the earliest examples was a cost-effectiveness analysis of hemodialysis in end-stage renal disease (20). This study, which projected a relatively low cost per year of life extension, probably influenced the decision by Congress to fund universal coverage under Medicare. A limitation of the study, to which we will return, was that it considered only the most favorable target group—the relatively young and otherwise healthy—and did not anticipate its expansion to older and sicker patients for whom the cost-effectiveness ratio is much higher. A barrier to applying cost-effectiveness analysis to new technologies generally is that decisions about adoption often are required before satisfactory data on effectiveness or even full cost are available.

Pharmaceuticals have probably received the most attention in cost-effectiveness analyses. Analyses of the drug cimetidine for peptic ulcer disease showed it not only to be cost effective but actually to give net savings relative to standard treatment (21,22). A study of the use of third-generation cephalosporins for hospital-acquired pneumonia also showed savings when compared to standard multiple-drug regimens, largely because of reduced costs of drug preparation and administration, monitoring, and side effects (5). Other drugs, although not cost saving, have been shown to have extremely favorable cost-effectiveness ratios in certain clinical uses. Beta-blockers following myocardial infarction, for example, have been shown to have a cost per year of life saved of from $2,400 for patients at high risk of subsequent infarction to, at most, $13,000 in patients at low risk. For other drugs, effects on quality of life are crucial, which has led to the use of quality-adjusted life years[1] as a measure of health outcome (23). Cost-effectiveness evaluations of antihypertensive drugs, for example, involve assessments of their effects on both quality of life and longevity (24). Diagnostic technologies have also been analyzed for their cost effectiveness. Unfortunately, many important imaging technologies, such as magnetic resonance imaging (MRI), have not been subjected to formal cost-effectiveness analyses because of the difficulty of attributing health benefits to the use of individual diagnostic modalities.

These and other examples illustrate a key lesson for cost-effectiveness research. A technology that is highly cost effective in one clinical situation can be extremely cost ineffective in others. Exercise tolerance testing is a cost-effective screening test for patients with chest pain (25) but not for asymptomatic patients (26). Coronary bypass graft surgery is relatively cost effective for patients with left-main coronary artery disease but not for patients with single-vessel disease (27). Cholesterol-lowering drugs probably are not cost effective for primary prevention of coronary heart disease in patients without other risk factors (28) but may well be cost effective, or even cost saving, in patients with established coronary artery disease or multiple risk factors in addition to high serum cholesterol.

The early lessons from the end-stage renal disease story suggest that even a clinically effective and cost-effective life-saving technology will diffuse into domains where it produces little additional health benefit at great additional cost. The Peter Principle says that employees will rise through the ranks until they reach their highest level of incompetence. The analog for diffusion of medical technology is that a technology will expand its use until it has found its way into medical applications that are cost ineffective. This presents a challenge for developers, utilizers, purchasers, and regulators of new technology: to permit adoption of cost-effective new technologies without allowing them to absorb significant resources for cost-ineffective uses.

## EFFECTS OF REIMBURSEMENT ON THE USE OF NEW TECHNOLOGIES

We return now to the central question: do the economic incentives in the U.S. health care sector promote diffusion of cost-effective technologies? Health care financing in the 1970s and early 1980s—characterized by cost-based hospital reimbursement, fee-for-service physicians, and generous insurance plans—promoted rapid diffusion of new technologies whether they were cost effective or not. Since providers knew they would be reimbursed for their services, there was relatively little concern over whether technologies were cost effective. As long as technologies were perceived to offer marginal benefits over existing practices, there was pressure in the system to adopt them. As policy makers began to address soaring health care costs in the 1970s, medical technology was singled out as an important source of the problem. The title of a major conference in 1977 asked whether technology was the culprit behind rising health care costs (1). Payers began seriously questioning whether the nation's investment in high-technology medicine was worth the cost. Articles appeared advocating the use of cost-effectiveness analysis for guiding resource allocation (17).

Most observers understood, though, that the culprit was not medical technology so much as perverse incentives that insulated patients and providers from the costs of care. By devising systems with more appropriate incentives, policy makers hoped that resources, including those for new technologies, would be allocated more cost effectively. The widespread reforms of health care financing in this decade, including the adoption of the Medicare Prospective Payment System (PPS) and the rapid growth of managed care insurance plans, have created markedly different incentives for providers to adopt and use new technologies. But while these systems establish incentives for providers to be more cost conscious, they do not necessarily ensure adoption of cost-effective technologies. Let us consider the current incentives for three major players in the diffusion of technology: hospitals, managed care insurance plans (including health maintenance organizations), and physicians.

## Hospitals

PPS may distort the adoption of cost-effective new technologies in several ways. Because it establishes fixed, predetermined payments per admission, PPS encourages hospitals to focus on short-run costs and reimbursement levels. But from society's point of view, the consequences of a new technology, in terms of its cost and health impact, are relevant for the duration of the patient's life. Under PPS, hospitals have a disincentive to provide new technologies that increase short-term costs, even if they save costs or offer substantial benefits in the longer run. From the hospital's perspective, diagnosis-related group (DRG) payment levels vie with, or even replace, health effectiveness as the measure of benefit associated with a new technology. PPS also creates an incentive for hospitals to shift services to outpatient settings, even if these services could be performed more efficiently on inpatients. Furthermore, the system favors capital-intensive technologies because capital continues to be reimbursed on a cost basis.

There are, of course, some countervailing incentives that tend to favor adoption of new technology in hospitals. Hospitals compete for patients and physicians by offering high-quality services that often depend on advances in technology. Ethical imperatives to give the best care to each patient and malpractice concerns tend to lead to use of technology. Physicians practicing in a hospital may be advocates for clinically effective technology regardless of bottom-line effects, but they may be as insensitive to cost as to revenue. Recent studies have shown that physicians are poorly informed about the cost of the services they order (29). The result is often conflict between administrators who are concerned with cost and revenue and physicians who are concerned with clinical effectiveness and satisfying patient and professional demands. Neither party reflects societal concerns for maximizing health outcome within budget constraints.

Two provisions of PPS—the annual update factor and recalibration of DRGs—mitigate disincentives to use costly new technologies, but they are likely to have little impact. The update factor, which increases the overall level of hospital reimbursement, increases per-patient hospital payments. But it fails to affect incentives at the margin because the additional funds are not necessarily earmarked to pay for the use of new technologies. The impact of the annual readjustment of DRG weights, which is intended to respond to the use of new technologies for specific diagnoses, is limited because of major time lags between the diffusion of new technologies and readjustment of weights. Since hospitals ultimately face the same DRG weight whether or not they use the technology, these updates do little to change the inherent distortions of the system toward underutilization.

There is limited empirical evidence about the diffusion of new technologies under PPS. The Prospective Payment Assessment Commission has reported that recent years have witnessed continued growth in the number of community hospitals offering lithotripsy, open heart surgery, cardiac catheterization, and organ transplants (30), but some evidence suggests that PPS has slowed the adoption of potentially cost-effective technologies. Kane and Manoukian (31), for example, reported that PPS has effectively halted the diffusion of cochlear implants, despite FDA approval and favorable reviews by the Office of Health Technology Assessment and several medical associations. The authors blame the underdiffusion on Medicare's decision to classify cochlear implant patients in a DRG for which reimbursement covers only a fraction of the cost of the device.

Like all fixed-price systems, PPS does not easily incorporate the changes in resource use that occur with new technologies. Some policy makers have advocated creating new or temporary DRGs, or add-on payments for such important new technologies as cochlear implants (32). But reimbursing technologies on a case-by-case, add-on-payment basis reestablishes a cost basis for payment and fails to remove the other distortions from cost-effective resource allocation noted above.

An alternative to prospective rate setting is global budgeting for hospitals, modeled after the Canadian system. Under global budgeting, hospitals or other entities are allocated a fixed budget and given the discretion to allocate it as they see fit. Because they do not associate fixed payments with the use of individual technologies, global budgets remove some of the incentive to focus on reimbursement levels. They also tend to expand the time perspective in which resource allocation decisions are made. As a result, they may create more appropriate incentives for hospitals to allocate scarce resources for new technologies. But global budgets do not remove all distortions. The hospital perspective is still limited to inpatients, for example. And the incentive to be efficient is attenuated because hospitals can receive a pass-through each year for legitimate cost increases, at least in the Canadian system. There is some evidence that new technologies do not diffuse as rapidly in Canada as in the United States, but it is not clear that the rate is more appropriate or that the most cost-effective technologies are adopted. Studies show, for example, that the United States has eight times more MRI units per capita than Canada, a difference unlikely to be accounted for by differences in disease or demographics (33). Whether the Canadian or the American utilization rate is the more cost effective remains to be determined.

## HMOs and Managed Care Plans

The perspective of health maintenance organizations (HMOs) is similar to the societal perspective in cost-effectiveness analysis in several important respects. Since HMOs receive a fixed payment per enrollee, they have incentives to consider the longer-term health and economic consequences of decisions about new technologies. In addition, capitated plans provide patient care in both the ambulatory and hospital setting.

However, the HMO and societal perspective differ in several ways. A major difference is that the HMO perspective is distorted by significant enrollee turnover; in other words, an HMO is not the closed system it may appear to be. The high rate of disenrollment in many capitated plans may have important consequences for the cost-effective adoption of new technologies. Technologies that increase short-run costs but save costs in the long run may be cost effective from society's point of view but not the HMO's, for example. An HMO's cost-effectiveness analysis regarding a new technology can be expected to discount costs, and to some extent health consequences, beyond the point of disenrollment. A second difference is that HMOs do not cover all health care services, such as stays in long-term care facilities. Technologies that affect these costs (e.g., which prevent nursing home stays) would not be as highly valued by the HMO. Third, the adoption of new technologies may be influenced by financial incentives, employed by most HMOs, that encourage physicians to restrict utilization (34). Recent evidence suggests that some financial incentives, as well as the type of HMO, influence the number of outpatient visits and the rate of hospitalization (35). As with hospitals, there are countervailing forces: competition for patients and physicians as well as ethical and malpractice concerns.

Because they receive a fixed amount per patient, capitated plans might be expected to adopt and use technologies at a lower rate than their fee-for-service counterparts. Some empirical evidence supports this hypothesis. One study found that Kaiser Permanente's utilization of computed tomography

(CT) examinations in the 1970s was substantially lower than that for California or the nation (36). Epstein and colleagues compared the rate at which patients with uncomplicated hypertension were tested by fee-for-service and large prepaid practices. After correcting for age, sex, and severity of illness, they found 50 percent more electrocardiograms and 40 percent more chest radiographs among patients in a fee-for-service system (37). Fee-for-service physicians believed both tests were associated with higher costs and profits, and the largest differences existed for tests where there was the greatest difference in profitability. Gold and colleagues recently found that HMOs are more likely than other plans to have drug utilization review programs, to mandate the use of generics, and to use formularies (38). Again, it remains to be determined which utilization pattern is more cost effective.

### Incentives for Fee-for-Service Physicians

The existing reimbursement systems for physicians have important implications for cost-effective adoption of new technologies. Because they are paid for services provided, fee-for-service physicians have incentives to use new technologies beyond the point at which marginal costs equal marginal benefits. Furthermore, current reimbursement levels have an inherent bias toward procedure-based services. Numerous studies have found that reimbursement is disproportionately higher for technology-driven services than for more cognitive services, such as clinical evaluation and management (39). Relative to resource costs, evaluation and management services are compensated at a lower rate than invasive, imaging, and laboratory services. There is also an inpatient bias to the system. Studies have found that services performed on ambulatory patients are compensated at substantially lower rates than if they are performed on inpatients (39).

The creation of a resource-based relative value scale (RBRVS) with an expenditure ceiling for physician services, recently approved by Congress, will affect the adoption of new technologies in several ways (39). The new fee schedule is intended to establish a "level economic playing field" for physicians based on resources used in providing services. Ideally, the effect will be to make medical decision making income neutral for the physician, leaving clinical benefit as the basis for resource allocation. Keeping the RBRVS up to date with current resource costs to the physician, however, may lead to short-term distortions affecting the use of new technologies.

## FUTURE DIRECTIONS: HOW TO ACHIEVE COST-EFFECTIVE DIFFUSION OF MEDICAL TECHNOLOGY

We have presented evidence that new technologies do increase costs on average, but that some technologies in some clinical uses may save more resources than they cost. We have also suggested that cost effectiveness is an appropriate criterion for guiding the adoption of new technologies, although other criteria, such as equity to the disadvantaged, must also be considered. Finally, we have described characteristics of the American system of reimbursement and health care management that do not always lead to the adoption of the most cost-effective mix of new and old technologies.

We conclude by suggesting some directions for the 1990s. First, new technologies must be evaluated as early as possible and should be reevaluated frequently. Both health and economic impact should be part of these evaluations. This country has not yet found a stable funding base for these kinds of evaluations, but this must be done to provide an adequate information base for policy formulation. Second, we must make the incentive structure facing health care insurers, providers, and consumers correspond more closely to societal goals and resource constraints. Physicians already have a commitment to improving health through effective medical care, and organized medicine has recognized and accepted the challenge of living within budgets. A system based more on global, flexible budgets than on piecemeal regulations would not be without problems, but it might bring improvement. In this regard, caution should be exercised in applying the standard HMO model, because HMOs do not bear the full costs or realize the full benefits of the technologies they employ. Therefore, any system of decentralized global budgeting should give managers financial responsibility for both external and induced costs and savings. The role of information and guidelines for cost-effective care would be enhanced in such an environment, and the research base for providing such information in real time should be expanded. Third, the current reimbursement system, especially the PPS under Medicare, tends to freeze the status quo. Cost-effective new technologies are at a competitive disadvantage relative to cost-ineffective existing ones. We need to level the playing field in this country, to encourage innovation, and to encourage, not stifle, the substitution of cost-effective for cost-ineffective clinical practices. Finally, the voice of the American public cannot be ignored. The people want cost containment, but they also want new technology if it can bring them better health. A system that rewards cost-effective health care and invites cost-effective new technology could accomplish both objectives.

## NOTE

1. The method of quality-adjusted life years assigns weights, ranging from zero to one, to states of health. Thus, 2 years at a quality level of 0.5 would be equivalent to 1.0 quality-adjusted life year.

## REFERENCES

1. Altman SH, Blendon RJ (eds). Medical Technology: The Culprit Behind Health Care Costs? Proceedings of the 1977 Sun Valley Forum on National Health. DHEW Publication No. 79-3216, Washington, D.C.: U.S. Government Printing Office, 1979.
2. Scitovsky AA, McCall N. Changes in the Costs of Treatment of Selected Illnesses, 1951-1964-1971. National Center for Health Services Research, Publication No. (HRA) 77-3161, Washington, D.C.: U.S. Government Printing Office, 1977.
3. Fuchs V. Essays in the Economics of Health and Medical Care. New York: Columbia University Press, 1972.
4. U.S. Congress, Office of Technology Assessment. Strategies for Medical Technology Assessment. GPO Stock No. 052-003-00887-4, Washington, D.C.: U.S. Government Printing Office, 1982.
5. Weinstein MC, Read JL, MacKay DN, Kresel JJ, Ashley H, Halvorsen KT, Hutchings HC. Cost-effective choice of antimicrobial therapy for serious infections. Journal of General Internal Medicine 1986;1:351-363.
6. Banta HD, Thacker SB. Assessing the costs and benefits of electronic fetal monitoring. Obstetrics and Gynecological Survey 1979;34:627-642.
7. Russell LB. Is Prevention Better Than Cure? Washington, D.C.: The Brookings Institution, 1986.
8. Weinstein MC, Stason WB. Cost-effectiveness of interventions to prevent or treat coronary heart disease. Annual Review of Public Health 1986;6:41-63.
9. Davis K. The role of technology, demand, and labor markets in the determination of hospital costs. In Perlman M (ed). Economics of Health and Medical Care. New York: Wiley, 1974.
10. Freeland MS, Schendler CE. National health expenditure growth in the 1980s: an aging population, new technologies, and increasing competition. Health Care Financing Review 1983;4:1-58.
11. Health Care Financing Administration, Office of the Actuary, Division of National Cost Estimates. National health expenditures, 1986-2000. Health Care Financing Review 1987;8:1-36.
12. Fineberg HV. Clinical chemistries: the high cost of low-cost diagnostic tests. In Altman SH, Blendon RJ (eds). Medical Technology: The Culprit Behind Health Care Costs? DHEW Publication No. (HRA) 79-3216. Washington, D.C.: U.S. Government Printing Office, 1979.
13. Scitovsky AA. Changes in the costs of treatment of selected illnesses, 1971-1981. Medical Care 1985;23:1345-1357.
14. Showstack JA, Stone MH, Schroeder SA. The role of changing clinical practices in the rising costs of hospital care. New England Journal of Medicine 1985;313:1201-1207.
15. Moloney TW, Rogers DE. Medical technology: a different view of the contentious debate over costs. New England Journal of Medicine 1979; 301:1413-1419.
16. Russell LB. Technology in Hospitals: Medical Advances and Their Diffusion. Washington, D.C.: Brookings Institution, 1979.

17. Weinstein MC, Stason WB. Foundations of cost-effectiveness analysis for health and medical practices. New England Journal of Medicine 1977;296:716-721.
18. Eisenberg JM. Clinical economics: a guide to the economic analysis of clinical practices. Journal of the American Medical Association 1989;262:2879-2886.
19. Riesenberg D. Economics is everybody's business (editorial). Journal of the American Medical Association 1989;262:2897.
20. Klarman HE, Francis JO, Rosenthal GD. Cost-effectiveness analysis applied to the treatment of chronic renal disease. Medical Care 1968;6:48-54.
21. Culyer AJ, Maynard AK. Cost-effectiveness of duodenal ulcer treatment. Social Science and Medicine 1981;15C:3-11.
22. Fineberg HV, Pearlman LA. Benefit and cost analysis of medical interventions: the case of cimetidine and peptic ulcer disease. Case Study #11 in Background Paper #2 in Case Studies of Medical Technologies. Office of Technology Assessment, U.S. Congress. Washington, D.C.: U.S. Government Printing Office, 1980.
23. Goldman L, Sia STB, Cook EF, Rutherford JD, Weinstein MC. Costs and effectiveness of routine therapy with long-term beta-adrenergic antagonists after acute myocardial infarction. New England Journal of Medicine 1988;319:152-157.
24. Weinstein MC, Stason WB. Hypertension: A Policy Perspective. Cambridge, Mass.: Harvard University Press, 1976.
25. Lee TH, Fukui T, Weinstein MC, Tosteson ANA, Goldman L. Cost-effectiveness of screening strategies for left main coronary artery disease in patients with stable angina. Medical Decision Making 1988;8:268-278.
26. Stason WB, Fineberg HV. Implications of alternative strategies to diagnose coronary artery disease. Circulation 1982 (suppl III);66:III80-III86.
27. Weinstein MC, Stason WB. Cost-effectiveness of coronary artery bypass surgery. Circulation 1982 (suppl III);66:III56-III66.
28. Oster G, Epstein AM. Cost-effectiveness of antihyperlipemic therapy in the prevention of coronary heart disease. Journal of the American Medical Association 1987;258:2381-2387.
29. Eisenberg JM, Williams SV. Cost containment and changing physicians' practice behavior: can the fox learn to guard the chicken coop? Journal of the American Medical Association 1981;246:2195-2201.
30. U.S. Congress, Prospective Payment Assessment Commission. Medicare Prospective Payment and the American Health Care System: Report to Congress. Washington, D.C., 1989.
31. Kane N, Manoukian P. The effect of the Medicare Prospective Payment System on the adoption of new technology. New England Journal of Medicine 1989;321:1378-1382.
32. U.S. Congress, Prospective Payment Assessment Commission. Report and Recommendations to the Secretary, U.S. Department of Health and Human Services. Washington, D.C., 1987.
33. Rublee DA. Medical technology in Canada, Germany, and the U.S. Health Affairs 1989;8:178-182.

34. Hillman AL. Financial incentives for physicians in HMOs: is there a conflict of interest? New England Journal of Medicine 1987;317:1743-1748.
35. Hillman AL, Pauly MV, Kerstein JJ. How do financial incentives affect physicians' clinical decisions and the financial performance of health maintenance organizations? New England Journal of Medicine 1989;321:86-92.
36. Willems JS, Banta DH, Lukas TA, Taylor CA. The computed tomography (CT) scanner. In Altman SH, Blendon RJ (eds). Medical Technology: The Culprit Behind Health Care Costs? DHEW Publication No. 79-3216, Washington, D.C.: U.S. Government Printing Office, 1979.
37. Epstein AM, Begg CB, McNeil BJ. The use of ambulatory testing in prepaid and fee-for-service group practice. New England Journal of Medicine 1986;314:1089-1094.
38. Gold M, Joffe M, Kennedy TL, Tucker AM. Pharmacy benefits in HMOs. Health Affairs 1989;8:182-190.
39. Hsiao WC, Braun P, Dunn D, Becker ER, DeNicola M, Ketcham TR. Results and policy implications of the resource-based relative value study. New England Journal of Medicine 1988;319:881-888.

# 3

# The Changing Economics of Pharmaceutical Research and Development

HENRY GRABOWSKI

These are interesting times for the research-oriented pharmaceutical industry. There have been several developments in recent years that are significantly changing the basic economics of pharmaceutical research and development (R&D). Since total investment and payback periods in pharmaceuticals now span three decades or more, it may be some time before all of the implications are apparent. However, some important changes in industry structure have begun to occur already.

This chapter provides an overview of several factors influencing the current and future environment for pharmaceutical R&D. The following section examines current trends in R&D opportunities, R&D costs, product life cycles, effective patent life, and prescription prices. The second section discusses some of the main results from a recently completed study of returns on past new drug introductions (1). This analysis provides a useful perspective for evaluating the impact of current industry trends. The final sections present conclusions and public policy implications.

## CURRENT TRENDS

### R&D Opportunities

The state of R&D opportunities in pharmaceuticals is no longer the source of concern that it once was. Industry R&D directors are very optimistic.

*Commentaries on the economics of pharmaceutical innovation can be found in Appendixes A and B.

**TABLE 3.1** New Drug Products Achieving $100 Million Sales in the U.S. Market Within the First 6 Years of Market Life

| | Number Discovered | |
|---|---|---|
| Period | Total | Outside United States |
| 1970-1974 | 2 | 1 |
| 1975-1979 | 8 | 2 |
| 1980-1984 | 12 | 7 |
| Total | 22 | 10 |

Note: Before performing this analysis, sales were transformed into constant (1986) dollars using the GNP price deflator.

Source: Compiled from sales audit data from IMS America Inc. (*U.S. Drug Store and Hospital Sales,* various issues).

The combined research efforts of academia, government, and industry have produced major advances in biomedical science, many of which offer promising clinical applications. Increased knowledge of physiological processes at the molecular level enable researchers to develop more selective and potent pharmaceutical targets. New research tools, such as electron microscopy and X-ray crystallography, and new research techniques associated with biotechnology have helped enhance the search for significant new compounds. Because of these advancements, pharmaceutical industry R&D now can be categorized more as a "discovery by design" approach, as opposed to the random screening of compounds that was once prevalent.

We have seen many more economically and therapeutically important drugs emerge from the R&D pipeline over the past decade. Table 3.1 provides an analysis of the number of drugs introduced between 1970 and 1984 that achieved 100 million dollars in annual sales in the first 6 years of market life. Using this definition of commercially important drugs, Table 3.1 shows that there were 22 such compounds over this period. The time trend shown is especially striking. There were only 2 such products in the 1970-1974 period, 8 in 1975-1979, and 12 for 1980-1984.[1]

This table also shows that foreign discoveries account for 10 of the 22 commercially important drugs in the United States during this period. This reflects the multinational character of the pharmaceutical industry. Pharmaceuticals discovered abroad have been a prominent source of U.S. market introductions over the past two decades. Conversely, sales of U.S.-discovered products in foreign countries have been important to earning satisfactory returns on R&D by U.S. firms.

It is also worth noting that while the relevant 6-year period for evaluating the sales of 1985-1989 introductions is still less than half completed, there already are eight compounds achieving $100 million in annual sales from this cohort.[2] This period is therefore likely to easily exceed the preceding one in terms of commercially significant compounds.

Another interesting development concerns the therapeutic orientation of these big commercial successes. The leading therapeutic category for these compounds during the 1970s was antibiotics and non-steroidal anti-inflammatory drugs (NSAIDs). For the 1980s the leading category was cardiovascular agents. This class of drugs accounted for over half the major compounds introduced. This trend reflects the changing orientation of pharmaceutical R&D.

The introductions of major new products for cardiovascular and other clincial conditions have begun to have a significant impact on clinical practice. Significantly fewer prescriptions are being written for older therapies such as diuretics. They have lost much of their share of the market to several products that were not even present during the 1970s. Newer product categories, such as the ACE inhibitors, the calcium channel blockers, and the cholesterol reducers, now account for a significant and rapidly growing share of the cardiovascular drug market. It is also important to note that the rate of deaths per capita in the United States from cardiovascular causes has decreased significantly over the past decade (2). This reflects, at least in part, the availability of new and better medicines (2-4).

Another measure of innovative performance that has received attention in the literature involves the diffusion of new chemical entities (NCEs) across major world markets. Drugs that have been adopted in a majority of these markets have been categorized as internationalized or consensus NCEs. This measure has been employed by Coppinger and Haas, Barral, Thomas, and in my own research on international competitiveness (5-8). Less than one-quarter of the new products introduced worldwide achieve the status of consensus drugs in these studies. There is also evidence of a significant statistical correlation between the international acceptance of a new drug and its therapeutic and commercial significance (6).

Figure 3.1 indicates that the U.S. pharmaceutical industry had the largest share of consensus NCEs for the period 1970-1985. The U.S. industry's share of consensus drugs—43 percent—is approximately double its 24 percent share of worldwide introductions over this same period. Furthermore, the United States has had as many consensus NCEs as all of the countries in Europe together. These data indicate that the U.S. industry has been at the forefront of the pharmaceutical innovation process. Whether this will continue in the 1990s and beyond depends on a number of technological, economic, and public policy factors.

## R&D Costs

There is strong evidence that the R&D process in the United States is becoming significantly longer and costlier. Figure 3.2 shows a plot of the average duration of the Investigational New Drug (IND) and New Drug

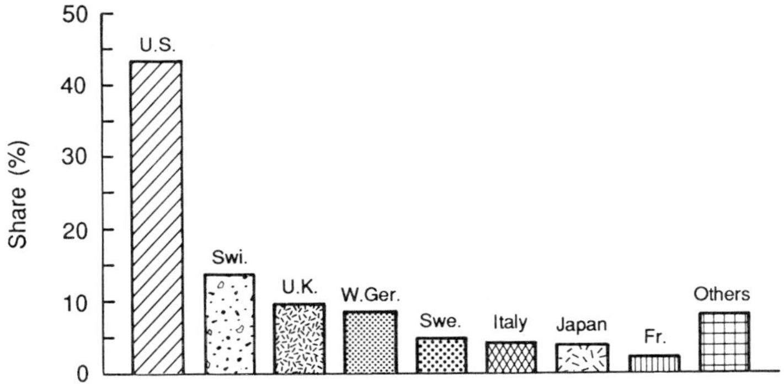


**FIGURE 3.1** Consensus new drug approvals by nationality of originating firm, 1970-1985. (Source: Grabowski H. An analysis of U.S. international competitiveness in pharmaceuticals. Managerial and Decision Economics, 1989, Special Issue:27-33.)

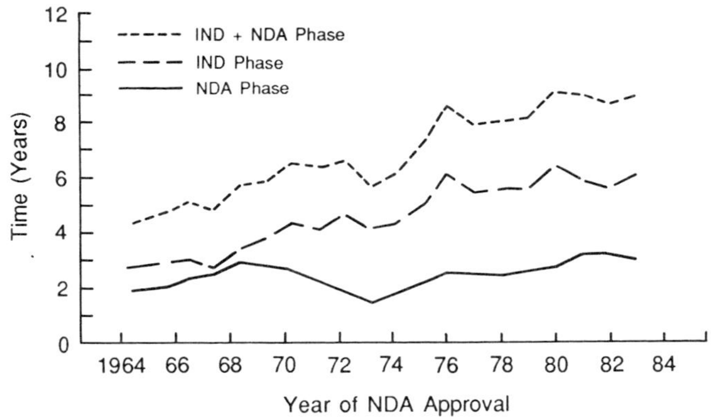


**FIGURE 3.2** Duration of IND and NDA phases, self-originated NCEs of U.S. firms. (Source: Center for the Study of Drug Development.)

Application (NDA) phases for annual new drug approvals between 1964 and 1984. By the mid 1980s, the IND or clinical investigational phase averaged over 6 years and the NDA or regulatory review phase was about $2^1/_2$ years. If we add to this a pre-clinical phase of 3 or more years, we obtain a mean total R&D time of over 12 years. This total R&D time has been trending inevitably upward.[3]

The bar graph in Figure 3.3 shows annual industry R&D expenditures, expressed in constant dollars.[4] The solid line shows the annual number of new drug introductions. This figure indicates that R&D expenditures have increased several fold, even after adjustment for economy-wide inflation. The increase in R&D investment is most dramatic in the past decade. At the same time, the annual number of new drugs has changed only moderately. While the issue of R&D costs is best analyzed at the level of individual drugs, the two series in Figure 3.2 suggest that R&D investment costs per new drug introduction are increasing significantly in real terms.[5]

The Center for the Study of Drug Development at Tufts University recently has completed a microeconomic study of R&D costs. The principal investigators in this study are Joe DiMasi, Ron Hansen, Lou Lasagna, and myself (9). This analysis is designed to estimate the average R&D cost for NCEs discovered and developed by U.S.-owned firms (i.e., their self-originated NCEs). Data were obtained on a random sample of 93 drugs first tested in humans between 1970 and 1982. In this analysis the costs of drug candidates that fail in pre-clinical and clinical trials are incorporated into the average costs of the new drug introduction. R&D expenditures also are capitalized to the date of marketing introduction to reflect the time costs associated with an investment in pharmaceutical R&D.[6] Our best estimate is that it takes an average of $231 million (in 1987 dollars) and 12 years to discover and develop a new drug. Of this total, $114 million is the out-of-pocket R&D costs and $117 million is the time cost associated with the 12-year average investment period. In addition, we find substantial variability around this mean cost estimate. Research is continuing with respect to how R&D costs vary by therapeutic category and other characteristics.

Our findings imply that average R&D costs per new drug introduction have been increasing significantly. An earlier analysis by Hansen (10) using the same general methodology found an average R&D cost of $54 million (in 1976 dollars). Hansen's R&D cost estimate is $100.7 mil-

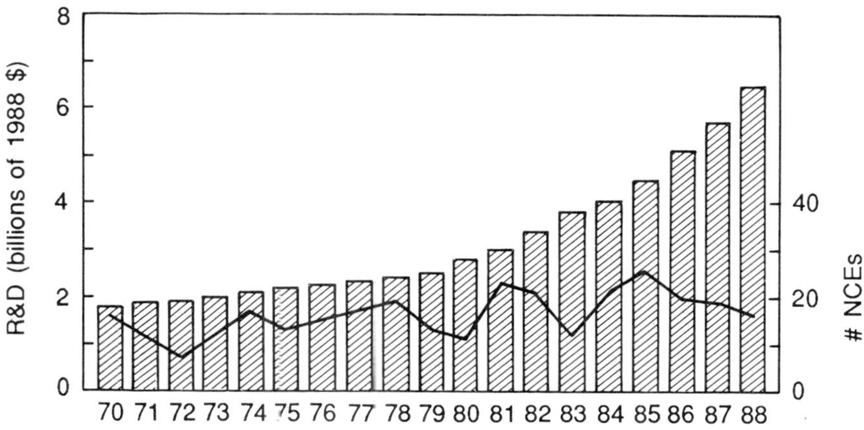


**FIGURE 3.3** FDA approvals versus R&D spending. (Source: data on new drug introductions from the FDA and pharmaceutical R&D expenditures data from annual surveys of the Pharmaceutical Manufacturers Association.)

lion expressed in 1987 dollars. Hence, in real terms total capitalized costs are about 2.3 times larger in our study than in the earlier period analyzed by Hansen.[7] What factors account for this increase in real R&D costs per new drug introduction? This is clearly an important issue for further research. Some key factors can be highlighted on the basis of our present knowledge. First, pharmaceutical R&D now entails significantly greater expenditures in the discovery phase. In addition, we found that the probability of success in the clinical phase has been increasing. These trends are consistent with a more science-based search process for new compounds. To date, however, the higher success rates at the clinical stage have not been sufficient to offset the greater costs expended elsewhere in the R&D process. A second factor associated with longer R&D times and higher costs per new drug introduction is the shift in research focus toward therapeutics to treat chronic clinical conditions such as cardiovascular disease and cancer. Chronic disease drugs require more long-term testing and greater overall resource investments prior to commercial introduction.[8] A third factor accounting for higher R&D costs is the rapid escalation in the out-of-pocket costs of clinical trials and the greater capital equipment requirements associated with current R&D activities in the pharmaceutical industry. There are striking changes in this regard emerging from our analysis compared to the situation of a decade ago. Understanding the forces underlying this rapid increase in out-of-pocket costs is an important topic for future research.[9]

## Product Life Cycles

Whereas R&D investment costs have been increasing, product life cycles have been getting shorter. This is the result of faster follow-on from competing new drugs and increased generic competition when patents expire. John Vernon and I have studied the life cycles of drugs introduced since the 1970s (1). It appears the sales volume of the average drug tends to peak somewhere around 10 to 12 years after market introduction. This research is ongoing, but there is definite information to suggest faster follow-on from competing drugs than in the past. The same factors that make the "discovery by design" research approach more effective, with higher probabilities of success, apparently also generate more intense competition from "fast followers."[10]

The biggest change in the commercial life cycle of a product in the 1980s, however, is due to increased competition from generics. Several years ago, when a patent expired, a manufacturer would lose part of the market share to generics, but at a fairly slow pace. A study by Statman (12) of the 1970s found that several years after patent expiration, the typical pioneering brand still maintained an 80 to 90 percent market share in terms of unit sales.

This situation changed dramatically in the wake of the 1984 Drug Price Competition and Patent Restoration Act and its related developments. One major part of this act shortened and simplified the regulatory process for generic drugs by allowing the submission of an abbreviated new drug application (ANDA). This allowed generics an easier and faster entry into the market. John Vernon and I recently examined the experiences of 18 economically significant drug products whose initial generic competition occurred in the post-1983 period (13). For these drug compounds, the average product was subject to 25 generic competitors and lost approximately half its market share within 2 years. There was a tendency for the rate of sales erosion to accelerate with more recent patent expirations. Compared to the period before the 1984 act, today's commercial environment is much more competitive with regard to generics.

## Effective Patent Life

Mindful that the 1984 act would result in greater generic competition and shorter times to recover R&D costs, legislators sought to grant brand manufacturers some relief by providing partial restoration of patent time lost during the clinical development and regulatory approval periods for new product introductions. Given this other objective of the 1984 act, what can be said about the effective patent life for current new drug introductions?

To date, most introductions have received partial benefits under the transition terms of the act.[11] Figure 3.4 shows some initial results for the transition period from a study by Kaitin and Trimble (14). In particular, it shows the impact of the 1984 act on the average effective patent life for new drug introductions from 1982 to 1986. For the post-1984[12] period,

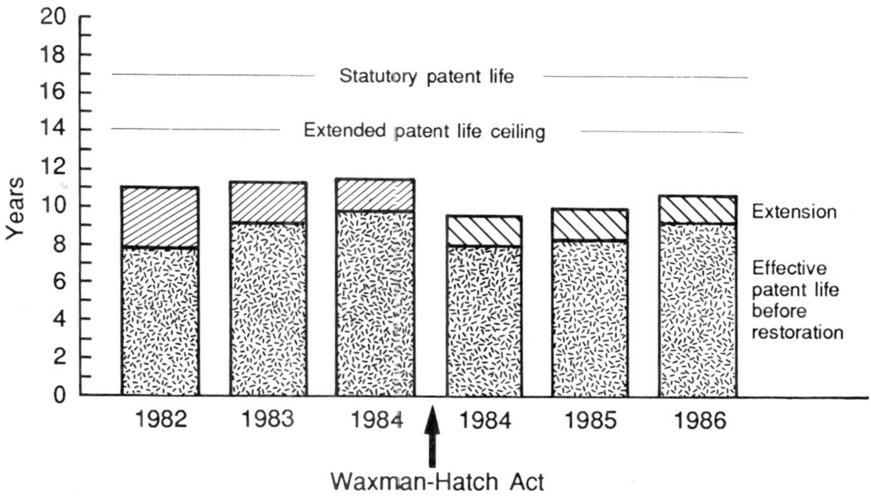


**FIGURE 3.4** Effective U.S. patent life. (Source: Center for the Study of Drug Development.)

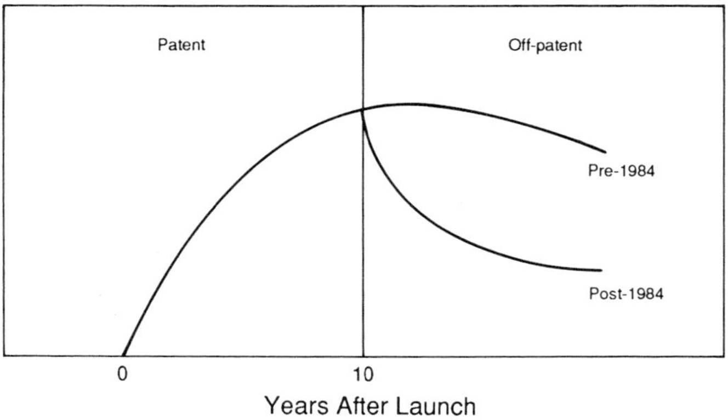


**FIGURE 3.5** Waxman-Hatch Act: generic impact on sole-source product sales.

Figure 3.4 shows what the average effective patent life would have been without any restoration (the black portion) and the additional patent life provided by the act (the hatched portion). The total patent life for a new drug introduction in the post-1984 period averaged around 10 years. Of this total, the average additional benefit provided by the act in restored patent life is 1½ years. These figures apply to the drugs in the transition phase, since most of these drugs were already patented and in clinical development when the act was passed.

We have also done some simulations at Duke on what the patent restoration periods will be when their benefits become fully effective. This involves restoring one-half of the time lost in the clinical development phase plus all of the time lost in the NDA approval process, subject to a cap of 5 years as well as other constraints. On average, recent introductions would get about 3 years of patent extension, based on our analysis. Some drugs will get the full 5 years and others will get none, depending on their status.

These analyses indicate that the average drug will probably have 10 to 12 years of effective patent life when the full patent restoration benefits from the 1984 act are implemented. The patent life may even be less if average development times continue to increase. In addition, when patents expire, there will be a rapid loss in sales and revenues of the pioneering product to generic imitators.

Figure 3.5 is a schematic diagram of the change that has occurred since the 1984 act was passed. Before 1984 loss of sales to generics was gradual; the erosion of sales in the post-1984 period has been much more rapid. This sharp decline in sales in the post-patent period is likely to intensify in the 1990s under the additional pressures of aggressive cost containment-driven generic substitution policies. In summary, manufacturers will most likely face an environment in which they must recoup their initial R&D

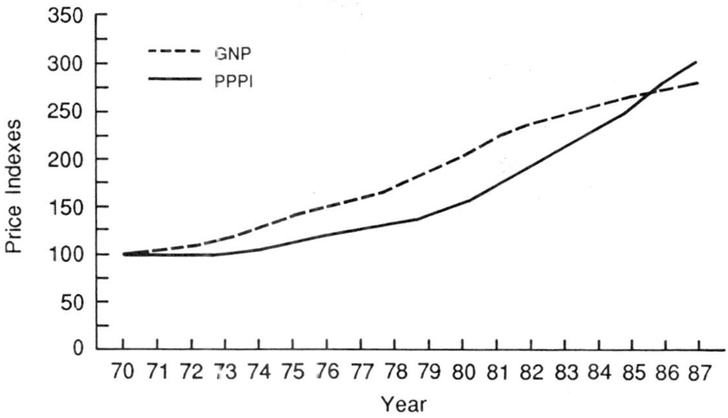


**FIGURE 3.6** GNP versus PPPI. (Source: original data from U.S. Bureau of Labor Statistics and Economic Report of the President.)

expenditures and earn the majority of their positive return during the first 10 to 12 years of effective patent life.

### Drug Prices

There has also been an important change in industry pricing behavior during the past decade. During the 1970s, U.S. prescription drug prices lagged inflation. At the end of the 1970s, however, prescription drug prices began to increase faster than inflation. This pattern persisted through the 1980s as illustrated in Figure 3.6, which shows a plot of the pharmaceutical producer price index (the PPPI)[13] versus the Gross National Product (GNP) price deflator. Both indices are valued at 100 in 1970 for comparative purposes. The GNP series advances faster during the 1970s, but the PPPI, with its faster growth in the 1980s, has a higher value than the GNP deflator by the end of this period.[14]

Increasing drug prices above the rate of general inflation has been one of the main strategic responses of the industry to higher R&D costs, shorter product life cycles, and increased generic competition. Analysis of the return on investment of new drug introductions, discussed in the next section, indicates that higher real prices in the 1980s had an important influence on industry's realized return on R&D investment.

## RETURN TO PHARMACEUTICAL R&D

John Vernon and I recently completed a study investigating the economic returns of new drugs introduced during the 1970s (1). Our analysis employs a sample of 100 pharmaceuticals introduced between 1970 and 1979.

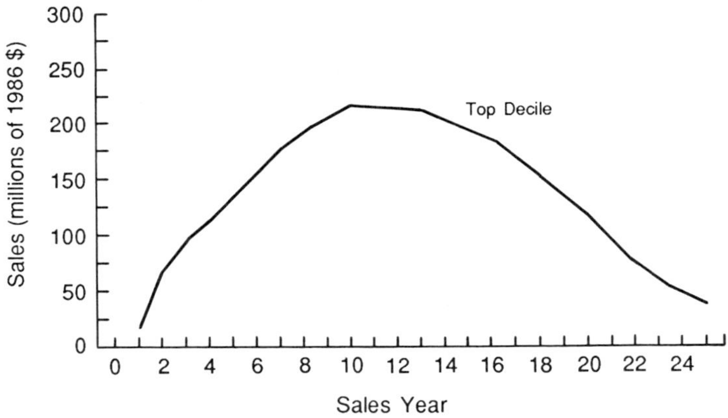


**FIGURE 3.7** Sales profile of 1970-1979 compounds. (Source: Grabowski H, Vernon J. A new look at the returns and risks to pharmaceutical R&D. Management Science, 1990, 36:804-821 [using original data from IMS America Inc.].)

The average R&D cost per new drug introduction is based on Ron Hansen's original research work (10), but his figures are adjusted to take account of the time period of our introductions. Cash flows are estimated from historical sales data and are also projected forward in time using representative life-cycle profiles. We have assembled between one and two decades of data on sales and related variables for each compound in our sample so that we can estimate the returns with some degree of confidence.

Figure 3.7 shows the sales profiles for the top decile of compounds ranked by sales. This is an estimate of dollar sales on a worldwide basis. For this group of drugs, sales peak in year 10 and diminish gradually over an expected economic life of 25 years. Discounted cash flows are estimated from each drug's sales profile, utilizing a number of parameters pertaining to both U.S. and foreign operations.

Some of the key results of this study are as follows:

1. The economic breakeven point occurs 23 years after market introduction for the mean compound.[15]

2. A real annual return of 9 percent is earned by the mean compound.

3. Returns are significantly influenced by the higher drug prices of 1980s.

4. The distribution of returns is highly skewed.

The first two findings are illustrated in Figure 3.8. The cumulative present value curve (gross of R&D outlays) for the mean compound is negative in the early years of product life owing to the large upfront capital investment and to market launch expenditures. It becomes positive by the

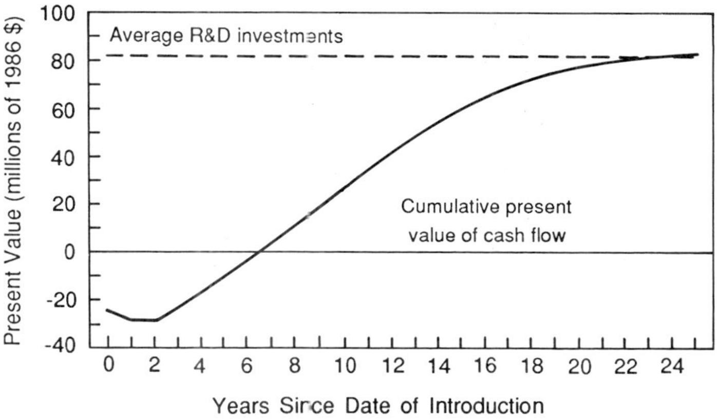


**FIGURE 3.8** Present value of cash flow versus R&D investment. (Source: Grabowski H, Vernon J. A new look at the returns and risks to pharmaceutical R&D. Management Science, 1990, 36:804-821.)

sixth year of market life and achieves equality with the average after-tax R&D investment in year 23 of market life.

The after-tax present value of the mean compound, which is gross of R&D costs, equals $83.5 million by the end of the drug's projected market life. Our estimated after-tax present value of R&D costs for this period is $81 million. Since both series are capitalized at 9 percent, their approximate equality by the end of the projected market life implies that the mean compound earned a real annual return in the neighborhood of 9 percent. This is in line with our estimates of returns for investments of comparable riskiness over this period.[16]

Another major finding is that the higher real drug prices in the 1980s had an important effect on the returns to the 1970s introductions. A sensitivity analysis indicates that if no real price increases had occurred in the 1980s, the cumulative present value of after-tax cash flows for the average drug in Figure 3.8 would have been reduced by 16 percent. Under this scenario, the typical new drug introduction would not have been able to achieve breakeven in economic terms within its expected market life.

Finally, it is important to note that the revenues from new product introductions are highly skewed. This is illustrated in Figure 3.9. This figure shows the distributions of present values of after-tax cash flows by deciles for the sample of 1970s new product introductions. The top decile has an estimated after-tax present value that is several times the average after-tax R&D investment. At the same time, only the top three deciles have present values in excess of average R&D costs.[17] These lower decile products may be important therapeutically and may also contribute economically in terms

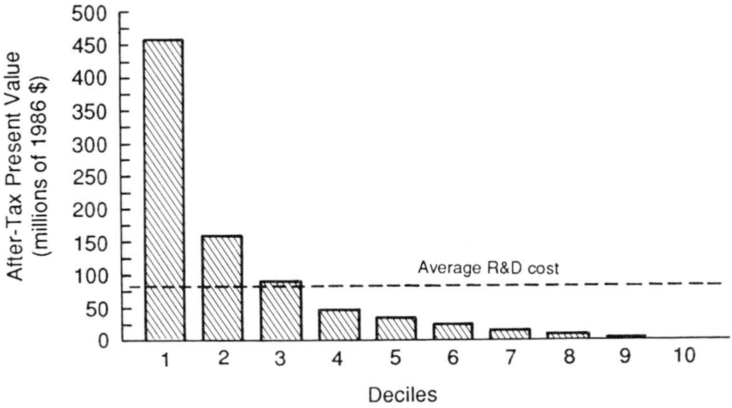


**FIGURE 3.9** Present values by decile. (Source: Grabowski H, Vernon J. A new look at the returns and risks to pharmaceutical R&D. Management Science, 1990, 36:804-821.)

of incremental cash flows. However, these results indicate that from a financial perspective, a firm must occasionally have a drug or two in the top decile of sales if it is to cover the large fixed costs of pharmaceutical R&D (i.e., common discovery costs and the costs of the compounds that fail in the development phase).

## IMPLICATIONS

If we turn now to a consideration of current and future returns to R&D, what insights can we garner from the above analyses? First, current new drug introductions will require, on average, substantially higher real R&D costs than previous introductions. Furthermore, these costs will have to be recovered over shorter product life cycles. New drugs introduced during the 1970s had an average patent life of 15 years and a gradual loss of sales over the assumed market life of 25 years. Current new drugs, whose patents expire in the 1990s or beyond, can expect an effective patent life of 10 to 12 years and a very rapid loss of sales in the post-patent period because of aggressive generic competition. Hence, a firm needs to realize most of its economic return from a new compound within the first 10 to 12 years of market launch. For pharmaceuticals launched during the 1970s, about one-third of their present value came from sales in the period between years 12 and 25. These revenues will have to be earned earlier in the life cycle by current new drug introductions, or imaginative strategies will have to be devised to extend the product life cycle.[18]

On a more optimistic note, the 1990s may see more commercially and therapeutically important innovations than in the past. Hopefully, the growing level of industry R&D investment portends continued success. Preliminary analysis indicates that sales revenues for new drug introductions in the 1980s have been increasing steadily.

In sum, current economic trends will place a greater economic burden on the industry to achieve higher sales levels and more breakthrough products than in the past. This will be true given the present environment of expanding R&D costs, shorter product life cycles, and increased generic competition.

Two other likely implications of this new environment for future pharmaceutical competition are worth mentioning—greater earnings variability and increased concentration of industry sales and assets. Even if the firms in the pharmaceutical industry are successful in developing significant innovations that achieve a healthy return on investment, they still face greater risk and volatility. There are going to be companies, even within a general industry climate of relatively successful research, that will have their mainstay products come off patent, without anything immediately coming out of the R&D pipeline to replace the missing sales. Earnings and, consequently, stock values are likely to fluctuate. There have been many examples of this already. This type of unstable situation will be prevalent in the 1990s and will likely produce an environment of more mergers and acquisitions and thus greater industry consolidation.

## PUBLIC POLICY CONSIDERATIONS

It is clear from the above analyses that R&D costs and returns on investment are highly sensitive to development and regulatory approval time. As we saw earlier, regulatory approval times currently average about 30 months for a new drug introduction. In some of our simulation analyses, we found that a 1-year decrease in regulatory approval times decreases breakeven lifetime by 3 to 4 years (15). This is due primarily to the fact that regulatory delays occur at the beginning of the product life cycle. If regulatory clearance times can be shortened, it would not only increase effective patent life, but firms would also realize their return on investment and subsequent profit at an earlier time. This would enable more drugs to cover their R&D costs and would therefore be a stimulus to further innovation. It is therefore worth examining current regulatory approval and clinical development procedures with an eye to accelerating what has become a very lengthy process. Making this process more efficient could have a high economic and social payoff.

Another factor influencing the returns to R&D is reimbursement policy. Many states now use formularies as criteria for Medicaid drug reimbursement. This process can result in significant time lags beyond those for Food and Drug Administration (FDA) regulatory approval before a drug is eligible for Medicaid reimbursement. Figure 3.10 shows the delays in formulary approval from a study of the Medicaid programs in six states (16). The

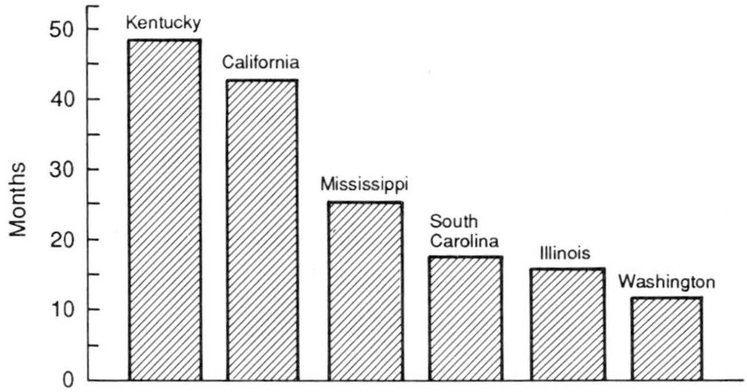


**FIGURE 3.10** Medicaid formulary delays. (Source: Grabowski H. Medicaid patients' access to new drugs. Health Affairs, 1988, 7:102-114.)

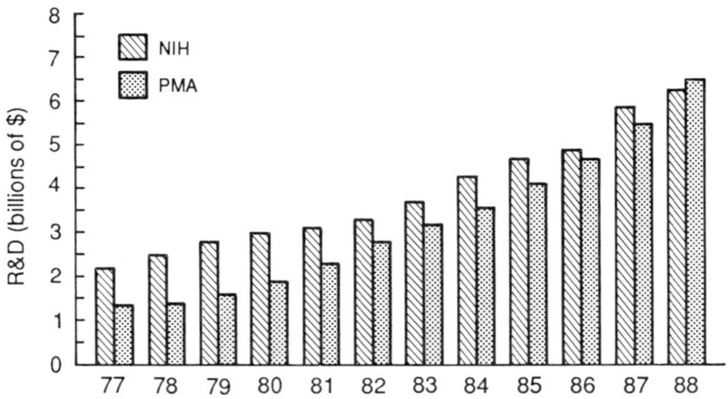


**FIGURE 3.11** R&D expenditures: NIH versus PMA members. (Source: Compiled from original data from NIH and PMA.)

average delays range from 11.6 months in Washington state to over 40 months in Kentucky and California. These delays in giving approval result in lost revenue and lower expected returns to new drug introductions. Furthermore, there was no observed tendency for drugs of greater therapeutic significance to be more available to Medicaid patients in these states.[19]

The use of formularies in state Medicaid programs, and more generally in private sector managed health care settings, appears to be increasing over time (17). This could have a significant negative effect on the incentives for drug innovation in the 1990s. It is therefore appropriate to study whether formularies are really cost beneficial to society and, if so, whether reimbursement and coverage decisions can be made on a more timely basis.[20]

A third policy concern is the slowing rate of public sector funding for biomedical R&D relative to that of the private sector. Publicly funded biomedical research promotes much of the fundamental knowledge on which the private sector search for effective new medicines is based. As discussed earlier, the rate of National Institutes of Health (NIH)-related biomedical R&D expenditures has been slowing. The drug industry has responded to these changes over the past decade by increasing its level of R&D investment. The relative changes over time are illustrated in Figure 3.11. In the late 1970s pharmaceutical industry R&D was about half that of the NIH. By 1988 the expenditures were approximately equal and proceeding on very different growth paths. The slower growth in public expenditures reflects the budget deficit problems of recent years. If left unchecked, this is likely to result in a downward pressure on both private and societal R&D opportunities in the 1990s. A vigorous public sector program in biomedical R&D is necessary to ensure that the search process for new medicines remains highly productive throughout this decade and that the United States remains at the forefront of this effort.

## NOTES

1. The products that meet these sales criteria are as follows: 1970-1974, Keflex and Motrin; 1975-1979, Naprosyn, Tagamet, Mandol, Clinoril, Lopressor, Mefoxin, Ceclor, and Corgard; 1980-1984, Capoten, Carafate, Proventil, Tenormin, Xanax, Cardizem, Feldene, Halcion, Lopid, Procardia, Zantac, and Augmentin.
2. Using sales data through 1988 for this cohort, the eight drugs exceeding $100 million in annual sales are Mevacor, Rocephin, Seldane, Pepcid, Vasotec, Activase, Cipro, and Prozac.
3. The comparable figure on total R&D time in the early 1970s was between 9 and 10 years.
4. To express each year's R&D expenditures in dollars of constant purchasing power (i.e., to correct for inflationary changes), nominal values are divided by the GNP price deflator. The latter provides a representative price index for the goods and services produced for the U.S. economy.
5. The R&D expenditures series in this figure are based on Pharmaceutical Manufacturing Association (PMA) data. They include foreign and domestic R&D outlays of U.S. owned firms, but only the R&D expenditures in this country of foreign-owned firms. The NCE series counts all United States introductions, including those originating in United States and foreign countries. A complete economic analysis of these data would need to make adjustments in these series to make them consistent. In addition, it would need to take account of the lag in time between R&D expenditures and NCE introductions (9).
6. Time costs reflect the fact that a dollar obtained earlier in time is worth more than one obtained later in time, since it can be invested and earn a positive rate of return. In this analysis we used estimates of the opportunity cost of capital for the pharmaceutical industry to capitalize R&D expenditures.
7. There is also an indication of rising real costs from other studies of R&D costs in pharmaceuticals surveyed in our article (9).
8. In addition, drugs based on biotechnology appear to require greater investments than the more traditional chemically based approach, judging from industry

R&D outlays and product successes to date. However, this is a topic that needs further research.

9. The executive of one major pharmaceutical company recently analyzed data from his firm's records relevant to this issue (11). These data indicate that the amount of information and the number of patients required to support an NDA increased significantly in the 1980s. He also mentions the complexity and scope of research and the adoption of expensive new technologies as important factors leading to rising R&D costs.
10. There is also case evidence consistent with this hypothesis. Consider Tagamet, which was quickly followed by Zantac, which in turn was followed more recently by products such as Axid and Pepcid. One also has Capoten, followed quickly by Vasotec, with many other ACE inhibitors now in the pipeline. Contrast that with older products like the diuretics of an earlier era, where there was a much longer period of dominance by the pioneer brands.
11. The full patent term benefits apply to drugs that were not yet in the clinical development stage or not yet patented when the 1984 act was passed.
12. The effect on drugs introduced prior to the 1984 act is not of major significance to this discussion because of a one-time retrospective patent extension provision in the law that applies to a limited group of pre-1984 introductions.
13. The PPPI reflects the annual change in the prices of a market basket of established pharmaceutical products.
14. Neither the PPPI nor the GNP price deflator adequately adjusts for quality changes that occur over time. For sectors with rapid technological advances, such as pharmaceuticals or computers, the comparison of these government-derived indices can be somewhat misleading because these indices would tend to overstate the *relative* degree of price inflation in research-intensive sectors.
15. The economic breakeven point is computed on the basis of capitalized values, using a cost of capital of 9 percent.
16. We estimated that pharmaceuticals had an opportunity cost of capital of 9 percent on the basis of an analysis of financial returns for investments of comparable risks over an extended period (1).
17. Not all the compounds will have R&D costs equal to the average compound, as emphasized in the prior section. However, the available evidence indicates that revenues are much more skewed than R&D costs and the two variables are imperfectly correlated.
18. In order to extend the life cycle for products coming off patent, firms are devoting more effort to new delivery systems and also to over-the-counter status for some pharmaceuticals.
19. In particular, there was no relationship observed in our analysis between a drug's ranking of 1A, 1B, or 1C by the FDA and its availability to Medicaid patients in these six states.
20. A major issue in evaluating the cost effectiveness of formularies is to examine their system-wide effect on health care costs. In particular, formularies may lead to lower costs for the restricted pharmaceuticals, but higher costs elsewhere in the health care system. This result has, in fact, been observed in a number of case studies (18-20).

## REFERENCES


1. Grabowski H, Vernon J. A new look at the returns and risks to pharmaceutical R&D. Management Science 1990;36:804-821.
2. Battelle Human Affairs Research Centers. The Value of Pharmaceuticals: A Study of Selected Conditions to Measure the Contribution of Pharmaceuticals to Health Status BHARC-01390/010, Washington, D.C., March 1990.
3. Goldman L, Cook EF. The decline in ischemic heart disease mortality rates. Annals of Internal Medicine 1984;101:825-883.
4. Weinstein MC, Stason WB. Cost effectiveness of interventions to prevent or treat coronary heart disease. Annual Review of Public Health 1981;2:363-395.
5. Coppinger P, Hass A. International patterns in the availability of important new chemical entities introduced since 1970. Paper presented at the 22nd Annual Drug Information Association Meetings, Washington, D.C., June, 1986.
6. Barral PE. Ten years of results in pharmaceutical research throughout the world (1975-1984), Puteau Cedex France, 1985.
7. Thomas LG. Spare the rod and spoil the industry: a ten nation study of competitive advantage in pharmaceuticals. Paper presented to the International Joseph Schumpeter Society Meetings, Charlottesville, Va., June 1990.
8. Grabowski H. An analysis of U.S. international competitiveness in pharmaceuticals. Managerial and Decision Economics 1989;Special Issue:27-33.
9. DiMasi J, Hansen R, Grabowski H, Lasagna L. The cost of innovation in the pharmaceutical industry. Forthcoming in the Journal of Health Economics, June 1991.
10. Hansen, RW. The pharmaceutical development process: estimates of current development costs and times and the effects of regulatory changes. In RI Chien, ed., Issues in Pharmaceutical Economics, Lexington, Mass.: Lexington Books, 1979, 151-187.
11. FDC Reports The Pink Sheet. Lilly estimates 3,300 person years go into development of successful new molecular entity; current antibiotic project is requiring 10,000 patients 1989, nos. 51 and 52:14.
12. Statman M. The effect of patent expiration on the market position of drugs. In Helms R, ed., Drugs and Health, Washington, D.C.: American Enterprise Institute, 1982.
13. Grabowski H, Vernon J. Brand Loyalty, Entry and Price Competition in Pharmaceuticals After the 1984 Drug Act. Duke University, Department of Economics, Discussion Paper Series, July 1990.
14. Kaitin K, Trimble AG. Implementation of the drug price competition and patent term restoration act of 1984: a progress report. Journal of Clinical Research and Drug Development 1987;1:263-275.
15. Grabowski H, Vernon J. The Regulation of Pharmaceuticals: Balancing the Benefits and Risks. Washington D.C.: American Enterprise Institute, 1983.
16. Grabowski H. Medicaid patients' access to new drugs. Health Affairs 1988; 7:102-114.
17. Gold M, Joffe M, Kennedy TL, Tucker M. Pharmacy benefits in health maintenance organizations. Health Affairs 1989;8:182-190.

18. Smith D, McKeicher P. The elimination of selected drug products from the Michigan Formulary: a case study. Hospital Formulary 1984;19:366.
19. Bloom B, Jacobs J. Cost effects of restricting cost-effective therapy. Medical Care 1985;23:872.
20. Reeder E, Lingle E. An evaluation of the South Carolina medical open formulary system. Reston, Va.: National Pharmaceutical Council, 1988.

# 4

# Public Policy and Access to New Drugs: The Case of Cancer Chemotherapy

LEE MORTENSON

Innovative therapies and their dissemination are threatened by more than just regulatory policies. Restrictive reimbursement policies are slowing the diffusion of new technology and diminishing the quality of care. These restrictions shorten the effective patent life of new products since physicians are blocked from using many of them for all the indications that the scientific literature recommends. This may seriously reduce the rate of return on investment for new drugs to pharmaceutical companies. The case of cancer research and clinical care is illustrative of the broad impact of reimbursement policies on the availability of new therapies.

A broad array of incentives and disincentives influence the actions and rules of the many players involved in health care. They influence the behavior of individual physicians and patients as well as that of institutional providers, payers, pharmaceutical companies, and regulatory bodies. These incentives are changing quite radically, altering the potential for delivery of innovative, quality care.

New and more restrictive reimbursement policies are among the most significant influences in today's health care system. In particular, they produce strong disincentives for the development and diffusion of new technologies. The cancer treatment community is experiencing more than just a temporary lack of payment for new drugs. It is seeing changes in the patterns of care by physicians and other health care providers as well as a shifting of incentives. Physicians who were trained to be innovators (or at least to stay current) now have strong incentives to be the last to adopt new technologies. These changes are pervasive and threaten to influence patient care negatively. This paper will examine cancer chemotherapy to illustrate these points.

## CANCER CARE: A SERIES OF INCREMENTAL INNOVATIONS

In the 1950s and 1960s cancer research and treatment changed radically with the discovery that combination chemotherapy could overcome tumor cell resistance and provide better patient survival than single-drug therapy. In the 1970s and 1980s investigators sought to determine the drug combinations that would be most effective against specific types and stages of cancer. Advances in cancer treatment were incremental, with different chemotherapy combinations being tested, improved, and promoted by a broad spectrum of clinical trials financed by what is now a $2 billion annual research budget (1).

A number of factors altered the patterns of cancer care in the 1970s. President Nixon's approval of the National Cancer Act in 1971 substantially increased the funding of university-based cancer research. This prompted the pharmaceutical industry to begin priority research into oncology and oncology-related drugs. Within a few years a profound change in cancer care occurred, advanced by significant federal and industry funding for cancer research and by the creation of a new profession—medical oncology. The locus and nature of clinical care for cancer patients changed significantly in this period. Surgeons dominated cancer care in the 1950s and 1960s. In the 1970s cancer patients began to be referred to the emerging specialists in medical oncology to receive the innovative therapies they were testing or that had been proven more effective than surgery or radiation therapy alone. Over the past decade medical oncologists have become the primary clinicians for patients with malignancies.

Universities played a key role in the evolution of oncology. They promoted awareness of oncology as a specialty through the creation of cancer centers that were given virtual departmental status. Cancer center directors were provided all the perks of medical school department chairmen. Cancer centers prospered because they had both money and manpower. They had large budgets with substantial basic and clinical research funds from the National Institutes of Health (NIH), pharmaceutical companies and other public and private sources, and significant clinical revenues, as well as the researchers and clinicians needed to staff the clinical trials and treatment units.

Community hospitals responded to the availability of new therapies and newly trained medical oncologists and began offering cancer chemotherapy services. Thus, community hospitals became involved in the rapid dissemination of new technology. A national cancer research machine developed that included community and university hospital components. National cooperative research groups formed, which had both university and community affiliates. These cooperative groups had access to vast numbers of patients eligible to participate in clinical trials. Affiliation with clinical research provided many community oncologists a source of professional prestige and current information helping them to compete for patients.

A culture was created in which clinical cancer research was seen as providing the best therapy for many patients and thus was made broadly available in the community. The development of the Association of Community Cancer Centers (ACCC) was based on the concept that community oncologists and hospitals should emulate university cancer centers and provide programs that included clinical research, use of the latest therapies, interdisciplinary cancer treatment planning, prevention, early detection projects, and public and professional education activities. One interesting effect of this change in "clinical culture" was that clinical research shifted from a university-based to a community-based activity. In the early 1980s about 5 percent of patients in National Cancer Institute (NCI) clinical trials were entered by community physicians; by the end of the 1980s, the community contribution reported by NCI national cooperative group chairmen was in excess of 60 percent.

The system had many factors favoring the rapid dissemination of research findings into clinical practice. Trained oncologists seeking practice opportunities in every community regardless of size provided many of the newest therapies to their patients, often through involvement in national clinical trials sponsored by the NCI. Significant peer and public pressure, fueled by massive media campaigns by the NCI and NIH, stimulated awareness of and desire for the newest cancer therapies. Peer pressure and training that emphasized the ethos of innovation as the standard of care to which oncologists should aspire also promoted rapid adoption of new treatments. In addition, a large number of oncology journals appeared, providing an accessible, widely read forum for the frequent dissemination of new research.

Of course, a variety of other factors affected the use of new technology in oncology. Competition between university and community hospitals increased as many academic centers, recognizing the need for clinical revenues to supplement declining federal support, sought to attract patients with state-of-the-art therapies. During the 1980s, NCI battled with the Food and Drug Administration (FDA) publicly and privately to speed approval of new cancer drugs. The development of the Group C and treatment investigational new drug (IND) categories served as alternate mechanisms to expedite the dissemination of new drugs into clinical use. Over the same period pharmaceutical firms invested in cancer and AIDS research and development (R&D) to develop the therapies of the 1990s. Indeed, both the success of new agents that have added months and years to the lives of cancer patients and the failure to find a "magic bullet" have drawn attention to oncology as an area requiring much additional work. However, the payoff of all of these changes in cancer treatment and care, in terms of patient survival and quality of life, scientific understanding of cancer, and financial return on investment, is far from complete.

## A PERIOD OF TRANSITION: FROM RAPID GROWTH TO STRICT CONTROL

The avidity with which new technologies are adopted has changed over the past decade. There has been a 7-year period of transition from liberal acceptance of innovations to our current situation in which the diffusion of new technologies is most often discouraged. In less than a decade we have moved from an era in which new technologies were heavily promoted to an era in which they are sometimes offered reluctantly and in which patients may have to sue their insurance companies to receive the new types of care. This has been the case for several patients desiring coverage for autologous bone marrow transplantation in the treatment of breast cancer (2).

During the same period, the health care system has changed from an environment in which it was hard for a hospital not to survive financially to one in which many hospitals are closing and many more are concerned about their economic position. Instead of attempting to regulate facilities, government health care policies have focused on setting average prices for diagnoses, letting health care providers figure out how to deliver care within those price constraints. Overall, the use of new technologies, often higher in price than older, less effective technologies, has been constrained and discouraged by changes in the philosophy and implementation of reimbursement systems.

## REIMBURSEMENT POLICIES AND THEIR EFFECT ON THE USE OF NEW TECHNOLOGIES

### The Effects of the Prospective Payment System

First signalled by the Federal Tax Equity and Fiscal Responsibility Act of 1982, changes in federal and private policies on prospective payment have diminished the use of new technology in the community. The diagnosis-related group (DRG) coding system, set up for Medicare's Prospective Payment System (PPS), has significantly changed patterns of care. Studies of changes in the coding of DRGs reveal a number of side effects that strongly discouraged innovation in patient cancer care. For example, patients previously coded by their inpatient disease diagnosis (e.g., lung cancer) and reimbursed as such are often recoded for their chemotherapy admissions not by disease diagnosis but by a single procedure code that is reimbursed at a lower rate. This policy does not take into account that patients with, for example, lung cancer admitted to the hospital for chemotherapy often have complications or require additional care; in reality, they consume more resources than those for uncomplicated intravenous infusion. However, DRG 410—chemotherapy—does not take into account the higher rates of resource use (3). In fact, DRG 410 is the lowest weighted of all the DRGs. Because of the low reimbursement rate and the recategorization of other diagnoses into this DRG, tens of thousands of cancer patients have had their care moved out of the hospital setting. Inpatient treatment that would have been adequately reimbursed under the old Medicare system now receives a lower level of reimbursement. As a consequence, chemotherapy on an inpatient basis quickly became a financial liability, as did inpatient treatment of a number of other cancer diagnoses. More recently, changes in the current procedural terminology (CPT) coding have disallowed payments for oncologists when they give chemotherapy in a hospital outpatient department but not when they administer it in their offices.

The overall results of PPS are dramatic: hospital administrators became wary of investing in additional hospital technology for cancer treatment, patients were treated in either hospital outpatient clinics or physician offices, hospitals rapidly invested in the home health and hospice businesses, freestanding radiation therapy centers sprung up across the country, and some administrators canceled federal research grants.

At the same time, managed care insurance plans began requiring preapproval of treatment regimens, often denying or delaying reimbursement for new technologies or their use for new indications. As private insurers attempted to battle cost shifting by hospitals (i.e., hospitals charging privately insured patients more to make up for the loss of federal revenues), they experienced their own losses and sought to reduce costs. These new costs, although only partially generated by new technologies, were perceived by payers to add to their total bill rather than substitute for outmoded or costly technologies.

### The Dis-Integration of Care

As the payment and coding system drives cancer care providers to deliver care at different locations for different types of cancer patients based upon differing insurance schemes, we are seeing dis-integrated care. This is especially tragic given the original thrust of modern oncology, which emphasizes interdisciplinary care. Cancer patients clearly benefit from coordinated, multimodality therapy involving surgeons, medical and radiation oncologists, and nursing personnel in a progressive management activity. However, instead of a coordinated single site for cancer care, we see patients moving from the hospital to freestanding radiation therapy centers to medical oncologists' offices and back again. I picture cancer patients on MX missile tracks, moving from one location to another, depending on the type of available reimbursement. In one notable case a health maintenance organization (HMO) insisted that a patient go to one hospital for surgery, another for inpatient radiation therapy, a freestanding center for outpatient radiation therapy, and another hospital for chemotherapy. So much for coordinated care.

## Growing Patterns of Denial of Payment

The ACCC recently surveyed oncologists across the nation about the prevalence and nature of reimbursement problems (4). The responses indicated that 90 percent of oncologists are spending more time than they were 3 years ago in attempting to get adequate third-party reimbursement, 90 percent said that they were having more difficulty getting reimbursed by managed care plans than 3 years ago, and 60 percent stated they were experiencing increasing difficulty within the last year receiving payment for previously reimbursed cancer therapies. Sixty percent indicated there had been a decline in reimbursement for cancer therapy over the previous year.

Of those surveyed, 55 percent reported one or more denials by an insurance company because a drug was not being used for its labeled indication, and 40 percent said they were experiencing denials because the insurance company claimed the drug was experimental. Perhaps the most disturbing report was that 23 percent indicated they were receiving some denials because a drug was being used as part of combination chemotherapy. Ninety percent of all cancer therapy, and our most effective therapy, involves a combination of drugs. While the FDA has a mandate to approve combinations of drugs, approval of all the current chemotherapy combinations and their addition to the FDA label would require a herculean effort well beyond the resources of the agency. If insurers deny payment for combination therapy because a drug is not approved for use in combination, we would see 90 percent of all effective chemotherapy disappear (5)!

When physicians were asked how much of their time was going toward trying to get reimbursement for denied claims, they said about half a day a week. In addition, the oncologist's staff was spending about 18 hours a week. This amount of time may be the maximum available to physicians for claims adjudication. Physicians who were interviewed remarked that they cannot afford to spend any more time fighting to get reimbursement.

We are also seeing significant pre-approval denials by HMOs and other insurers of any new drug use outside the standard profile for a particular disease. Physicians are saying the constant battles with insurance companies for the right to use current drugs or biologicals are not worth the costs in their time, in the time of their staffs, and in the delays and denials they are experiencing in reimbursement. In some cases it is simply easier to use older, if less effective, drugs. Indeed, in some cases, given the amount of time that current reimbursement problems require, they simply cannot maintain a practice and battle for the drugs they desire to use.

## Off-Label Use and New Indications

Reimbursement policies over the past 18 to 24 months have become more stringent as insurers have faced increasing competition, a decline in profit margins, and a significant loss of reserves. In order to minimize outlays, payers have established stricter standards for payment. One of these standards is the FDA label—the package insert specifying the clinical indications for which FDA has approved the drug. This is the same set of indications listed in the *Physician's Desk Reference*. Whether the FDA agrees to it or not, the FDA's label has become a standard that some insurance companies are stating is their exclusive standard for what is or is not "experimental." FDA staff members have been quite forthright in saying that they do not expect every legitimate clinical use of a drug to be listed on the label. Indeed, one of their frequently cited bulletins states that FDA recognizes that standard clinical use of any drug will exceed the labeling (6).

The prospect that all off-label uses will be reclassified as "experimental" is frightening to oncologists because 46 percent of all the chemotherapy they now deliver is off label (Figure 4.1). Thus, about half of all cancer care is off-label (5,7). Parenthetically, often physicians did not have the foggiest idea what is or is not on the label. This is not surprising since they are far more used to consulting the medical literature than the package insert drug label. Table 4.1 illustrates the eight top cancer drugs and the percentage of their off-label use in an audit of 165 oncologists' offices. Another way to understand the implications of these findings is to consider the potential number of treatments that could be denied if only the drugs

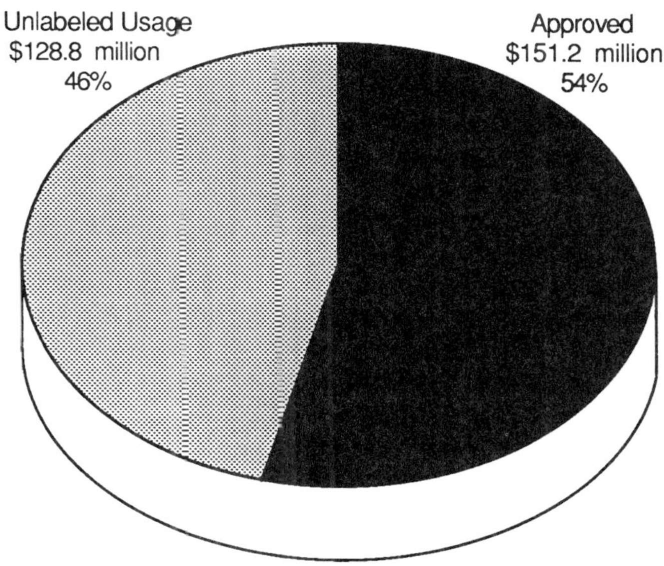


**FIGURE 4.1** Percentage and total annual sales of approved versus unlabeled usage of eight common chemotherapy drugs, 1986. (Note: Dollar amounts are in millions. Source: Association of Community Cancer Centers.)

**TABLE 4.1** Out-of-Package Insert Use for Eight Common Chemotherapy Agents

| Agent | Unlabeled Diagnoses | 1986 Projected Treatment | 1986 Percent Unlabeled Use |
|---|---|---|---|
| Adriamycin | G.I./digestive cancers | 68,182 | |
| | Other malignancies | 35,444 | 15 |
| Cytoxan | G.I./digestive cancers | 5,972 | |
| | Lung cancers | 182,384 | |
| | Other malignancies | 30,200 | 22 |
| Fluorouracil | Lung cancers | 33,310 | |
| | Metastatic adenocarcinoma | 12,584 | |
| | Metastatic prostate cancer | 28,650 | 4 |
| Methotrexate | G.I./digestive cancers | 72,834 | |
| | Ovarian cancers | 18,912 | |
| | Other malignancies | 28,688 | 12 |
| Mutamycin | Rectal cancers | 56,364 | |
| | Lung cancers | 16,782 | |
| | Breast cancers | 82,200 | |
| | Ovarian cancers | 3,420 | |
| | Other malignancies | 12,142 | 84 |
| Oncovin | G.I./digestive cancers | 16,132 | |
| | Breast cancers | 133,348 | |
| | Lung cancers | 151,304 | |
| | Other malignancies | 71,900 | 41 |
| Platinol | G.I./digestive cancers | 7,528 | |
| | Lung cancers | 38,344 | |
| | Metastatic thyroid cancer | 4,336 | |
| | Malignant melanoma | 2,580 | |
| | Metastatic uterine cancer | 3,432 | |
| | Other malignancies | 34,596 | 68 |
| Vepesid | G.I./digestive cancers | 2,540 | |
| | Ovarian cancers | 4,556 | |
| | Brain cancer | 660 | |
| | Hematologic malignancies | 33,722 | 31 |

SOURCE: Association of Community Cancer Centers

that were being used for their FDA labeled indications were reimbursed. In the case of the drug Oncovin, there would be 372,000 denied treatments.

Congress, in the recently repealed National Catastrophic Act, recognized three compendia (the U.S. Pharmacopeia, the AMA's Drug Evaluation, and the National Hospital Formulary) as a more appropriate set of standards for payment. These compendia are means by which scientists and physicians evaluate drugs from information in the scientific literature the FDA cannot use at the time of labeling. As a consequence, the U.S. Pharmacopeia's *Drug Information* volume includes 25 percent more uses for FDA-approved drugs than are listed by the basic FDA label.[1] The compendia's review panels have long served to establish the standard acceptable use of most drugs.

Insurance companies defend their reliance on the FDA label by claiming that they are confused about which current therapies are legitimate. If they cannot count on the FDA label, what can they rely on? Moreover, they add, why not just insist that the other indications also be approved by the FDA? There are several very practical reasons why these notions are impossible to entertain. First, under such a scheme the FDA would face an enormous deluge of supplemental new drug applications (NDAs) if the agency had to review all current therapies that are standard practice and add them to the label. The task would crush the already overworked and understaffed agency. Second, pharmaceutical companies would need to sponsor lengthy and expensive clinical trials required by the FDA for each clinical condition for which the drug is used. Since many of these drugs have now gone generic, there would be no incentive for a pharmaceutical company to sponsor the trials. The costs of multiple trials is so high that many drugs would remain with obsolete labels. Third, there is no congressional mandate for the FDA to review supplemental NDAs in a timely fashion. In addition, since the FDA is currently behind in reviewing regular NDAs, a flood of supplemental NDAs would easily cripple the system. Proposals to undertake massive FDA review of currently accepted therapies might also be unacceptable on the grounds cancer patients would needlessly die while providers waited for the review process to recognize the effectiveness of drugs that have been standard treatment for years.

Oncologists are experiencing repeated payment denials when they use new drugs or use a drug for a new indication. At the minimum they are experiencing lengthy delays before payment, with significant time required to reverse denials. Some oncologists report delays of 18 to 24 months (8). I have been particularly vocal about the policies of some insurance companies which insist that FDA labeling be required for every use before they are willing to pay. The Blue Cross and Blue Shield Association has stated that it will now "consider" payment for cancer chemotherapeutic drugs that are being used in off-labeled indications (9). The Blues have heralded this recent pronouncement as an "advancement" in their policy, but, in fact, it is a significant step backward. They wish to move away from the three compendia that Congress recommended in the Catastrophic Act, perhaps because new indications are being listed too regularly. On the other hand, the Health Insurance Association of America has issued a more enlightened policy recommending that its over 300 member commercial payers recognize the three compendia for determining the legitimate use of drugs (10).

## Payment for Investigational Therapies

For years the medical benefits contracts of nearly all payers, public or private, contained clauses prohibiting reimbursement for patients receiving investigational or experimental therapies. However, this nonpayment clause was not enforced until recently. Improvements in computerized insurance claims systems and increased use of utilization review have allowed payers to more easily identify patients receiving experimental therapies. Following the Health Care Financing Administration's (HCFA's) precedent, other third-party payers have focused on the expensive hospitalizations of patients in clinical trials and denied these claims. Many, if not all, of the charges associated with a clinical trial are being disallowed. The trend toward more expensive new therapies will increase as more potent and potentially toxic agents are being developed to treat unresponsive cancers. This means that experimental and, later, standard therapies will include more intensive and expensive inpatient stays in the hope that life-threatening cancers can be eradicated by heavy-hitting chemotherapy.

Treatment IND and Group C categories, used by Medicare to identify experimental drugs that should receive payment, are designations from which insurers are veering away. They fear that other drugs will be reclassified into one of these two categories, forcing payment. Treatment INDs and Group C drugs are experimental drugs not yet approved by the FDA but which the FDA and NCI regard as a significant improvement over existing therapies. Many of these agents later receive full approval. Interestingly, the HCFA has agreed to pay for these experimental therapies, even though it states that there is a congressional mandate that it cannot pay for experimental therapies.

There has also been a series of recent pronouncements by third-party carriers about research. Before the National Committee to Review Current Procedures for Approval of New Drugs for Cancer and AIDS (the Lasagna Committee), the Health Insurance Association of America announced a new policy that recommended payment for Group C and Treatment IND drugs (10). Representatives stated their belief that, at least in some cases, patients in clinical trials should have their costs reimbursed. However, at the same meeting the Blue Cross and Blue Shield Association stood by its official policy of not paying for Treatment IND or Group C drugs, nor for any experimental therapies (9). The HCFA representatives have said that they are interested in paying for as little as possible, given their interpretation of the original Medicare law, which they believe precludes use for experimental therapies. Therefore, there have been rumors that they would like to stop paying for Group C drugs.

## EFFECTS OF REIMBURSEMENT POLICIES ON INNOVATION

### The Impact of the PPS on Clinical Research

With the institution of the DRG payment system, denials of payment for patient care costs associated with clinical research have grown (8). Denials of payment for patients on research protocols are sufficiently frequent to imperil the entire enterprise of clinical research (11). John W. Yarbro and I expressed concern that new clinical trials were being halted by hospital administrators because their high costs exceeded allowed DRG payments. DRGs are formulated to provide reimbursement for today's average treatment, not the potentially higher costs of experimental treatments given in clinical trials. Thus, major cancer centers have experienced major cost overruns for new therapies that hold significant promise for prolonged survivals and cures but that are far more expensive than today's average treatment (12,13). Hospitals have continued to be involved with cancer research, but some hospital administrators have closed down clinical research programs because they felt reimbursement was inadequate (14-17).

Obviously, we cannot investigate just those technologies that are less costly than current technologies. Efficacy should be our only concern during the research phase. Cost may vary widely when a new technology is in actual use. As many studies have indicated, new technologies are likely to be more expensive in the experimental stage. In addition, a new technology may substitute for less efficacious standard therapies.

A related problem is that the HCFA has a national policy that precludes payment for patients on research-protocols, a policy that has been enforced erratically. While the HCFA states that it is a national policy, it allows local intermediaries to determine if, how, and when it will be enforced. As a byproduct of their own financial problems, more and more of these intermediaries are seeking to determine whether patients are involved in experimental therapies, especially if the patient care costs are higher than expected, so that they can disallow the physician and patient care costs. We have a very interesting national research policy that one can characterize only as schizophrenic. We have one group, NIH, with a congressional mandate to promote research. We have a second group, HCFA, with a congressional mandate not to pay for congressionally mandated NIH clinical research. The implications of such contradictions are serious.

## Decreasing Effective Patent Life

Loss of reimbursement effectively shortens pharmaceutical patent time and lowers return on investment, threatening investment in cancer innovations. Projections of the economic return on a product will be significantly overestimated if the manufacturer assumes (which many do) that the product will be used for all its major indications throughout its patent life. Clearly this does not happen. While one or two indications might be put on the label, it seems unlikely that all will be worthy of full approval-oriented clinical trials. Furthermore, payment for those indications not on the label will be denied by insurers. Thus, total usage will be less than anticipated. Moreover, given the incentives to add every indication to the label, FDA is likely to receive an ever-increasing number of supplemental NDAs. As the stack grows, so will delays in processing and reimbursement. Thus, instead of having the full patent life for all indications, a manufacturer may be faced with three-quarters of the patent life for one indication, half for another, and none for the remaining indications.

Pressures to curtail and constrain payment for new and experimental drugs effectively shorten the patent life and pose an additional long-run obstacle to R&D investment. Certainly, the impact of low use of new products needs to be taken into account in calculating the costs of R&D. This problem will be compounded if the pharmaceutical industry must also spend additional dollars to conduct NDA-quality clinical trials to receive additional labeling for new indications.

Whereas previously research conducted through the national cancer research groups was sufficient to promote widespread use of a cancer drug for a new indication, this will not matter nearly as much as receiving FDA approval for a particular indication. This, I think, will lead to a deluge of NDAs that will pile up at FDA and will cause companies to concentrate on developing pharmaceuticals for those types of cancer with the largest numbers of patients. Research on drugs for less common cancers will come to a virtual halt. Most cancer trials would focus almost exclusively on the Big Four: breast, colon, prostate, and lung cancer.

The drug interferon provides an example of this phenomenon. There are 12 indications for interferon, but the pharmaceutical company went for its initial FDA labeling indication for a rare form of cancer called hairy cell leukemia because of impressive clinical evidence of efficacy for this cancer. Fewer than 500 people are diagnosed with hairy cell leukemia each year. This was a typical strategy: go for approval and initial labeling for a small select patient population for which you have very solid clinical data demonstrating improved efficacy, and then go for other indications or allow the NCI cooperative research groups and the scientific literature to document the additional uses. Unfortunately, insurance companies decided that hairy cell leukemia was the only indication for which they would pay for interferon. This is the first major variance from the customary system of allowing physicians to use drugs for indications off the official label.

The result is history. Pharmaceutical companies that made interferon were amazed at how slowly this widely publicized product was put into use. Even now the use of interferon is well below its reasonable market potential. In response to a question from a pharmaceutical representative about why interferon is not being used more frequently, a leading oncologist said he did not have the time to fight for reimbursement every time he was going to use the drug. The product manager asked about a new service his company had set up to assist in getting payment for denied claims. The physician said it still took significantly more of his and his staff's time every time he prescribed the product and it was unbearable to be disputing claims denials constantly. The pharmaceutical representative remarked, "This is where 75 percent of our use is lost!" In fact, a number of reports indicate that payment still is being denied for the labeled indications of interferon. Obviously, this pharmaceutical manufacturer will not use the smallest indication the next time around.

Moreover, we should expect that treatments for many medium-size or small patient population clinical conditions will never be researched actively. The research and labeling process will be too expensive, and the return on the investment is likely to be small. As drugs enter their generic phase and prices drop quickly, use for new indications that emerge in the literature will not be disseminated very quickly or very widely. Since generic manufacturers are unlikely to see the financial value of research to document additional indications, these new uses for established products will never be labeled by the FDA and therefore will never be reimbursable.

## GROWING DISINCENTIVES TO PROVIDING STATE-OF-THE-ART CARE

Clearly, the incentives have changed. It costs time and money for an oncologist to use the latest therapies, and it costs more time and money to participate in clinical trials. Many oncologists are involved in these clinical trials, despite their complex and time-consuming nature, because they are rewarded by the prestige, satisfaction, and peer recognition that such pursuits provide. Many of them also wish to offer their patients the best, most modern therapy and still believe that research offers the best hope for patients and the future of cancer care.

But the incentives for oncologists to continue doing this are shifting. Now, they have a better chance of surviving economically if they use less effective, older technologies. By eschewing new, potentially controversial practices, oncologists will spend less time on the phone with the insurance company clerk and will be more likely to receive complete and timely reimbursement. Incentives for physicians now dictate waiting 24 to 36 months to use a new therapy—until it has become more accepted by insurers. Furthermore, there are strong incentives to practice in an office setting, separate from the hospital, even though high-quality, multidisciplinary care is more easily available when the medical oncologist practices in the hospital, in close contact with radiation therapists and surgeons. Even rural outreach programs, providing oncology clinics in small communities, are being hit hard by the current reimbursement pressures.

In addition, primary care physicians and general internists are increasingly reluctant to refer cancer patients to specialists because they perceive their job to include gatekeeping—to mitigate against the use of specialists and costly technologies. This strategy often results in the patient missing a therapeutic opportunity for cure because of lack of expertise or delay in time of referral. One really needs to be a specialist to keep up with the literature in this information-intensive, rapidly changing field of oncology. Moreover, oncologists are far more likely to treat a patient aggressively, inducing potentially toxic reactions, to increase the chance of a cure. Thus, whereas some of the older chemotherapeutic regimens may be somewhat effective and somewhat less toxic, there are opportunities for aggressive management with greater potential that a general practitioner is far less likely to know of or be willing to try. There are also significant disincentives for oncologists who wish to participate in clinical trials. Their patients, their hospitals, and even their fees are likely to be denied if a third party audits the records.

Pharmaceutical companies soon will recognize a whole new series of disincentives to support innovation. Reimbursement may effectively shorten patent life. Larger indications are likely to be the first, and perhaps only, subjects of research and use. Since smaller indications are likely to have modest or small paybacks, we may see the pharmaceutical industry disinclined to sponsor the necessary research to obtain FDA labeling for less common types of cancer.

## PROSPECTS FOR THE FUTURE

Given this set of disincentives and dynamics, I predict that the pace of research will slow. The diffusion of new technologies will also slow. Ironically, we are retraining a group of physicians, who were trained during medical school to be innovators, to become technologic laggards. We are giving them direct disincentives to provide innovative care. It is also likely that we will see poorer care delivered as oncology programs become more disaggregated.

Of course, the key question is, "What can be done?" On the pessimistic side, we have less money for research, less money for care, more insurance company financial problems, and no easy solutions. The FDA certainly has explicitly resisted being involved in regulating clinical practice and setting standards for reimbursement. With all its other mandates, it seems unlikely that the FDA would become the authority on effective and appropriate use of medicines. Nor does it desire this role. The schizophrenia in Congress regarding more research but less money together with competition among providers has tended to destroy the maintenance of timely, integrated multidisciplinary care.

That leaves us with only a few things we might consider as possible solutions. First, with public pressure and congressional and state legislation, we could advocate the universal adoption of the three drug compendia as standard references on indications that are acceptable for payment. These compendia are more complete and current than the FDA label. However, legislation citing the three compendia as standard references would be insufficient since, as it is written, the growing numbers of self-insured firms would be exempt. Reaching this group will require enormous public awareness on a series of very complex issues that must be conveyed to corporate leaders or their third-party administrators.

We might try to remedy congressional schizophrenia on the issue and pass legislation that says that the HCFA should pay for the patient care costs associated with NIH and FDA clinical trials. It is also worth educating people that clinical trials offer the best care for current and future patients. It should not be too difficult for people to understand that support for medical innovation is an investment in everyone's health and future.

Lastly, there are unusual solutions that could be tried. For example, the President could sign an international treaty, as one group has suggested, that would recognize statements of drug approval from regulatory bodies in other countries. This would lower the work burden on our own FDA and reduce the duplication of research and evaluation efforts that occur worldwide. Without some of these novel solutions, we are likely to see increasing problems for practitioners, patients, and innovators in the years ahead.

## NOTE

1. K. Johnson, Director of Research, United States Pharmacopeia Drug Information: personal communication, September 1989.

## REFERENCES

1. 1991 Budget Estimate: National Cancer Institute, 1989.
2. Howe RF. Blue Cross ordered to cover treatment. Washington Post, April 19, 1990. A1, C5.
3. Mortenson LE. Cancer Diagnosis Related Groups. Washington, D.C.: Association of Community Cancer Centers, 1985.
4. Mannisto M. Readers report increasing reimbursement constraints: survey. Oncology Issues 1989;4:19-23.
5. Mortenson LE. Audit indicates half of current chemotherapy users lack FDA approval. Journal of Cancer Program Management 1988;3:21-26.

6. Food and Drug Administration. New angina drugs. FDA Bulletin 1982; 12:4-5.
7. Mortenson LE. Audit indicates many users of combination therapy and unlabeled. Journal of Cancer Program Management 1988;3:33.
8. National data show significant denials for the treatment of cancer with alpha interferon. Oncology Issues 1989;4:11-12.
9. Tennenbaum D. Statement of the Blue Cross and Blue Shield Association before the National Committee to Review Current Procedures for Approval of New Drugs for Cancer and AIDS, Washington, D.C., October 25, 1989.
10. Plocher D. Statement of the Health Insurance Association of America before the National Committee to Review Current Procedures for Approval of New Drugs for Cancer and AIDS, Washington, D.C., October 25, 1989.
11. Yarbro JW, Mortenson LE. The need for DRG 471—protection for clinical research. Journal of the American Medical Association 1985;253:684-685.
12. Antman K, Schnipper L, Frei E. The crisis in clinical cancer research: third-party insurance and investigational therapy. New England Journal of Medicine 1988;319:46.
13. Mortenson LE, Young JL, Ney MS. Variations in cancer DRG profit and loss by hospital size and region of the nation. Journal of Cancer Program Management 1988;3:16-19.
14. Davis C. The impact of prospective payment on clinical research progress. Journal of the American Medical Association 1985;253:686-687.
15. Horn SD, Sharkey PD. A study of patients in cancer-related DRG. The Journal of Cancer Program Management 1986;1:8-14.
16. Katterhagen JG, Mortenson LE. Clinical research patients generate significant losses under diagnosis related groups (DRG). Seminars in Oncology 1984; 11:330-331.
17. Lee C, Mortenson, LE. Clinical research patients exceed costs of cancer patients within the same DRG category. Cancer Program Bulletin 1984:6-7.

# 5

# The Impact of Public Policy on Medical Device Innovation: A Case of Polyintervention

SUSAN BARTLETT FOOTE

As a nation, we have come to expect innovation in drugs, devices, and clinical procedures. This chapter examines innovation in the medical device industry. Although traditional models of innovation are relevant to an understanding of the industry, they do not tell the whole story. Public policies have wrapped themselves around the innovative process at virtually every stage. Numerous government institutions intervene in the process to accomplish a variety of public goals. I have coined the term "polyintervention" to describe this type of policy environment.[1] The challenge is to determine how this constellation of policies affects innovation in the medical device industry.

Polyintervention is analogous to polypharmacy—a problem familiar to health care professionals. Polypharmacy can occur when a patient takes a number of prescription drugs. Each may have been prescribed for a legitimate ailment, but over time medications can conflict in purpose, thus producing harmful interactions. Some drug interactions may be unexpected, some may be predictable and tolerable, and some can be fatal. Doctors often will request that patients bring all their medications into the office for a global evaluation of the patient's medication regimen. The rationale for each drug and the appropriateness of each dose can be checked, as well as the presence of unwanted side effects or unanticipated and potentially dangerous interactions. Polyintervention in the arena of medical devices requires similar scrutiny.

Let us pursue the medical analogy by characterizing the medical device industry as the patient. The goal is to assess the effect of the prescriptions, that is, public policies, on innovation in the industry. This paper presents a framework for evaluation of polyintervention in the medical device industry, with a specific focus on the two important prescriptions of government regulation and reimbursement. After an evaluation of current interventions, treatment options will be discussed.

Although drugs, devices, and procedures all are forms of medical technology, the policy environment for each category is very different. The device environment is perhaps the most complex. The primary policy hurdle for drugs is Food and Drug Administration (FDA) regulation. For procedures, there is no federal regulation, but much depends on the payment policies of third parties. Devices are subject to both influences to varying degrees. Although this paper discusses devices only, the framework for policy analysis could be used to evaluate drugs and procedures as well.

## THE ASSESSMENT: PUBLIC POLICIES AND MEDICAL DEVICE INNOVATION

### The Limits of the Traditional Models of Innovation

The medical device industry is subject to many of the same economic forces that affect all highly innovative industries. Device producers must make reasonable profits, ever vigilant of the commercial strategies and technological advances of competitors. A rich scholarly literature on innovation has developed models of the innovative process. Scholars have identified essential stages of innovation, which appear in Figure 5.1 (1).

The process begins with pure science—the systematic study of phenomena to add to the total of human knowledge. The technology stage is directed toward use and includes the process of invention and development. Invention is the first confidence that something should work and the first tests to demonstrate that it does. Development involves a wide range of activities that measure the chances of success of the product. Finally, the market stage includes adoption of the innovation and its diffusion into the stream of commerce. The steps can be distilled into two categories: the early stages affect the research and development (R&D) of innovative products; the later stages seek to influence adoption and diffusion of such products.

Much of the medical device industry can be understood by referring to the traditional innovation literature, which describes the links between these stages of innovation; how technology is transferred from one stage to another; how firms are organized to facilitate the transfer of technology; and other issues of competitiveness, strategy, and profitability. However, this literature takes a limited view of the environment in which innovation occurs. In particular, it often ignores the role of government in the process. Traditional theorists often assume that innovation is driven primarily by the play of free-market forces in the private sector. And, by traditional measurements, the medical device industry is highly innovative. First, the industry reinvests a high percent of sales in R&D (7.5 percent). The total number of patents

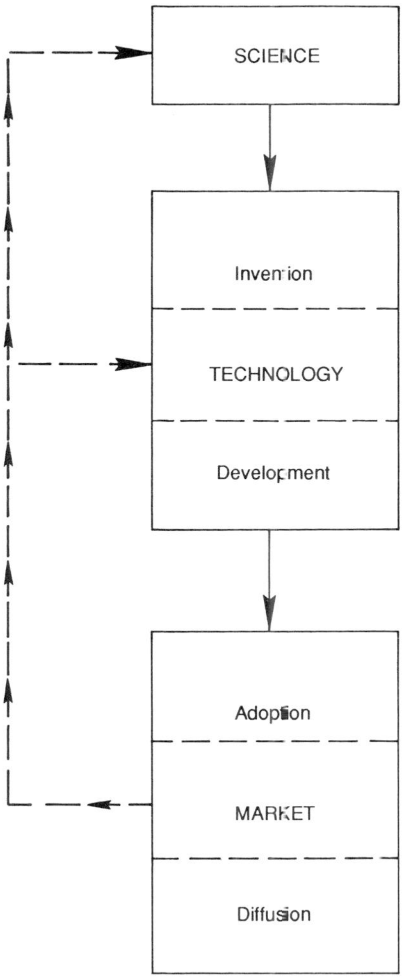


**FIGURE 5.1** The stages of innovation.

issued to innovators has increased, and shipments of medical devices are growing, with sales growth projected into the 1990s (2). But medical device innovation does not take place in a vacuum. Public policies impact the process at every stage. Conventional measures of innovation—industry R&D spending, number of patents issued, annual sales and shipments—may not tell us much about the role and impact of government intervention.

## The Pivotal Role of Public Policy

Public policies such as federal regulation, product liability statutes, reimbursement rules, and government funding for basic research have had a significant impact on the production and diffusion of new medical devices.

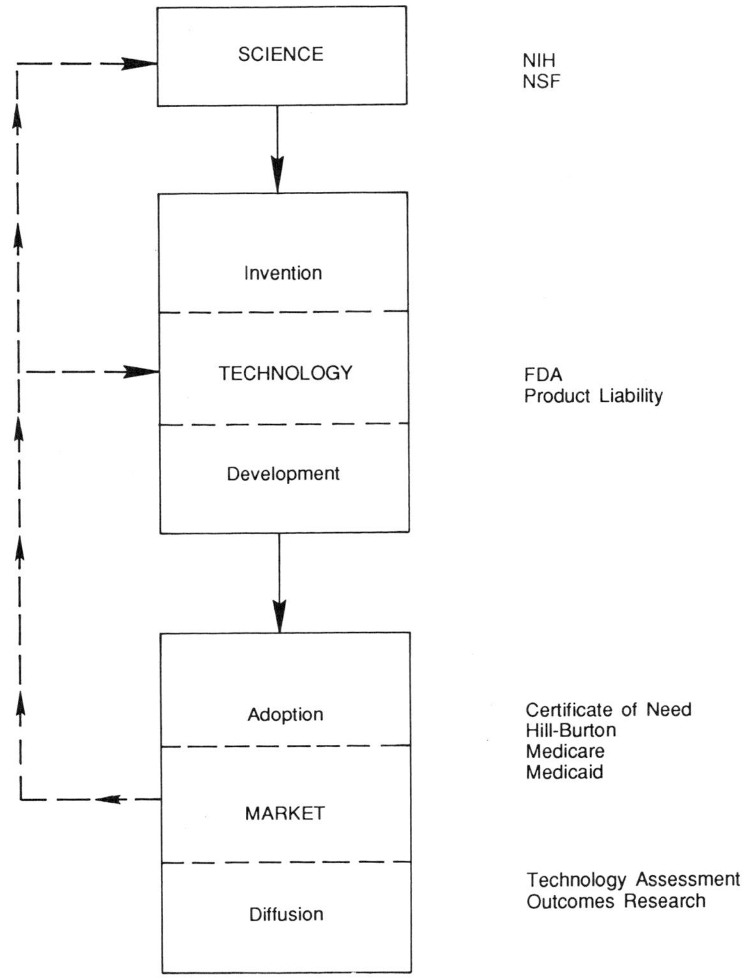


**FIGURE 5.2** The stages of innovation: impact of institutions.

Figure 5.2 notes some of the many federal and state institutions and activities that can affect innovation in the medical device industry.

This chapter emphasizes federal regulation and reimbursement, two of the most important policies that affect medical device producers. As Figure 5.2 illustrates, there are other important policies as well, and reference is made to them throughout. For example, the National Institutes of Health (NIH) funds intramural and extramural projects that deeply affect the quality and quantity of biomedical scientific research. Product development and marketing strategies inevitably weigh the legal product liability environment, and government's actual or proposed interest in technology assessment may affect adoption and diffusion in the marketplace.

Such a diversity of government influences almost guarantees polyintervention, but before turning to an evaluation of this condition, the unique characteristics of the patient—that is, the medical device industry—must be explored.

## THE MEDICAL DEVICE INDUSTRY AS PATIENT

A comprehensive policy analysis is complicated by the diversity of the medical device industry. An estimated 7,000 firms make over 1,700 types of medical products. In contrast, the pharmaceutical industry is composed of considerably fewer large, established companies. The firms within the device industry vary greatly. Some are single-product firms or have a small product line, such as IOPTEX Research, an innovative intraocular lens firm. Others are giants in computers and electronics, such as Hewlett-Packard, known for its sophisticated monitoring equipment, and General Electric, with its eight medical product subsidiaries, some of which are leaders in diagnostic imaging modalities. Still others are billion-dollar pharmaceutical firms with medical product divisions. For example, Pfizer, Inc., one of the world's largest drug firms, has a small laser subsidiary (Pfizer Laser Systems, with 50 employees and 3 products), a subsidiary producing hospital supplies and orthopedic implants (Howmedica), and a dental supply producer (Austenal). Medical device companies draw upon diverse fields of science and technology, and their products range from big-ticket capital equipment, such as lithotripters to crush kidney stones, with price tags over $1 million, to more mundane hospital supplies, such as surgical gloves and syringes. Finally, the commercial markets themselves cover a broad spectrum—from hospitals to physicians' offices, laboratories, and the home.

An assessment of the impact of government policies on device innovation must note that the medical device patient is many patients. Indeed, as we look at public policies, we must understand that the impact of policy prescriptions may vary significantly from segment to segment of this industry. Despite this diversity, however, I will not shy away from efforts to generalize in pursuit of greater understanding of the total policy environment.

## THE EVALUATION: THE IMPACT OF POLYINTERVENTION

How does one analyze the impact of policies on innovation when there is so much diversity and fragmentation, both in products and firms in the private sector and among the public policies? One familiar approach is the case study. A case study examines how a policy or several policies affect the invention, development, adoption, and diffusion of a particular product or procedure. Case studies make up a large portion of the work on medical devices, provide essential data for the analyst (3-5), and can be used to illustrate specific relationships and interactions. This paper takes a different approach. Our analysis starts on the policy side of the equation. The

| | PROMOTE | INHIBIT |
|---|---|---|
| Research and Development | 1. National Institutes of Health (NIH)<br>Space (NASA)<br>Defense (DoD) | 3. FDA regulation<br>Product liability laws |
| Adoption and Diffusion | 2. Construction funds (Hill-Burton)<br>Medicare<br>Medicaid<br>VA + defense medical programs | 4. Certificate of need<br>cost containment<br>technology assessment |

**FIGURE 5.3** Public policies that promote or inhibit innovation.

search is for patterns, relationships, and interactions among the policies. The result is a more systematic examination of the total policy environment.

The matrix in Figure 5.3 aggregates the public policies on two dimensions: (1) whether they affect R&D of devices or adoption and use of devices, thus situating them along the innovation continuum (the vertical axis), and (2) whether the policy goal is to promote or to inhibit innovation (the horizontal axis). The boxes are numbered and represent a rough chronology based on the time when the relevant policies were introduced (6,7). In developing this matrix, several important themes emerge. First, while the thrust of policies in the 1950s and 1960s was to promote innovation, policies initiated in the 1970s and 1980s tended to inhibit them. Second, the matrix illustrates that the number of these policies has built up over time. Although some policies have been modified in response to changing social and political forces, very few are discontinued. New policies are rarely substituted for older ones. Rather, policies accumulate, and the effect is a stratification or layering of them. These policies are intended to influence all stages of the innovation process, and they have different goals. Some promote innovation; others inhibit it. By focusing on these trends in the policy environment, we can begin to see the collective effects on the industry. This global view helps identify the potential for conflict or duplication and leads the way to rational policy reform.

The first box in the matrix focuses on how government policy promotes R&D. The primary vehicle for promotion is support for basic scientific research by NIH (8-10). Much NIH support involves funds for basic science rather than product development and may not have a direct impact on specific device technologies. However, NIH activities, such as the Artificial Heart Program, have targeted specific devices. The National Aeronautics and

Space Administration's (NASA's) R&D programs have also supported technologies with device-related applications, primarily products that rely on electronic monitoring, control, and miniaturization. Research at the Defense Department encouraged work on ultrasound and lasers, technologies with valuable medical applications. The heyday of federal biomedical research support occurred in the 1950s and 1960s. More recently, support for biomedical science has leveled off, while funds for defense-related R&D have expanded (11). In addition, when the federal and state governments began to support health services through Medicare and Medicaid programs, political interest in research support began to wane. Politicians could point to support for health services, which had more immediate and direct benefits to constituents than the less direct and long-range research goals.

Box 2 identifies government promotion of demand for medical devices. The passage of Medicare and Medicaid in 1965 ushered in the biggest boom the medical device market had ever known. Although these programs did not support the device industry directly, they greatly expanded demand for its products. The impact was dramatic. Government programs injected billions of dollars into the medical marketplace every year, financing the adoption of medical technology. As federal spending accounted for an ever-increasing share of health expenditures, the acquisition of capital-intensive medical devices soared. This was especially true in the hospital sector, which was insulated from price in its decision making because payment policies allowed for capital cost pass-through to the federal government. The incentives under federal programs created price insensitivity, leading to near-maximum growth rate. By some estimates the government pays for over 40 percent of all new medical technologies (12). Government policy has changed the face of medical care. For example, capital- and technology-intensive facilities such as intensive care units, composed of sophisticated and expensive life-support and monitoring equipment, were virtually unknown in 1960; by 1984 they comprised 8 percent of all hospital beds. In the 1980s there has been dramatic growth in capital- and technology-intensive diagnostic imaging facilities.

Government policies that promote use of such devices continue. NIH maintains support for basic science—over $7.5 billion in 1990—which provides a strong foundation for some aspects of new device development. However, the amount in constant dollars has leveled off from the heyday of federal support in the 1950s and 1960s. Private spending now accounts for a much larger share of total R&D in the industry (11). Some special programs to promote small innovative businesses, as well as efforts to target product development through NIH, such as the Artificial Heart Program, have continued to support medical device innovation in its early stages.

In contrast, the policies of the late 1970s and the 1980s attempted to constrain the production and use of medical devices. Box 3 includes the two primary inhibitory policies: federal regulation and product liability statutes. Although regulation of food and drugs dates back to the turn of the century, and the FDA had some jurisdiction over medical devices as early as 1938, it was not until 1976 that the FDA acquired extensive pre-market and post-market regulatory authority over medical devices.

The stated goal of the Medical Device Amendments of 1976 was to "provide for the safety and effectiveness of medical devices intended for human use" (13). The law created a three-tiered classification scheme based on the degree of health risk presented by a device. Devices that pose the most significant safety risks are placed in Class III, the most restrictive classification, and must receive pre-marketing approval. Class II devices must meet performance standards, and all devices are subject to the general controls of Class I. These include reporting of defects, plant inspections, and other post-marketing restraints (14). This system acknowledges the variety of medical devices and is quite different from the requirement by the FDA that all new drugs must undergo pre-marketing approval.

FDA's implementation of the complex device law has been controversial. FDA has subjected only a tiny fraction of the thousands of medical devices to pre-marketing approval; the vast majority of devices have entered the marketplace virtually unregulated. Congress regularly has expressed dissatisfaction with the FDA's implementation of the law (15). Recent General Accounting Office (GAO) reports have criticized the FDA for shortcomings in both pre-marketing review and post-marketing surveillance (16,17). For the last several years the subcommittees of the House Committee on Energy and the Environment noted "regulatory gaps and loopholes" and "inadequate agency scrutiny" of new medical devices (18).

In the final hours of the last Congress, new medical device legislation was enacted (19). The new law streamlines the device classification process and expands FDA's authority to track devices, recall defective products, and impose civil penalties on the industry. It also extends reporting requirements to hospitals and other facilities.

Although it had antecedents in early common law rules, there was an expansion of product liability law in the 1970s. The goal of liability law is to compensate injured users for product-related harm and to deter the production of unsafe products. Judgments imposing liability even in the absence of fault on the part of manufacturers (known as strict liability) and huge jury awards, including the imposition of punitive damages, led to proliferation of lawsuits and immense legal uncertainty for innovators (20). This uncertainty is exacerbated by the lack of uniformity in the separate state jurisdictions. Because each state develops its own set of liability policies in its legislature and courts, the legal environment is complex and relatively unpredictable. Many medical devices have been caught up in the liability environment—most notably, intrauterine devices, heart valves, pacemakers, and anesthesia equipment (21,22).

Box 4 identifies government policies that inhibit the adoption and diffusion of medical devices. Although concerns about costs date back almost to the advent of Medicare and Medicaid, cost containment became a central focus in the late 1970s. From 1975 to 1980 the percentage of Gross National Product (GNP) spent on health care rose from 8.4 to 9.2 percent. This is relatively small compared with the post-1980 changes: from 10.7 percent in 1985 to 11.1 percent in 1987, with projections to over 11.5 percent for 1990 (23). Medicare payments to hospitals nearly quadrupled from 1980 to 1987, rising from $25.9 billion to $100 9 billion.

In 1982 Congress passed legislation that began the process of payment reform for Medicare (24). In 1983 the final plan established the Prospective Payment System (PPS), replacing the cost-plus payment rules that allowed providers to set the amounts for reimbursement. Under PPS, payment rates are set in advance, with all procedures placed in 467 separately priced diagnosis-related groups. The hope was that this type of payment system would make expenditures more predictable and hospitals more efficient, ultimately controlling escalating costs.

Although these and other efforts to control costs have not succeeded in reducing overall expenditures, they have had an impact on how and where health care dollars are spent. The incentives of this complicated system have slowed the growth of inpatient hospital costs, although the increase in outpatient costs has outpaced inflation. There is an extensive and growing literature on how PPS has changed resource allocation, locus of care, and health care spending generally (12,24).

As one might expect, PPS also has had an idiosyncratic effect on medical technology. The system appears to discourage big-ticket items, especially those used in hospitals. Under the old rules a portion of capital expenditures could be passed through to the Medicare system—that is, hospitals bore very little of the true costs of the purchased equipment. PPS intends to limit or eliminate this pass-through provision, but that policy has not yet been implemented. When it is, there will be even greater constraints on hospital technology purchases. Given the financial pressures for hospitals to control spending, PPS has been hard on technologies that require costly support systems. Innovations such as angioplasty equipment (lasers and other catheters to unplug arteries) require highly trained specialists and a high-cost hospital setting. To date, PPS applies only to hospitals (Part A of Medicare); thus, there has been an incentive to produce new technologies that can be used outside the hospital, leading to growth of mobile units and freestanding diagnostic and surgical centers.

There is no doubt that efforts to control spending are here to stay. The question is how those efforts will affect the market for medical devices. At the very least, the marketplace will be uncertain as new or additional proposals appear in the challenging process of cost control. Uncertainty alone may deter innovators. At the very most, these efforts, coupled with limits on market size or constraints on profits through payment policies, will dampen innovation in this industry significantly.

Each public policy that has been described, standing alone, has the potential to inhibit innovation in medical devices. However, their effects are exacerbated by polyintervention. Uncertainty is magnified when changes in a number of public policies can alter the incentives to produce or market a product. As we have seen, these policies have different goals, emanate from different agencies and institutions, involve different decision-making processes, and change at different times, generally without consultation or coordination. In addition, stratification of rules and regulations can lead to redundancy, conflicts, and deleterious interactions. Managing this complex environment requires constant, careful, and costly vigilance. Two case studies illustrate the interactions between innovators and the policy environment.

## Case Study: Lithotripsy

The introduction of extracorporeal shock wave lithotripsy (ESWL) in 1984 illustrates dynamic innovation in the private sector and its relationship to public policies (25-28). Kidney stones in the urinary tract (urolithiasis) develop when minerals, primarily calcium and oxalate, form crystals rather than being diluted and passed out of the body. More than 300,000 patients a year, 70 percent of them young to middle-aged males, develop kidney stones. For many, treatment with fluids and painkillers is sufficient; in 20 to 40 percent of cases, however, the stones cause secondary infections, impaired kidney function, or severe pain, warranting more aggressive intervention, but until the past decade, surgery was the only form of medical help in most cases.

The first major advance included percutaneous endoscopic techniques developed in the early 1980s that permitted stone extraction or disintegration and reduced the morbidity associated with conventional surgery. The second major advance was ESWL. Its most exciting feature was that it offered a noninvasive way to treat kidney stones. The first ESWL devices required the patient to be placed in a water bath. After X-ray monitors positioned the patient, intense sound waves were generated by a high-voltage underwater spark. The resultant sound waves disintegrated the stone into fine bits of sand that could easily pass out of the body. Subsequent technological modifications eliminated the need for the water bath, and mobile units were developed. Currently, devices that use optical fibers as conduits for pulses of laser light that fragment stones are in experimental stages of development.

Although ESWL is an exciting innovation, several factors might have led to skepticism about its likely commercial success. The equipment was very expensive (early models cost at least $1.5 million), there was a viable surgical alternative, and the patient base was small and likely to remain so. When the constraints of public policy—regulation and cost containment—are added, the successful adoption of the technology becomes even more doubtful. The device was subject to the highest form of FDA regulation—Class III—requiring pre-marketing approval by the FDA. In addition, payment incentives seemed to be against its rapid adoption by hospitals. Only a small percentage of kidney stone patients are covered by Medicare, and current Medicare payment levels for outpatient ESWL do not adequately cover the costs of the treatment for those patients who receive it.

Despite these barriers, the product took only 13 months to receive FDA approval and then diffused rapidly. There were 200 lithotripters in operation within 2 years of introduction. The market now includes 220 devices and is basically saturated. There are 10 firms in the market. Only four have received FDA approval, and the others have devices in investigational stages. The market leader is Dornier Medical Systems, the first to receive a pre-marketing application (PMA), along with Medstone, Diasonics, Technomed, and Northgate Research.

The next generation of machines is already in development. In a relatively short period there have been major improvements in the original device; other designs, such as the use of laser technology, are on the horizon. There have been a number of creative marketing solutions to the problems of high cost and low patient volume. Entrepreneurs have put together joint ventures with physicians and hospitals that ensure a broad patient base, lower the unit cost of treatment, and amortize the cost of the device. Some freestanding centers have developed symbiotic relationships with providers of other forms of kidney stone treatment so that comprehensive services and alternative treatments to lithotripsy are all available in one center.

What lessons about innovation in the device industry can be learned from this case? How can we explain the success of this expensive, highly regulated technology? One explanation is that truly useful technologies usually succeed despite the barriers placed in their paths. There is, no doubt, truth to this conclusion. However, it may be that the dynamism and creativity of the industry are based on the expectation of enormous market expansion through the application of this technology to patients with gallstones, a much more prevalent clinical condition.

There are 20 million gallstone patients in the United States, with 487,000 gallbladder removals in hospitals every year. The treatment of gallbladder disease is a $5 billion market (23). If lithotripsy could be applied to many of these patients, hospitals could avoid much of the costs associated with surgery, and the firms could compete for this greatly expanded market.

Whether that expansion will occur is now in doubt. Here is where the policy process reenters. In October of 1989, an FDA advisory panel recommended that the agency disapprove the PMAs filed by Dornier Medical Systems and Medstone International for biliary (gallstone) lithotripters. The panel members expressed concern about the safety data in the PMAs. Questions also were raised about the effectiveness of lithotripsy for destroying all gallstones. Preliminary evaluations reveal that only a small percentage of patients with gallstones may benefit from EWSL (29). The delay in marketing approval will allow competitors to catch up with the two leaders, although the ultimate clinical usefulness of biliary lithotripsy remains uncertain. Manufacturers have been slow to gather data because the lack of any third-party reimbursement for this new procedure has limited the number of patients who have received it. In addition, because the drugs used in conjunction with the treatment work slowly, studies often take a long time to complete.

The failure to receive FDA approval may be only a temporary and minor delay. It may also mean that the technology is inappropriate for the proposed use and that the FDA sagely is placing safety concerns ahead of the desires of the innovative firms to rush to market. Or we may be seeing a regulatory failure in that the FDA is inappropriately obstructing the entry of a valuable innovation into the marketplace. FDA's decision delays reimbursement from third-party payers, including Medicare, which will rarely pay for unapproved technologies, further burdening the innovators. Nor does FDA approval necessarily guarantee Medicare coverage of the procedure. The Health Care Financing Administration (HCFA), Medicare's payment authority, makes its own assessments of new technologies for coverage and payment decisions, often independent of FDA findings.

At this point, the lithotripsy industry remains dynamic, highly innovative, and very competitive. However, the market for kidney stone treatment is not expanding. No improved technology to date has left the others outmoded. Whether the expansion for use in gallstone treatment will occur depends upon the public sector—the FDA and third-party payers (primarily Medicare). The marketplace must wait for the policy process to resolve the debate.

## Case Study: Intraocular Lenses

Millions of Americans, particularly the elderly, suffer from eye diseases causing impaired vision. Cataracts, opacities of the lens of the eye, are often a result of degenerative changes in old age or of such diseases as diabetes. The symptoms include gradual loss of vision. The usual treatment is removal of the diseased lens and implantation of an intraocular lens (IOL) (30-34).

Ophthalmology in general, and IOLs in particular, represent one of the largest and most dynamic health care markets. IOLs are regulated by the FDA. Because most of the implant candidates are elderly, the market is strongly tied to Medicare policy as well. The interaction of regulation and reimbursement has the potential for significant impact on the industry.

IOLs are one of the few ophthalmic products that the FDA has placed in

Class III. Regulated since 1979, IOLs are subject to special requirements imposed by Congress and enforced by the FDA. FDA reviews data on safety and efficacy for all Class III devices in the PMA stage. During the experimental stage, Class III products may receive an investigational device exemption (IDE) that allows them to be used in controlled studies while the manufacturer gathers and evaluates data about safety and efficacy. The collection of data supporting a PMA is expensive and time consuming and may represent a significant barrier to entry for innovative firms. For IOLs, however, a special exception was made. Producers could charge for the costs of the implanted lenses in the IDE stage. This exemption facilitated the development of IOLs during the 2 or more years of device testing required in clinical practice.

The vast majority of IOL implants are done on elderly patients with cataracts or other degenerative eye problems. Indeed, the availability of Medicare payment guaranteed a large, stable market for lens removal and IOL implantation. The average cataract patient is 68 years old, so Medicare is virtually the only payer for cataract surgery. The numbers of implants grew rapidly in the 1980s. There were 177,000 implants in 1979 and 888,000 in 1986. In 1987 there were 1.1 million implants in the United States and another 1 million internationally. IOL sales have been estimated at $400 million annually.

Cataract surgery costs the federal government close to $1.5 billion a year. It is the largest item in the Medicare program. During the 1980s, much of the treatment shifted from hospital to outpatient surgery centers or physicians' offices, which are covered under Part B of Medicare. Medicare provides the funding; growth can be attributed to advances in technology, including cataract management, anesthesia, surgical technique, and postoperative care. New IOL technology includes soft lenses that can be implanted with smaller incisions (the one-stitch lens is popular), bifocal implants, and other specialty lenses.

There are a number of companies in the IOL market, ranging from large firms such as Johnson & Johnson (IOLAB), Coopervision (acquired by Alcon/Nestle), and Allergan (purchased by Smith Kline in 1989), to such smaller firms as IOPTEX Research, a small, privately held industry leader, and Chiron Ophthalmics, a subsidiary of Chiron Corporation, a biotechnology firm. There are foreign IOL makers from West Germany, France, Belgium, Israel, and Japan as well.

Changes in Medicare policy as well as FDA regulations present some threats to the market for IOLs. Congress has reduced federal Medicare payments for cataract surgery twice since 1986. HCFA has lowered the amount of payment to physicians for the procedure, which had increased 61 percent in a 3-year period. HCFA also plans to establish a new payment rate for an IOL implanted during the cataract extraction. This proposed rate of $200 would mean an average decrease of at least $100 on the former IOL rate. Some have advocated a tiered rate to accommodate the higher costs of newer specialty lenses. To date, the proposed flat rate of $200 stands.

The FDA has also imposed new requirements for data collection. For new bifocal and multifocal products, 50 implants have to be studied for a year, and then the studies can be expanded to 500 implants. Overall, it is likely to take nearly 4 years before a new lens will receive its pre-market approval. The guidelines have made it difficult for new companies to introduce competitive products.

This longer period for approval is less onerous if the innovator receives at least partial payment for experimental lens implants. Rumors have been circulating that the exemption allowing payment for IOLs under IDEs soon will be rescinded. The HCFA officials say that this will encourage producers to move from the IDE to PMA stage. They assert that companies have been allowing products to languish under IDEs because the exception reduces the economic incentive to go to market. The device is paid for in either case. However, the longer testing requirements and threatened withdrawal of payment during the investigational period probably will have an inordinate impact on newer, less well-capitalized entrants.

The changes in Medicare payment rates and FDA regulations could each have an adverse effect on innovation. The collective impact, however, is likely to be even more significant, particularly on smaller or newer firms. Clearly, cost containment and safety are important considerations. There have been serious concerns about overcharging for the implant procedures and the products as well as suspicions about unnecessary implants and concerns about the safety of some designs. However, it remains to be seen how the pursuit of safety, efficacy, and cost containment will affect innovation in this dynamic segment of the device industry.

## TREATMENT OPTIONS: IMPROVING THE PUBLIC POLICY ENVIRONMENT

The public wants innovations that improve the quality of medical care. Many government policies have promoted innovation, including Medicare payments and federal support for biomedical research. However, the public supports other values, such as safety, in medical technology. Although it is hard medicine to swallow, there is a recognition that cost containment in some form is also necessary. Can we have it all? Probably not. However, an understanding of the policy environment can prevent unnecessary constraints on innovation, particularly those caused by the interaction among the many overlapping policy interventions. The following discussion suggests some ways of approaching policy reform. It is meant to be illustrative and thought provoking; it is beyond the scope of this chapter to map a detailed blueprint of comprehensive change.

## Fine-tuning Individual Policies

As policy makers implement their goals, they should be sensitive to the potential impact on innovation. A brief look at regulation and reimbursement illustrates this point. If proposed reforms make regulation more stringent, as pending bills appear to do, certain precautions are essential. The well-documented drug lag occurs when regulation delays entry of innovative pharmaceuticals onto the market (35). Recent efforts by the FDA to speed up the regulatory process, particularly for drugs for life-threatening conditions such as AIDs and cancer, should be applauded. Similarly, tightening controls on medical devices must never be allowed to create a "device lag." Congress should consider this possibility and make appropriate legislative accommodations, including adequate resources for timely device evaluation. Congress should also consider better use of post-marketing controls to monitor devices in use. These regulations do not delay entry into the market and are less burdensome on innovation than pre-marketing regulation. However, given the intense criticism of FDA's post-marketing surveillance system, Congress is skeptical of FDA's commitment to this form of regulation. The general point to be made is that the FDA should balance the desire for innovation with its goal of promoting safety and efficacy in medical devices. Lessons learned from the pharmaceutical experience should help develop an appropriate balance between safety and innovation.

Policy makers in the business of containing costs should also be sensitive to the value of innovation. Many have expressed concerns about stifling innovation, but because it is an elusive concept to measure and costs are spiraling ever higher, it is easy to overlook this value in pursuit of another. Proposals that support innovation include allowances for scientific advances or pass-throughs for certain new technologies during some designated trial period; automatic temporary approval for coverage by third-party payers of all FDA-approved technology for designated periods of time; and allowances for experimental treatments and technologies in designated centers of excellence to gather information on costs and benefits of innovations. Innovation need not increase costs, although many innovations do, particularly when first introduced. Premature decisions about the value of innovations may inhibit more thoughtful and accurate evaluations that can come only with experience. The system must permit more flexibility in order to protect innovations, particularly when public payment policies to do otherwise influence such a sizeable share of the potential market.

## Understanding Polyintervention

It is also possible to conceptualize reform among the various policies, particularly to control duplication and overlap in the polyinterventionist

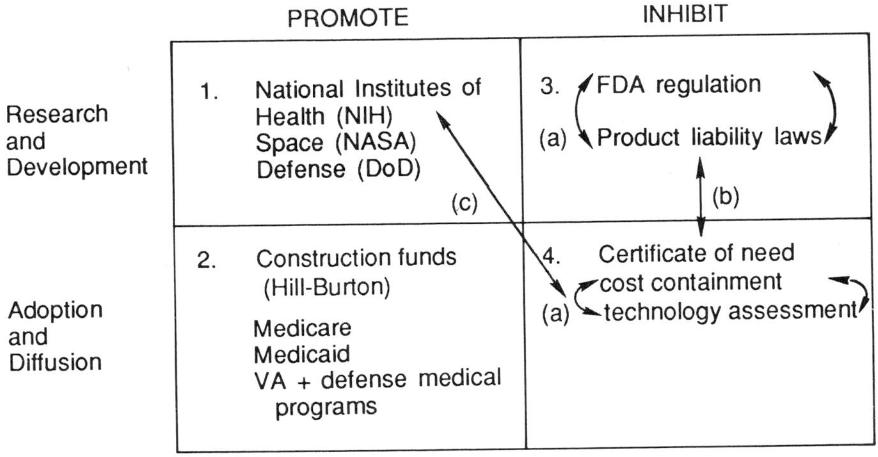


**FIGURE 5.4** Interaction of public policies that affect innovation.

environment. To illustrate, Figure 5.4 takes another view of the policy matrix.

Three types of interactions are denoted by lowercase letters: "a" represents the interactions within boxes, "b" represents interactions between boxes on the vertical axis, and "c" represents interactions across boxes on the horizontal axis. Again, a cautionary note is appropriate. The discussion that follows is meant to highlight how the analysis might proceed; it is not intended to propose comprehensive policy reform.

Policies within one box on the matrix, "a," presumably intend to accomplish similar goals (to inhibit supply or promote demand, for example). In some cases there is policy duplication and overlap, often imposing unnecessary costs and constraints on innovators. I have written a detailed discussion of the interaction between regulation and product liability with suggested proposals for reform (21). The general point of that article can be summarized succinctly. Both regulation and liability are systems designed to promote safety. Although their goals overlap, the institutions that carry out these policies employ vastly different methods and evaluate safety in different ways. The value of device safety can be protected without two elaborate institutions. Reform of the system depends on a wide range of factors. The ultimate goal would be to preserve or improve the pursuit of safe medical devices while eliminating overlapping, inconsistent, and irrational attributes of both systems. Similarly, one can evaluate more rational coordination of policies in box 4—for example, linking technology assessment mechanisms to HCFA's cost controls.

It is also possible to coordinate policies between boxes on the vertical axis, represented by "b." These policies share common goals—to inhibit or to promote innovation—albeit at different stages of the innovative process.

Coordination might make the policy environment more coherent for manufacturers and might reduce costs of federal intervention in the process.

An illustration of such cooperative efforts by the FDA and HCFA is the Cardiac Pacemaker Registry. Following controversies about unnecessary implantation of pacemakers and serious safety violations by some pacemaker companies, the FDA and HCFA proposed a joint rule to establish a registry. Physicians and providers requesting or receiving Medicare payment for implantation or removal of a pacemaker must provide product safety and performance information to the pacemaker registry database. The final rule permits HCFA to deny Medicare payment to providers who fail to submit required information to the registry (36). The FDA's independent jurisdiction extends only to manufacturers, not providers. By developing a cooperative scheme, the FDA can acquire information about pacemaker performance to which providers, not manufacturers, have direct access. The link to payment is a strong incentive for compliance.

It is also important that the two agencies do not duplicate evaluations. There is a current controversy about whether the HCFA should engage in safety evaluations of products that have received FDA approval. Some believe that these efforts are redundant and that safety determinations need to be made only once by one federal agency; FDA approval should be sufficient for other agencies. Others accuse the HCFA of using safety inappropriately as a pretense to deny coverage and reimbursement for medical technologies that it does not want to pay for. Regardless of the merits of these accusations, it is legitimate to question federal duplication of safety evaluations.

It is also possible to coordinate policies even when the goals are very different—that is, promotion of R&D and inhibition of diffusion and adoption. This is represented by "c" on the matrix. For example, NIH, or other sources of federal research money, could be used to promote products that would specifically reduce health care costs. It is legitimate to ask, for example, why NIH promotes artificial heart research when it is unlikely that Medicare would ever be able to pay for the procedure for all the elderly that might want or need it. It is interesting to note that some NIH officials tried to curtail the program in 1988, but Congress prevented that action. The fight to save the program was led by Senator Orrin Hatch (R-Utah), in whose state much of the funded research takes place.

## CONCLUSION

Polyintervention describes an environment in which there are many different policies imposed by a variety of institutions. This multivalent policy environment is rooted in our federal system, with the separation of powers across the branches of the federal government and the existence of 50 sovereign states. Moreover, it is inevitable that important products such as medical devices will attract many levels of scrutiny because of the great social costs and benefits associated with health care.

This diversity and complexity of policies can be frustrating to innovators, particularly if they do not appreciate the intricate history of health policy in the United States. It must not be forgotten that multiple sources of public policy may be beneficial as well. The system permits experimentation and flexibility and prevents the likelihood that one institution or individual could unilaterally ban or promote a technology. Nevertheless, polyintervention is particularly acute for the medical device industry and can have an adverse impact on innovation. While innovation is important, other values, including safety, universal access, and cost controls, cannot be overlooked. Some of these values may compete with innovation. Our ultimate goal should be to reconcile the competing societal values wherever possible. When it is not possible, we must be explicit about the conflicts and make the hard policy choices fairly and rationally. Innovators and patients deserve no less.

## NOTE

1. The medical device industry is not the only one subject to polyinterventionary effects. Others include the oil industry, the automobile industry, and the nuclear power industry. For each, the configuration of public policies varies according to the history of the industry, the values of the public, and the perceived importance of the issues at stake.

## REFERENCES

1. Jewkes J, Sawers D, Sillerman R. The Sources of Innovation. London: Macmillan, 1969.
2. Pollard MR, Persinger GS. Investment in health care innovation. Health Affairs 1987;6:93-106.
3. Rettig R. The politics of organ transplantation: a parable of our time. Journal of Health Politics, Policy and Law 1989;14:191-227.
4. Rettig R. Lessons learned from end stage renal disease experience. In Egdahl RH, Gertman P (eds). Technology and the Quality of Health Care. Germantown, MD: Aspen Systems 1978: 153-174.
5. Plough A. Borrowed Time: Artificial Organs and the Politics of Extending Lives. Philadelphia: Temple University Press, 1986.
6. Foote SB. From crutches to CT scans: business-government relations and medical product innovation. In Post JE (ed). Research in Corporate Social Performance and Policy. Greenwich, Conn.: JAI Press, 1986.
7. Foote SB. Coexistence, conflict, cooperation: public policies toward medical devices. Journal of Health Politics, Policy and Law 1986;11:501-523.
8. Shannon JA. Advancement of medical research—a twenty year view of the role of the National Institutes of Health. Journal of Medical Education, 1967.

9. Harden V. Inventing the NIH: Federal Biomedical Research Policy 1887-1937. Baltimore: Johns Hopkins University Press, 1976.
10. Spingarn N. Heartbeat: The Politics of Health Research. Washington, D.C.: Robert B. Luce, 1976.
11. Brooks HR. National science policy and technology innovation. In: Landau, R, Rosenberg, N (eds). The Positive Sum Strategy. Washington, D.C.: National Academy Press, 1986:119-167.
12. Garrison LP, Wilensky GR. Cost containment and incentives for technology. Health Affairs 1986;summer:46-58.
13. Preamble to MDA Pub. L. no. 94-295, 90 Stat. 539.
14. Foote SB. Loops and loopholes: hazardous device regulation under the 1976 medical device amendments to the Food, Drug and Cosmetic Act. Ecology Law Quarterly 1978;7:101-135.
15. United States House of Representatives, Committee on Energy and Commerce, Subcommittee on Oversight and Investigations. Medical Device Regulation: The FDA's Neglected Child. Washington, D.C.: U.S. Government Printing Office, 1983.
16. General Accounting Office. Medical Devices: The FDA's Implementation of the Medical Device Reporting Regulation. Washington, D.C.: U.S. Government Printing Office, 1989 (GAO/PEMD 89-10).
17. General Accounting Office. Medical Device Recalls: An Overview and Analysis 1983-1988. Washington, D.C.: U.S. Government Printing Office, 1989 (GAO/PEMD 89-15BR).
18. United States House of Representatives, Committee on Energy and Commerce, Subcommittee on Health and Environment. Hearings on health and safety issues related to medical devices. Testimony of the Honorable John D. Dingell. Washington, D.C.: U.S. Government Printing Office, November 6, 1989.
19. Pub. L. no. 101-629, 1990.
20. Mahoney RJ, Littlejohn SE. Innovation on trial: punitive damages v. new products. Science 1989;146:1395-1399.
21. Foote SB. Product liability and medical device regulation: proposal for reform. In: Ekelman K (ed). New Medical Devices: Invention, Development, and Use. Washington, D.C.: National Academy Press, 1988:73-92.
22. Mastroianni L, Donaldson PJ, Kane TT (eds). Developing New Contraceptives: Obstacles and Opportunities. Washington, D.C.: National Academy Press, 1990.
23. Reinhart, UE. Somber clouds on the horizon. Health Week Forecast '88, December 23, 1987.
24. Russell L. Medicare's New Hospital Payment System. Washington, D.C.: The Brookings Institution, 1989.
25. Biomedical Business International, July 15, 1988;11:98-100.
26. Alder HC, Murray ML. Operating characteristics of U.S. lithotripter facilities. In American Hospital Association, Hospital Technology Series Special Report, July 1987.
27. Weiss M, Freiherr G. Romancing the market for stones. Healthweek, December 4, 1989:18-26.
28. Citrin DB. Extracorporeal shock wave lithotripsy. Arthur D. Little Decision Resources, 1987;Sec. 2:85-88.

29. Costly shock wave machines fare poorly on gallstones, disappointing hospitals. Wall Street Journal, February 9, 1990: B1, B6.
30. United States House of Representatives, Committee on Ways and Means. Medicare Reimbursement for Cataract Surgery. Washington, D.C.: U.S. Government Printing Office, 1985;35:99-37.
31. Editorial. The role of the Food and Drug Administration in ophthalmology. Archives of Ophthalmology, August 1986;104:1145-1148.
32. Worthen DM, Boucher JA, Buxton J, Lowther G, Talbott M. Update report on intraocular lenses. In American Academy of Ophthalmology 1981;88:381-385.
33. McCarthy E, Pokras R, Moien M. National trends in lens extraction 1965-1984. Journal of the American Optometric Association 1988;59:31-35.
34. Biomedical Business International, May 16, 1989;12:69-72.
35. Kaitin K, Mattison N, Northington F. The drug lag: an update of new drug introduction in the United States and the United Kingdom, 1977 through 1987. Clinical Pharmacology and Therapeutics 1989;46:121-138.
36. Federal Register. Vol. 52, No. 141, July 23, 1987, 27756-27765.

# 6

# The Dynamics of Medical Device Innovation: An Innovator's Perspective

ALAN KAHN

Innovation in the medical device industry is very different from that in the pharmaceutical industry. There are major differences in who does the research and development (R&D), the nature of that R&D, and the public policies that affect it. For example, if we compare the device industry to the drug industry, we see smaller companies taking the lead, a more fluid innovation process, and looser regulations on medical devices. This chapter addresses the major differences between device and drug innovation and their implications for public policy.

## PATENTS

The significance of patents as incentives to innovation is influenced by the different natures of drug and device R&D. Drug patents tend to be more useful, for it is very difficult to design a drug that simulates all the efficacies and side effects of another drug. A further difference between patents in the two industries lies in which aspects of the innovation lead to patentable claims. An example in the drug industry is the use of antihistamines to treat allergies. The basic principle of using antihistamines is not patentable, but the specific drugs are. In the device industry it is often just the opposite. The basic principle can be patentable, but specific devices usually are not. Generally speaking, it is possible to design a medical device for a specific application in a number of different ways. The innovation often lies in the underlying principle being used in the particular application. For example, the concept of pulse oximetry was patentable, although specific implementations of the idea were simply design exercises and did not provide patentable material. In instrumentation products, patenting the design of the instrument itself is a futile exercise because it is not difficult to design another instrument in a different way that performs in exactly the same manner. An instance illustrating this difference took place when we started a medical device division in Hoffmann-LaRoche, a drug company. The Roche attorneys insisted on patenting the circuit diagrams of the equipment because of their similarity to the structural formulas for drugs. This, however, was a false analogy.

Patents appear to be of relatively less importance in many segments of the device industry. Once a product is introduced, competition usually follows quickly. However, patents play other roles in the process of innovation. Until the recent changes in the income tax laws, the patent application played a significant role in determining whether royalties paid to the inventor would be treated as ordinary income or capital gains. The simple fact that a patent had been applied for signaled the Internal Revenue Service (IRS) to treat the subsequent royalties as capital gains. Another situation in which the patent plays a role surfaces when a small company needs investment capital. Potential investors usually are concerned with whether the new development is covered by one or more patents. The patents can be trivial, but the investors feel reassured.

## WHO DOES R&D?

The development of new medical devices generally takes place in small, entrepreneurial companies. Once an introduction is made, larger corporations tend to buy up the smaller innovative companies and their products, or the corporations may introduce their own version. There are several reasons why small companies take the lead in innovation in the medical device industry while large companies are dominant in the drug industry. The drug industry is relatively more restrained by its risks and regulations. That restraint is not nearly as important in the device industry, on the part of either the regulators or the technology. A small company can bring a new product to market in a fraction of the time required by a large company. In the small company the innovator usually is also a key decision maker and can take risks based upon his first-hand knowledge of the technology and its applications. In a larger organization the decision makers often are several management layers removed from the innovators and cannot feel the reassurance provided by direct involvement in the process. Without this involvement these decision makers do not have the tools to assess the risks and tend to avoid the risks altogether. On the other hand, in the past, large corporations have tended to set up expensive research divisions in order to generate innovation. Researchers within these divisions find an environment permitting creativity but without any of the urgency of the entrepreneur to develop applications in a timely manner. Many of the large corporations have become disenchanted with this kind of R&D and have found it much more profitable to purchase innovations developed by the small companies.

Another difference between the two industries that helps explain why small device companies lead in innovation is that the market for new devices is not always well defined. This is illustrated by the history of the cardiac pacemaker. When this device was first introduced, a market survey revealed a total of about 1,000 patients around the world who needed the device, about 500 of them in the United States. This tiny market was of no interest to major corporations. A small company—Medtronic, Incorporated—with only $2 million in annual sales, agreed with the inventors to develop and market this product for this orphan device market. As we now know, the market turns out to be in the order of 200,000 units a year in the United States alone. Arnold Beckman tells a similar story of his experiences in introducing the pH meter. The estimated market size was so small that is was only of interest to the tiny company that Beckman organized. The market turned out to be many orders of magnitude greater than that estimate and was the stimulus for the establishment of Beckman Instruments, Incorporated. The point of these examples is that an evaluation of the market before a device is diffused into clinical practice can grossly undervalue the technology to a degree that only very small companies would find the prospects interesting.

These differences help explain why, in certain segments of the market, large medical device companies generally are not innovators in the early development of medical devices. Innovations such as pacemakers customarily are developed and introduced by small companies. Such innovative devices are invented or optimized by individuals and are not the result of the really intensive team efforts that take place in the large drug companies. The exceptions to this small-company rule lie in a few selected areas, such as medical imaging, where devices are complex and costly. The cost of developing these large, expensive systems is outside the level investors and innovators are comfortable with. These kinds of systems tend to be developed and introduced by the larger companies.

## FINANCING OF INNOVATION

Lest one get overenthusiastic about the opportunities of entrepreneuring, it should be pointed out that a majority of the small entrepreneuring companies end up as business failures. The reasons can too costly a technology, a lack of marketing ability, too small a market, or undercapitalization. Entrepreneuring in this area is becoming more difficult as the regulatory environment becomes more demanding and venture capital becomes more limited. The investment community is not as enchanted with the medical device industry as it once was. New technology is no longer welcomed in the hospitals unless cost effectiveness can be demonstrated early in the product cycle.

In many areas of the device industry, public sector financing has played a relatively small role in supporting the R&D process leading to device innovation. A major portion of these new developments is pursued in the small business environment where public sector support usually is not readily available. Although public support does finance basic research in universities and clinics, these are not where the invention and reductions to practice generally take place. Financing of these companies is accomplished through investment capital from individuals and venture capital firms. In a few instances the federal government has been instrumental in providing support to small businesses for such technologies as the artificial heart, but these are exceptions to the rule.

One source of public funds available to small companies is the Small Business Innovation Research (SBIR) program. This program was instituted as a result of a public law requiring that branches of the federal government providing research grants and contracts must allocate a certain proportion of this budget to small business. As a result, SBIR grants are available from the National Institutes of Health (NIH), Department of Defense, and other agencies. A typical SBIR grant is allocated in several phases. The Phase I award, typically around $50,000, supports an exploratory phase of about 6 months' duration in which feasibility of a technology is assessed and established. Upon successful completion of that phase, an application is made for a Phase II grant, which is typically in the order of several hundred thousand dollars. It is the purpose of this phase to develop the application to a point where a product or service will result. The timing on these phases is such that a rather long period of 6 months to a year or more separates the completion of Phase I and the initiation of Phase II support. While the SBIR program has been responsible for stimulating some new developments, it is generally unsatisfactory for several reasons. First, some granting agencies require so much administrative and reporting procedures that the cost to a small company does not justify the $50,000 awarded in Phase I. In addition, the time period between the funding of Phase I and the funding of Phase II is often so long that a small company could not possibly wait that period to continue with its product development efforts lest it run out of funds in the interim. As a result, other moneys are used to continue the development begun in Phase I. No company can consider waiting for a year to continue its development projects, especially a small company operating on limited capital.

## REGULATORY DIFFERENCES

Drugs and devices are regulated differently because the two fields are so disparate. Traditionally, the technologies associated with drug products have been based on chemistry and biochemistry, and the Food and Drug

Administration (FDA) has been able to develop a significant expertise in these technologies. In contrast, devices are based on a wide variety of technologies, such as biomaterials, electronics, optics, mechanics, fluidics, and so on. Even our largest corporations embrace only a portion of these technologies, and it is not feasible for the FDA to become expert in all of them. This factor makes it far more difficult to assess and regulate medical devices. This concern is balanced by the fact that most medical devices do not have the potential for profoundly influencing body processes and generating potentially damaging short-term and long-term effects. As a result of these two factors, many medical device technologies are subject to less restrictive regulations than are drug products. In fact, the FDA has made use of the 510(k) provision, originally intended for allowing continued marketing grandfather devices at the time the current law was passed, to maintain surveillance of the introduction and market penetration of medical device products that did not perform functions that could be potentially dangerous. Recently, the use of the 510(k) provision for regulation of medical devices has been curtailed significantly.

An important difference between drugs and devices lies in the ability and propensity to make changes in the device product during clinical evaluation and after it has been marketed. A drug product is usually in its completed form prior to marketing and is described by its chemical formula, and the dosage form remains stable for most of the life of the product. In contrast, devices constantly are being modified to remove defects, improve performance, and add features throughout the product life. These changes occur frequently and are driven by competition among the manufacturers in order to offer the best product performance and features. Prior to the advent of the microprocessor, these changes were implemented through hardware redesign. These types of changes are expensive and were done relatively infrequently. Many of today's device products are operated by microprocessors, and most of their functions are dictated through the internal software. Software changes are very easy to make and to test. As a consequence, product changes are now very frequent and almost impossible to track by a regulatory agency. These changes are especially frequent during the first 6 months after the introduction of a product, during which time the broader clinical exposure exposes minor defects and limitations. The FDA has initiated a program to gain better regulatory control of device software.

Another important difference between medical devices and drugs lies in the product life. Once introduced into the market, a drug will enjoy a product life of at least 5 years; indeed, some drugs have been around for 50 years or longer. The continuous product changes that devices undergo eventually render the product obsolete, often within 2 years or less. Device manufacturers must bring products to market more rapidly than drug manufacturers in order to keep up with this high rate of product obsolescence.

## THE ROLE OF LIABILITY

All of the players in the delivery of health care are subject to significant financial liability. Device manufacturers are at somewhat less risk than drug manufacturers, since many of the products are less apt to affect the body functions of patients. The concern about liability on the part of the physicians and hospitals has had a significant effect on the medical device industry. Many medical devices provide the physician and the hospital with the means for testing and monitoring patients in order to decrease the likelihood of morbidity and mortality. As the concern about liability and malpractice has increased, new laboratory tests and monitoring procedures have been welcomed as a safety net by physicians and hospitals. The risk of litigation has played a significant role in the direction of the development of new technologies in medical devices in recent years. Monitoring patients provides the clinical staff with documentation that provides evidence for the quality of care provided. Since the burden of proof of adequate care falls on the health providers in malpractice cases, this documentation is helpful.

A specific example of this trend can be seen in the increasing use of various monitoring technologies by the anesthesiologist. It is, of course, most important to have a record of the patient's status during periods when critical changes are taking place and emergency situations arise. However, it is just during these periods when the anesthesiologist is busy with the patient and has no time to generate records of the patient's status. Automated systems for performing measurements and collecting information fill this gap and provide substantiation of the management of the patient. This is of particular importance to the anesthesiologist, because in the absence of proof of competent administration of care, awards are usually given to the plaintiff.

## REIMBURSEMENT

Another factor that influences the direction and energy applied to innovation in a particular technology is the likelihood that the providers of care can get reimbursed for the application of the technology. This is a particularly difficult area for device manufacturers because the third-party payers will not directly reimburse the new technology until it has proven itself in the marketplace. Since new technologies often take several years to prove themselves and, in addition, may prove themselves in an area of care not originally intended, theoretically new innovative technologies will not be reimbursed. However, it is common practice to code these new technologies within the framework of existing codes in order to generate reimbursement during the early periods of introduction. Eventually, the payers will establish a new code for a new, successful technology. An innovation novel enough to be difficult to fit within the existing codes has an especially difficult acceptance by the health care system. An ideal new device product will be reimbursable within existing codes, decrease the likelihood of malpractice suits against the health care provider, decrease the cost of managing the patient, and, perhaps, improve the quality of care.

## CONCLUSIONS

Although most of the attention of this publication is directed toward the pharmaceutical industry, these discussions seem incomplete without considering the medical device industry as well. The concerns of the device industry are different from those of the pharmaceutical industry in the areas of R&D, patents, regulation, liability, and reimbursement. In particular, policy makers will need to take into account differences between drug and device innovation, as well as the importance of the small business community in generating devices.

## SELECTIVE BIBLIOGRAPHY

1. Ekelman K (ed). New Medical Devices: Innovation, Development, and Use. Washington, D.C.: National Academy Press, 1988.
2. Kessler DA, Pape SM, Sundwall DN. The Federal Regulation of Medical Devices. New England Journal of Medicine 1987;317:357-365.
3. Roberts EB. Technological Innovation and Medical Device Innovation. In Ekelman K (ed). New Medical Devices: Innovation, Development, and Use. Washington, D.C.: National Academy Press, 1988.

# 7

# Reimbursement and the Dynamics of Surgical Procedure Innovation

SOPHIA W. CHANG* and HAROLD S. LUFT

While the economic environment has important effects on medical practice, we focus here on a single part of the picture: the interaction between payment and the diffusion of surgical procedure innovation. In doing so, we make the distinction between reimbursement (i.e., the repayment of costs incurred) and payment (i.e., compensation that may be more or less than incurred costs). The former entails few cost-saving incentives, whereas the latter may have powerful cost containment effects. It is also important to distinguish surgical procedure innovation—the development of a new procedure—from its application and dissemination. Although we discuss the former, most of our focus will be on the latter. We will also attempt to contrast the characteristics of surgical procedure innovation with those of pharmaceuticals and medical devices.

Surgical innovation often has a significant relationship with new drugs and devices. For example, the expansion of transplantation surgery was facilitated by the development of better chronic immunosuppressive drugs (e.g., cyclosporine). New devices, such as fiberoptic endoscopes, have made possible a wide range of surgical procedures, from arthroscopies to laser atherectomies. The development of total hip replacement relied on such new materials as methylmethacrylate, a plastic cementing mixture allowing better fixation of the prosthetic hip joint. The complexities of these relationships are deep and far reaching. In a study by Comroe and Dripps (1),

* Sophia W. Chang, M.D., was supported by a NCHSR National Research Service Award HS0026-04 postdoctoral fellowship.

the development of cardiac surgery was traced to a series of 25 "essential bodies of knowledge" that enabled Gibbons to perform the first successful open-heart surgery with bypass. The gamut of technologies ranged from antibiotics to electrocardiography to pump oxygenators. Thus, if new payment systems affect innovation in the drug and device arenas, there may be indirect and unanticipated effects on surgical innovation.

Unlike pharmaceuticals and devices, which are often developed by industry with specific marketing goals or strategies, surgical procedure development occurs in a more diffuse and less "market-oriented" fashion. Similarly, the entry of drugs and devices into the market is regulated heavily by formal and often costly and time-consuming procedures. Surgical procedure development and diffusion are subject to little or no regulation and appear to be more influenced by payment strategies.

Our discussion focuses on how payment affects the development and diffusion of new surgical procedures and secondarily on how these innovations affect medical costs. To understand this dynamic better, we first discuss different types of surgical procedure innovation. Still focusing on the innovative process, we look at how procedures are developed and the incentives inherent in their development. We then examine the diffusion process and discuss how procedures are paid for, with an emphasis on payer recognition and coding practices. This is followed by a consideration of the interaction between competition and diffusion of surgical innovations. Finally, we speculate about the possible effects of the new payment environment on innovation in surgery.

## DEVELOPMENT OF NEW SURGICAL PROCEDURES

### Types of New Surgical Procedures

Surgical procedures generally are based on a "vocabulary" of basic surgical techniques. For the individual surgeon, mastering surgical procedures requires facility with an array of techniques that, when combined in different ways and in different settings, result in different operative procedures. Some procedures, such as appendectomies, remain relatively simple and have undergone little or no change in the past decade. There is little variation in how the procedure is performed throughout the United States. Greater expertise, as well as greater support from a team of providers, is required to execute the larger array of techniques that comprise more complex surgical procedures. For example, whereas simple procedures such as suturing of lacerations can be performed by any surgeon, such operations as cholecystectomies require the help of anesthesiologists and nurses, and cardiac surgery requires specialized nurses, anesthesiologists, pump technicians, and intensive care specialists.

New procedures generally fall into one of two categories: new themes and variations on a theme. New themes are considered to be a leap in technological innovation. They result from the invention of new techniques or application of existing techniques in a new context. One example is coronary artery bypass surgery, which when first performed using saphenous vein grafts was a new theme; a related technique using the internal mammary artery can be considered a variation on a theme. Because the complex development of new technologies relies on previous discovery, the distinction between new themes and variations can be blurred somewhat. However, costly changes are more likely to be considered new, whereas less costly changes are usually considered to be variations.

The process of surgical innovation includes a broad spectrum of activities that range from relatively simple changes, such as using a new type of suture material, to modifying a surgical technique and to developing a transplantation program. Although some changes require little or no financial investment and might actually decrease costs (by improving outcome, decreasing hospital stay, or decreasing anesthesia time), others require significant investment. Thus, procedures can be classified as either "little-ticket" or "big-ticket" items. Big-ticket technologies usually require institutional (rather than individual professional) support for development and adoption. A liver transplantation service, for example, requires a team of specialists, both medical and surgical (2). Such expensive big-ticket technologies often are used when a disease is life threatening and there is no effective alternative treatment. Some big-ticket procedures, however, can also be cost saving in the long run. In the case of end-stage renal disease, for instance, the costs of renal transplantation generally are less than those of chronic hemodialysis, especially when social costs are included (3).

Not all new theme procedures are big-ticket technologies. Certain new procedures, such as the arterial switch procedure for repair of congenital transposition of the great vessels, require no new devices or personnel. This particular procedure does not increase operative time and has better patient outcomes than its previously used alternative (4). Similarly, biliary lithotripsy, a noninvasive therapy for gallstones, is being introduced at centers that already own renal lithotripsy units (5). Although some changes in adjunct equipment are required, most renal lithotripters are adapted easily to biliary treatment and allow their more efficient utilization.

Variations are often little-ticket technologies that may increase surgeon efficiency and/or improve patient outcome. Different vagotomy techniques for treatment of peptic ulcer disease, which ligate specific portions of the vagus nerve, can be considered variations. Selective approaches are more time consuming than truncal vagotomy, and there is mixed evidence concerning their relative efficacy (6). Blood cardioplegia, which adds some of the patient's own blood to the "paralyzing" solution used during open-heart surgery, is an example of a variation that improves patient outcome without incurring much expense (7).

### The Development Process for Surgical Procedures

New theme procedures generally begin with an experimental phase that is carried out primarily at academic centers with animal models. Research at this stage focuses on the new procedure's technical feasibility and evidence of efficacy without undue risk. Once these surgical procedures are improved or perfected, they are performed on selected human subjects who might benefit from them. Results of animal and human surgery are reported in peer-review journals and/or at professional meetings, usually as case reports. Other forms of peer review occur internally through institutional review boards (required prior to human experimentation) and at morbidity and mortality conferences, where individual cases with poor or unexpected outcomes are discussed among colleagues.

At this stage of development, with relatively small numbers of patients involved, it is possible to detect only large differences in outcomes. Furthermore, ethical precepts generally preclude the use of sham operations or the randomization of patients to a new procedure unless there is some evidence that it is at least as good as the standard treatment. The acceptance of a procedure as standard or nonexperimental occurs more readily when the disease is life threatening and there is no effective treatment. The first cardiac transplant at Stanford, for example, did not undergo institutional review for clinical experiments. Shumway maintained that he was trying to save someone's life—not conduct an experiment (8). Indeed, in such critical situations it is difficult for surgeons (and the public) to withhold experimental therapies.

In the past, once a series of patients underwent a procedure with some perception of "good" outcome, the procedure became accepted as standard practice. Clinical acceptance of a procedure generally occurred informally through its adoption by colleagues. In the case of coronary artery bypass graft (CABG) surgery, the procedure was first reported in 1969 and disseminated rapidly. By 1973 to 1974, before publication of any clinical trial results, it had become the established treatment for angina pectoris with known two- or three-vessel disease (9). In many cases major innovations have become accepted and paid for without formal evaluation, as is required for new drugs and devices. Some of these practices, such as gastric freezing for the treatment of peptic ulcer disease and gastric balloon placement for the treatment of morbid obesity, have since been shown to be ineffective or even potentially dangerous (10,11). The importance of surgical procedure evaluations should not be underestimated. For example, the $9 million federally funded, randomized extracranial/intracranial arterial bypass trial found that a procedure deemed efficacious and widely practiced for 16 years actually had worse outcomes than nonsurgical treatment. It is estimated that the study saved the United States $11 million in charges for professional and hospital services not provided to those patients randomized to medical care during the trial (12). The potential reductions in cost and morbidity of applying these results to the general population are far greater.

Recently, increased concern and emphasis on more rigorous methods of technology assessment has helped preclude the rapid diffusion of certain procedures based only on case reporting. A recent case in point is that of neurosurgical transplantation of adrenal medulla tissue into the brain (caudate) of patients with severe Parkinsonism. The inability of investigators to replicate the early reported results essentially has stopped this practice (13). On the other hand, there are occasional egregious examples of highly questionable procedures being undertaken for years by selected surgeons without any formal review (14).

New procedures that are variations often undergo an even less formal development process. Certain new procedures might be performed by necessity in patients undergoing reoperations or with slightly different underlying anatomy. Decisions to perform a variation of a procedure often are made during surgery. The resulting new procedures might be disseminated to peers as case reports in professional journals and then used by other practicing surgeons. Other changes are more explicit attempts to improve surgical efficiency and patient outcome (15). In either case, formal or systematic review of the procedure is uncommon. Untoward outcomes might be discussed with peers at morbidity and mortality conferences; otherwise, results are simply added to the participating surgeon's anecdotal experience with that particular procedure.

## Comparison of the Development of Drugs, Devices, and Procedures

In order to better understand the development process of surgical procedures, it may be useful to examine the apparent differences among surgical, pharmaceutical, and medical device innovation. Table 7.1 presents some observations on the characteristics of innovation in drugs, devices, and procedures. The cost of developing a new drug is often enormous as measured in both money and time. Many surgical procedures are developed without external funding. Those with outside sources of support typically are small in scale compared with the cost of pharmaceutical development. New medical device innovation is in an intermediate category of cost. In part, development costs for new drugs and devices reflect regulatory requirements for testing, whereas little formal testing is required of a new procedure. However, even without Food and Drug Administration (FDA) regulations, drug and device development would likely still be orders of magnitude more expensive than that of most surgical procedures.

It is not surprising that these cost differences are balanced by differences in the ability of the developer to capture the rewards. The patent process allows the developer of a new pharmaceutical or medical device to recap-

**TABLE 7.1** Aspects of Innovation in Drugs, Devices, and Surgical Procedures

| Characteristics | Drugs | Devices | Procedures |
|---|---|---|---|
| Cost of development (regulatory hurdle) | High | Moderate | Low |
| Patentability | Yes | Maybe | No |
| Uniformity | High | Moderate | Low |
| Evaluation | | | |
| Double Blind | Yes | No | Rare |
| Controllable | Yes | Yes | No |
| Link between evaluation and diffusion | Yes | Yes | No |
| Diffusion | Corporate | Corporate | Professional |
| Local monopolies | No | Sometimes | Frequent |
| Coverage | Once approved (usually) | Once approved | May not even seek approval |

ture the investment over a period of time. Surgical procedures are not patentable. Although the surgical innovator may gain national renown, higher fees, and more patients, it is impossible to earn licensing fees for procedures performed by others.

The drug manufacturing process is designed to assure a uniform product. The same is true for devices, although problems of calibration and maintenance may reduce uniformity. Surgical procedures, in contrast, depend on the technique and the skill of the surgeon, patient factors, and sometimes the skill and cooperation of the rest of the care team. Thus, while it is reasonable to assume that a given drug would be equally effective in different hospitals, the same cannot be assumed of surgical procedures.

Evaluation of new surgical procedures remains much less formal than evaluation of drugs and devices. Drugs are classically evaluated through a double-blind, randomized, controlled trial. New devices may be evaluated in the same fashion, although it is much more difficult to blind the investigators and use placebos. With surgical procedures, randomization and blindedness are very difficult under reasonable ethical guidelines. The number of cases evaluated also is typically far smaller than for drug and device evaluations. Correspondingly, the detectable differences in outcomes must be far greater in magnitude. Other outcome research methods, such as meta-analysis, are being developed to synthesize formally the disparate results of clinical reports and trials that often differ in design, size, and findings. Most importantly, the timing of the evaluation process in relation to product diffusion differs. FDA guidelines for drugs regulate market entry by mandating product evaluation before dissemination. Although less standardized, the evaluation of medical devices has a similar timing. Post-marketing surveillance is becoming more common (especially for devices), however, regulation requires that some known efficacy be demonstrated prior to diffusion. Surgical procedures, on the other hand, generally are not evaluated prior to diffusion, making their evaluation more difficult once they have been accepted professionally as "standard of care." Surgical procedures are evaluted only with post-diffusion clinical trials, if at all.

The diffusion process for various innovations also differs. New pharmaceuticals and devices are marketed actively by manufacturers at professional meetings and through sales representatives. New surgical procedures generally are first discussed in the professional literature. Then, if necessary, the techniques are demonstrated in continuing medical education courses. In general, new drugs are available to all the relevant physicians at roughly the same time. Thus, with the exception of experimental drugs, there are no local monopolies. Some devices, by virtue of their high capital cost or regulatory constraints, may be available only at selected hospitals, but most centers are unlikely to be local monopolies. Sites of new surgical procedures, such as transplants, may be local monopolies for similar reasons, but even when the procedures are widely diffused, local surgeons can develop reputations for being more skilled (or having better outcomes) and thus may attract a disproportionate share of patients.

Once a new drug has been approved by the FDA, it is usually covered by most third-party payers. There are some important exceptions for payers that use formularies to select drugs. The same situation generally holds for devices, although explicit formularies are less likely. For surgical procedures recognition and approval for funding are even more closely linked. However, many innovative surgical techniques are thought to be billed with the use of preexisting codes, making them unrecognizable to payers as innovations.

## Incentives in the Innovation Process

The allocation of research funds can have a direct impact on the nature of innovation. This is most clear in the development of new drugs and devices, which is influenced directly by the priorities of the companies involved. At the other extreme, the classic National Institutes of Health (NIH) model of investigator-initiated research allows the pursuit of science, rather than external priorities, to determine the focus and funding of new research.

Academic surgical departments generally have relied on several funding sources, including federal agencies (especially the NIH), industry, private foundations, and clinical revenues/teaching funds (16). The level of funding for surgical innovation is difficult to estimate, for most information concerning biomedical research funds does not specify the amounts allocated to surgery departments nor to research focusing on surgical procedures. Funds generated within academic surgical departments include institution-wide funds for "teaching cases" and clinical revenue.

A shrinking share of NIH research funds is being spent on clinical trials and clinical research, with a growing share spent on molecular research (17). Private foundation research funds often are disease or organ specific in orientation and have generally echoed the NIH trends in supporting basic science rather than clinical pursuits. Industry support of surgical research has been restricted primarily to procedures related to devices, such as cardiac pacemakers or new artificial graft materials.

There is a longstanding tradition of surgical research and development (R&D) in university medical centers. Innovation is often the route to academic prestige (18). For the academic surgeon this translates into tenure evaluation criteria that emphasize journal publications and the development of new procedures. Although there is little literature on the personal incentives for surgical innovation, it appears that surgical innovators, like those in other areas, are driven more by a desire for knowledge and improvement of patient care than a desire for money. Issues of payment and competition become more prominent in the adoption and diffusion of surgical innovations.

Outside of academic centers, practicing surgeons continue to be pushed by the need to remain proficient with old skills and to keep up to date with newer developments. These community-based surgeons rely on a handful of mechanisms to receive knowledge of new procedures. The most common way to stay current is to read surgical journals. However, a large number of newly reported procedures are published in journal supplements that generally are not peer reviewed. Specialty society meetings, grand rounds at individual hospitals, and short courses at innovating centers are other means of disseminating new procedures through "continuing medical education." New surgical procedures involving medical devices often are taught by manufacturer representatives on artificial models and in the operating room. For some of the less complicated, smaller-ticket changes in surgical procedures, the individual surgeon can try to implement a new procedure in his or her own practice without formal instruction.

The pressure on surgeons to innovate and adopt innovations has been exacerbated by the loss of surgical "turf" to nonsurgical specialists who have developed less-invasive substitute procedures. For example, radiologic computerized tomography (CT)-guided percutaneous biopsy and drainage procedures have replaced some surgical open-lung biopsy and intraabdominal abscess drainage procedures (19,20). Endoscopic papillotomies performed by gastroenterologists have replaced open common bile duct exploration for the most part (21). Other therapies, such as ulcer treatment with oral H2 blockers, have further decreased the rate of surgery for peptic ulcer disease (22). Thus, with traditional surgeries becoming less common, the surgeon is pressured to adopt newer procedures in order to maintain a busy practice and to compete successfully with nonsurgical specialties.

Incentives for hospitals to remain competitive parallel those for surgeons. In general, the public focus on new life-saving procedures has meant that the world-renowned doctor is more often a surgeon than an internist. This is based in part on the surgeon's more clearcut and dramatic intervention and the public interest in curative treatments. To some extent the reputation of an individual surgeon or surgical team casts a "halo" on the whole hospital and is seen as beneficial to the institution. From the hospital or institutional standpoint, surgical innovation is highly prestigious. Public recognition as an innovator in one field often is equated (justifiably or unjustifiably) with institution-wide high-quality care. A reputation for providing the latest in technology can often provide the type of institutional advertising that can increase the hospital's competitive edge. A favorable reputation boosts referral patterns benefiting the institution's providers. More patients will use hospital services, not only for the innovative procedure, but also for more routine services. A perhaps apocryphal example of this phenomenon is a story of a survey of Louisville, Kentucky, residents. In it they identified Humana Hospital Audubon, the site of Humana's artificial heart program, as having the best obstetrical service. In fact, the hospital had no obstetrical service. Even if the story were not true, it nonetheless reflects the belief that high technology brings significant rewards.

A recent example of the symbiotic relationship between hospitals and surgeons is the report of a new twist to outpatient herniorrhaphy using laparoscopically guided internal stapling. The innovative surgeon claimed that the benefits for the practitioner of the new, yet not well-evaluated, procedure included shorter operating time, improved productivity, and less risk of complication. The projected benefits to the hospital included more efficient use of hospital operating rooms, less need for operating room support staff, increased hospital revenue with shorter lengths of stay, and the "marketing advantage of a much less invasive procedure" (15). Reported at a professional meeting, knowledge of this new procedure spread rapidly when it was noted in the *Journal of the American Medical Association*, with a circulation of over 350,000 in the United States.

## PAYMENT FOR SURGICAL PROCEDURES

A surgical innovator desiring payment for his or her new procedure can follow one of two general approaches. One is to record the new procedure as a minor variation of a standard and accepted procedure and thus be paid at the same level. Under this approach, no new name is given to the procedure; for payment purposes, nothing is recognized as having changed. The other approach is to identify the procedure as new or as a significant variation and seek a different payment (usually a more generous one). In general, this requires a third-party payer to make an explicit coverage decision. Historically, coverage evaluation criteria focused simply on whether the new procedure was a "reasonable" and "necessary" form of treatment. Concern over rising medical costs has since led to the development and integration of more rigorous technology assessment criteria into coverage decisions.

The Health Care Financing Administration (HCFA), the federal agency responsible for the administration of Medicare, claims that its consideration of a procedure as "reasonable" and "necessary" must be based on evaluation in the literature showing it to be "safe, effective, and not experimental" or "generally accepted in the medical community as safe and effective for the condition for which it is used" (23). The implementation of this relatively vague terminology is complicated further by the fact that coverage decisions are made on a case-by-case basis. Over 150 entities contract with HCFA to review and adjudicate claims for Medicare services. The contractors, known as intermediaries (for Medicare Part A or hospital services) or carriers (for Medicare Part B or physician services), include Peer Review Organizations, health maintenance organizations (HMOs), commercial insurers, and Blue Cross/Blue Shield plans.

The distinction between payments for hospital services versus physician services is most clear under the Medicare program, in which different payer authorities review different aspects of the claims generated by the same clinical episode. However, even when the same payer is involved as a private insurer, hospital service claims are handled differently from physician service claims. The hospital claim focuses on the patient's diagnosis and the specific charges for services rendered, such as room charges, operating room time, and medications. The specific procedure performed, however, is of secondary importance and may not even be coded. On the other hand, professional fee claims focus primarily on specific procedures and their coding. Submitted code numbers and charges for procedures are scrutinized, since there are screens for reasonable fees for each procedure and different rates for similar yet distinctly coded procedures.

## Determining Coverage for New Procedures

The first step in the coverage decision process is procedure identification. New procedures are sometimes recognized only after a claim is filed. However, carriers are now being approached by some physician and hospital providers (as well as manufacturers) to consider a new procedure and make an explicit ruling prior to billing. This generally occurs when the new procedure is likely to incur substantially higher costs. Reviews of provider claims can also detect new procedures based on the absence of codes or the presence of unrecognized codes and through excess charges for an accepted service (24). The ability of this process to identify new operations is limited by the sheer volume of individual claims processed. In fiscal year 1987, the HCFA estimates that 400 million claims were processed by its contractors (23); we have no estimate of the number of claims processed by other payers outside the Medicare insurance program, but we can assume that it is even larger.

Most coverage decisions are made by local fiscal intermediaries or carriers. However, if a contractor cannot resolve a coverage question satisfactorily or believes a national coverage decision may be necessary, the issue is referred to the central HCFA office, specifically the Bureau of Eligibility, Reimbursement and Coverage (BERC). BERC formally reviews 20 to 30 services each year, most of which are referred by contractors. "In general, the more expensive a service is or promises to become, either in an individual case or in the aggregate, . . . the more likely it is to be referred" (23). BERC will review procedures meeting any of the criteria, which include being a significant scientific advancement, a new or costly product, a procedure having potential for rapid diffusion, or a procedure considered to be outmoded or under question concerning its safety and effectiveness. Generally, HCFA will postpone making a national policy decision if the service involves a new or emerging technology or practice for which there are limited clinical data.

Individual contractors maintain significant autonomy in deciding what procedures are reimbursed. They generally focus on the appropriate use of a technology in a specific setting (e.g., does this patient require inpatient care for an elective herniorrhaphy?) and do not carry the burden of following strict technology assessment criteria. Coverage of those procedures that are truly novel and are referred to BERC can be left unresolved if there is inadequate information for a national coverage policy decision. Furthermore, there are no formal checks on the compliance of contractors in following national guidelines; most decision making remains at the local level. If a procedure does not appear to be markedly new or expensive, it might easily be considered eligible for reimbursement by some local contractors.

In the past, the HCFA led the way in the recognition of new surgical procedures. Once Medicare accepted a procedure for payment, commercial payers generally followed suit. In general, private payers are contractually bound to cover accepted procedures, and the Medicare stamp of approval signified a new technology as legitimate. However, large private insurers recently have led the way in the coverage of new surgical procedures (e.g., cardiac and liver transplants). This acceptance has put greater pressure on HCFA to provide Medicare payment for these procedures (25). All third-party payers must rely primarily on claims reporting to identify new surgical procedures. Evaluations of procedures generally are performed in house by private insurers, with direct consultation from physicians (e.g., the Blue Cross/Blue Shield National Association Medical Advisory Panel) and specialty groups. Although not necessarily less rigorous, the process of private insurer technology assessment is generally less formal and can be implemented more quickly than national Medicare evaluations. Other public programs, such as state-administered Medicaid programs, remain highly divergent in their range of coverage policies and criteria. The Oregon Medicaid program, for example, has chosen not to pay for any transplants (excluding renal transplants, which are covered by Medicare), whereas California's program will not pay for any hospitalization during which an "experimental" procedure is performed.

## Issues of Coding

Unless a surgical innovation is a variation on a theme that is coded under the traditional procedure, the designation of a new code may have a crucial impact on the procedure's payment and dissemination. It is important, however, to consider the implications of coding and coverage separately for physicians and for institutions.

### *Physicians*

Professional fee billing for surgical procedures uses codes determined by the American Medical Association (AMA), published as the Current Procedural Terminology (CPT). CPT codes are the primary tools used to describe physician services and are used for private insurance claims, for most Medicaid claims, Medicare Part B claims,[1] and for all outpatient hospital surgical procedures. Like diagnostic codes, surgical procedures are organized primarily by organ groups and are relatively specific. For example, there are 18 specific codes under surgical knee arthroscopy, including "with meniscectomy (medial AND lateral)," and "with meniscectomy (medial OR lateral)," "with meniscus repair (medial OR lateral)," and "with meniscus repair (medial AND lateral)." The codes, however, are not uniformly specific. In contrast to arthroscopy, there is only a single code for a supratentorial craniotomy, which can describe a range of neurosurgical procedures requiring anywhere from 1 to 12 hours of operating time.

Unspecified procedures are billed as "unlisted procedures" with an additional descriptor (e.g., "unlisted procedure, vascular surgery"). A special report normally is included that provides pertinent information concerning the nature, extent, and need for the procedure. Payers use this information to determine the medical appropriateness of the procedure and whether to pay for it. Modifiers can also be appended to a listed CPT code, and operations coded as such can be paid at a different rate. A commonly used modifier for a new or altered procedure is that of "unusual services." This can include a range of circumstances, from a difficult reoperation to a wholly new surgical technique.

While the existence of a billing code for a new surgical procedure does not necessarily guarantee its coverage, the development of a new code signals a recognition of a distinct new procedure and allows the possibility of more generous payment. CPT codes are generated primarily by medical specialty societies, which send proposals to the AMA for review. After a new procedure is deemed to need a new code, based on its dissimilarity from existing codes and on the FDA approval status of any involved drugs or devices, an advisory committee consisting of delegates from medical specialty societies evaluates the appropriateness of the proposed new code. The AMA's editorial panel makes the final decision on a quarterly basis. Aside from the specialty society route, individual physicians may also propose new procedure codes. These direct inquiries have increased markedly over the last several years, with most generated by university-based physicians and a few by community-based practitioners. With the traditional usual, customary, and reasonable (UCR) fee-for-service system, surgeons were rewarded financially for performing new surgical procedures that had no charge precedents. Especially if relatively few surgeons performed the procedure, individual practitioners were able to "forge" professional fees because whatever they charged became the UCR fee (26).

Currently there are approximately 7,000 separate CPT codes; there were over 500 code changes in 1988 alone. Most billing is performed by secretaries or other medical assistants who generally are not trained in the use of CPT codes and may not fully understand the surgical procedure itself. Miscoding is frequent. For example, Blue Shield of California estimated a 15 percent error rate in claims coding. It also estimates that 1 percent of that 15 percent is due to the coding of new procedures under old procedure codes (27). Commonly cited examples of miscoding include chemonucleolysis labeled as diskography and percutaneous transluminal coronary angioplasty (PTCA) billed as coronary angiography. In response to cost containment efforts by payers, surgery practices have begun to turn to independent billing agencies to maximize billing efficiency and revenues. The growing recognition of the potential use and abuse of codes has led to greater concern on the part of payers.

There is concern that a certain amount of "upcoding"[2] occurs within the CPT structure, with physicians selectively choosing to bill procedures under more remunerative codes. Among arthroscopic procedures, for example, similar but differentially reimbursed techniques can be billed as "meniscectomy," "synovectomy," "chondroplasty," "debridement," "patellar shaving," "patellar plasty," or "lateral release." There is more serious concern about the "unbundling"[3] of surgical services in professional billing. Some carriers, for example, allow the separate billing of Swan-Ganz catheter monitoring during coronary procedures, whereas others consider it a part of the procedure. Similarly, a cholecystectomy can be billed as a series of professional charges, including preoperative care, abdominal exploration, freeing of adhesions within the abdomen, doing a related procedure such as an appendectomy, and, finally, the cholecystectomy itself. It is estimated that the unbundling of services might be present in as many as 50 percent of claims, but a more realistic estimate is 10 to 20 percent (28).

Listed surgical procedure codes are meant to be "global" or inclusive of "normal, uncomplicated follow-up care" (29). However, there remains significant variation in interpretation with specific codes. A study conducted by the Physician Payment Review Commission (PPRC) found that the fee for transurethral resection of the prostate (TURP) in one region covered the basic operation, up to 2 weeks of postoperative care, and, if necessary, surgical repair of one specific complication. In another area, however, the fee covered preoperative evaluation (including up to 3 days of preoperative visits); the operation, including any of seven ancillary procedures performed at the time of TURP; 3 months of postoperative visits; and, if necessary, surgery for complications (30).

*Hospitals*

New hospital codes for surgical procedures generally are developed by HCFA once a procedure is recognized for payment. Hospitals identify procedures and diagnoses based on the ICD-9-CM (International Classification of Diseases, Ninth Revision, Clinical Modification) code. The ICD-9-CM Coordination and Maintenance Committee, cochaired by HCFA and the National Center for Health Statistics, determines how the procedure will be specified and, therefore, how it will be reimbursed.

Once a new surgical procedure is deemed reimbursable by HCFA, it is assigned to a new or existing DRG. Each DRG is an aggregate of ICD codes and includes the primary operative procedure, the presence of comorbidities (e.g., diabetes mellitus), patient age (e.g., less than or greater than 18 years), and patient discharge status (e.g., death). The DRG system of hospital reimbursement assumes that hospitalization costs within a DRG group are, on the average, similar across patients and institutions. Therefore, each DRG has its own weight relative to a standard index of resources consumed by the average U.S. Medicare inpatient. As of 1988, there were 219 distinct surgical procedure DRGs. The system generally relies on existing classifications. A new classification is formed when a procedure does not fit into existing classifications (e.g., heart transplantation) or will be used frequently enough to specify a separate resource weight (e.g., cardiac pacemaker replacement versus only generator replacement).

The HCFA remains sensitive to the potential impact of rate setting on the diffusion of a new technology. Recently, policy analysts have argued that cost-increasing forms of technology introduced since 1985 have been placed in underpaying DRGs. A 1989 case study of cochlear implants claims that DRG underpayment has become a significant financial disincentive that hinders the adoption and diffusion of new devices (31). It must be noted, however, that the HCFA was aware of this potential problem and had intentionally included cochlear implants in an "inappropriate" DRG, that of "major head and neck procedure," as it was the heaviest weighted ear, nose, and throat surgery DRG.

Physicians and hospitals may differ on the importance of increased payment levels for specific procedures. If the procedure allows better survival rates but requires an increased use of resources, such as longer lengths of hospital stay or more costly technologies, then hospitals will be interested in receiving more generous reimbursement for that hospitalization. In cases where a hospital must invest in a new drug or device, the hospital will have a clear interest in having the procedure placed in a more generously reimbursed DRG [e.g., cochlear implants and thrombolytic therapy using tissue plasminogen activator (TPA)]. In fact, very costly and capital-intensive new surgical procedures, especially those that require special equipment and staffing, may not be adopted by providers (both physician and hospital) until a new procedure code is developed.

## Payment Problems with New Procedure Classifications

Of particular interest in reviewing surgical innovation is whether new procedures substitute for older ones or are additions to the surgical repertoire. The HCFA's intent in imposing the DRG payment system was to encourage the use of less costly hospital resources—that is, to substitute more efficient practices. Specific technologies, such as renal lithotripsy, were encouraged under PPS in the belief that despite the significant initial capital investment, the use of this less-invasive treatment for renal calculi would be more cost effective.

The Prospective Payment Assessment Commission (ProPAC) is responsible for recommending adjustments of the DRG payment system to the Congress and HCFA. ProPAC has an advisory, rather than a decision-making, role. The reassessment of DRG rates expressly provides for changes in technology and surgical practice but is generally limited by the time lag in available information. Reevaluation is based on the most recent available charge data, which in December 1989 were data from fiscal year 1988. Thus, adjustments to the DRG payment system remain perpetually a year or two behind and are relatively insensitive to real-time changes in costs. While the HCFA and the public are relatively quick to hear about technologies that are perceived to be underpaid, providers are unlikely to complain of overpayment. In addition, while the system of financial incentives arising from fixed payments works in favor of the more efficient hospital or surgeon, it may also serve to discourage the introduction of less generously reimbursed innovations.

It is clear that changes in surgical procedures are likely to be undetected without the development of a new code. New procedures that fit under an old code are simply left in that category. Generally, it can be assumed that if the new procedure is just as costly, if not less costly than the older coded procedure, there is little incentive for providers to change the code. Well-known examples of procedures that were reimbursed at high rates but became less costly with time include intraocular lens implants and CABG. When complex surgical procedures are evaluated at an early stage of their development, costs and charges are often high; with time and experience, costs may decrease yet charges remain high (VA Rinkle, personal communication, November 10, 1989).

The transition of a surgical procedure from an experimental to an accepted one is crucial in the reimbursement process. In the past this process was quite informal. Now it is subject to more explicit review. For a new surgical procedure to become recognized as an "accepted, standard procedure," technology assessment guidelines rely on peer review, which includes literature review and consultation from specialty groups. Generally, this means that there must be some experience with the surgical procedure. Especially for very expensive procedures, this includes definite guidelines for patient eligibility and some record of morbidity and mortality from the procedure.

For a big-ticket surgical procedure, the development of institutional experience is therefore necessary to obtain reimbursement. The question is who pays for these procedures during this experimental/developmental phase? Professional fees generally have been waived at academic institutions; hospital costs cannot be ignored so readily. With the increasing pressure on hospitals to control costs, little margin has been left to pay for uncompensated care, whether for uninsured or new surgical procedures. Many teaching and research institutions have limited the discretionary funds previously available to help pay for some of this care. In some cases hospitals or institutions have opted to absorb the cost, presuming that the procedure will be a successful and potentially lucrative one.

At the other extreme it is clear that much surgical innovation occurs in a more incremental and less obvious way. Yet, even little-ticket procedures have developmental costs, particularly when some third parties refuse to reimburse hospital costs associated with an admission for a procedure deemed experimental. Some academic centers, such as the University of California, San Francisco, have become increasingly aware of the expense incurred by the push for new medical technologies and have instituted internal reviews of proposed new services. They require a report of new programs by each department, with information concerning the number of procedures expected to be performed, whether the procedure is additive or a substitute, and a projection of how the procedure will be covered. It is hoped that such reviews will allow earlier detection of new procedures (VA Rinkle, personal communication, November 10, 1989). There is no evidence that such reviews have led to the abandonment of fruitful areas of investigation, but surgeons are getting the message that experimental and development costs will have to be paid for in some fashion.

### Interaction of Diffusion and Competition

One manifestation of hospital competition is avid adoption of high-technology procedures to remain competitive and attract patients (24). This impetus for the diffusion of new surgical techniques has come from both the hospital and the individual practitioner (33). With the recognition of technology as a competitive tool, nonacademic institutions are rapidly adopting new surgical procedures. The spread of new procedures to nonacademic settings also reflects the success of training programs, which have produced larger numbers of surgeons to compete as providers (34). Without the financial commitment to support research and teaching costs that academic centers must make, many community-based institutions are able to attract well-trained surgeons and offer better prices for specific operations. This can, in turn, reduce the patient load at innovative centers. At Stanford University, for example, which is world renowned for its cardiac surgery service, the number of CABG procedures fell from 623 to 378 between 1983 and 1986 with the proliferation of neighboring competitors (data derived from discharge abstracts made available through the California Office of Statewide Health Planning and Development). Furthermore, surgical case loads are decreasing on average, making it harder for surgeons to remain proficient at routine procedures. From 1982 to 1985 the average number of operations performed annually by general surgeons decreased by 25 percent (35).

The development of a major new program, such as a liver transplant service, requires a substantial institutional investment of space, faculty positions, and other resources in addition to funds. Such decisions are clearly made at the highest levels in the institution. Not all decisions are in favor of new technology adoption; after 2 years of in-house debate, the trustees of Massachusetts General Hospital chose not to adopt a cardiac transplantation program. Reasons for their decision included costs (with one transplant consuming the resources of six to eight open-heart surgery cases) and the paucity of new knowledge the proposed clinical program was thought to add. It was a clear (and perhaps unusual) case of an institution overriding professional desire to implement a new surgical innovation (36).

CABG surgery is a commonly cited example of a rapidly diffused technology. Although substantial investment in equipment and personnel is required to perform this operation, hospitals project a positive cash flow in several months and profitable operation of an open-heart surgery unit within a year or two. These rosy projections do not even take into account the fact that a cardiac surgery unit enables a hospital to provide the required backup for the performance of percutaneous transluminal coronary angioplasties, another major source of hospital revenue. Having a cardiac surgery unit also projects the image of being a state-of-the-art hospital. These competitive pressures are so great that the number of heart surgery units continues to grow despite controversies about the appropriateness of CABG surgery relative to aggressive medical management for many patients (37) and evidence that hospitals with low volumes of CABG surgery tend to have worse patient outcomes (38).

Given the concerns about the potentially excessive diffusion of CABG surgery, it is instructive to examine the roles of market competition and regulatory forces. Hospitals with more local neighbors (who are likely to be competitors) are much more likely to offer open-heart surgery. Furthermore, the more neighboring hospitals with open-heart units, the higher the probability that a competing hospital will offer CABG surgery. Thus, there appears to be a "medical arms race" in which the presence of cardiac surgery services in one hospital results in an escalating availability of the service among local competitors (39). In some states, however, regulatory agencies have sought to constrain this type of behavior. For example, New York State has a stringent certificate of need approval process for new beds and open-heart surgery units. In 1986, with a population of 17.8 million, New York had 27 hospitals offering CABG, with an average volume of 362 operations per hospital per year. In contrast, California has a very lenient approval process. This state, with a population of 27.7 million (1.5 times that of New York), had 89 hospitals offering CABG (three times that of New York), with an average volume of 201 procedures per hospital per year. Los Angeles alone had over 40 hospitals offering the procedure, none more than 7 miles from another (40).

## Selective Contracting for Surgical Procedures

With interest in containing costs while maintaining quality care, one payer response has been selective contracting.[4] Although the concept of selective contracting has been in existence for decades (e.g., coverage for specific services at designated hospitals by Crippled Children's Services), there is a recent national proliferation in this approach to payment. It is useful to distinguish two types of selective contracting. In one approach a payer establishes certain standards that must be met by a provider before payment will be made. The second approach combines standards with the notion that even among providers meeting the standards, only certain ones will be selected for contracts.

The primary example of selective payment for a high-cost surgical service is cardiac transplantation. In 1983 California Blue Shield began providing payment for cardiac transplantations on a case-by-case basis at Stanford University, based on the view that the procedure was standard accepted care for that community.[5] With the diffusion of the procedure to other centers, pressure for reimbursement by Medicare increased, and by 1985, the HCFA made a concerted effort to evaluate the procedure, including issues of cost effectiveness (41). The evaluation of cardiac transplantation made it clear that the institutional program, with its interdisciplinary team and ancillary support services, was just as important as the performance of the procedure itself. Furthermore, the costs and outcomes of the surgical procedure were highly dependent on the postoperative management of the transplant recipient (41). Medicare announced coverage of cardiac transplantation in 1986 and, for the first time, included institutional criteria for coverage. Although it has been argued that these criteria are not strict enough nor sufficiently sensitive to truly discriminate among centers (42), it was nonetheless a policy move that acknowledged a concern over too rapid diffusion of high-cost technology. A policy of selective contracting sought to limit rapid growth by setting limits on whom HCFA would pay for specific services. The shortage of available organs in the case of cardiac transplantation also concerned policy makers, who feared that the spread of the procedure to a large number of institutions could lead to a less than optimal matching of organs and recipients. These selective payment programs have placed a greater onus on the hospital or institution to make significant investments to develop experience with a new surgical procedure prior to receiving coverage approval.

Despite efforts to control their growth, transplantation programs have continued to diffuse at a rapid rate. Community hospitals see transplantation programs as potential big moneymakers and have made the initial investments to start their own programs. These hospitals generally are able to attract academically trained transplantation surgeons to a nonuniversity setting by offering better remuneration, less teaching responsibility, and, generally, less pressure to pursue surgical research. This is causing increased tensions as academic centers are competing not just with each other but with community hospitals that do not invest in research, development, and training. These rivalries are exacerbated further by the fact that many of the community surgeons trained at or were previously on the faculty of academic centers.

Supporters of "standards-based" selective contracting have been somewhat disappointed in its results. The initial hope was to significantly limit the diffusion of high-cost surgical technologies and improve patient outcomes by restricting new procedures to sites meeting specific criteria with respect to staffing levels, support, and patient outcomes. However, there has been continued growth in the number of transplantation centers, and institutions have carefully selected patients to ensure a good outcome rate for reimbursement (RW Schaffarzick, personal communication, November 2, 1989).

In essence, the standards-based approach does not necessarily limit the number of institutions that are eligible; it merely specifies what any center must do in order to qualify. By rewarding programs that achieve favorable results through selection of healthier patients, this policy provides incentives for providers to avoid difficult patients who might have the most to gain from the new procedure.

The second type of selective contracting sets minimum criteria for entering the "game" and then selects certain institutions from among those eligible.

These more restrictive modes of payment have begun to introduce cost consciousness and occasionally price competition in lieu of non-price competition (43-45). With the current emphasis on competitive bidding and an increased focus on price and possibly on quality or outcome, the next wave of selective contracting may be for new surgical procedures. We are already witnessing competing price bids by large institutions for such accepted procedures as CABGs. For example, the Texas Heart Institute established a subsidiary corporation in 1984 to offer CABG surgery at a package rate that included the hospital, surgeon, cardiologist, and other associated costs (including transportation) for $13,800, in contrast to the Medicare rate of $24,588 (46).

The HCFA is now developing a program of selective contracting with "centers of excellence" to provide big-ticket surgical services for Medicare beneficiaries. Similar programs have been developed by commercial insurers, such as Prudential's program of centers of excellence and Metropolitan Life's centers of quality. Self-insured employers, such as Honeywell, have made similar arrangements for certain high-cost, schedulable procedures. Larger payers generally are able to bargain for better quality and price because they purchase a large volume of services for a large number of beneficiaries. This buying power has enabled HMOs to contract selectively for specific surgical services. HMOs select the providers and often specify their own criteria for deciding whether the procedure should be done. In this way they are able to control not only the cost of the procedure but also the frequency of its use.

## Limitations of Selective Contracting

The criteria used to evaluate centers that provide new surgical procedures are relatively limited. Mortality and morbidity rates, while informative, may not provide sufficient information to assess a program's quality. Factors such as patient selection become highly important; certain institutions may choose only patients who are likely to have good outcomes but who may not be most in need of the procedure.

With low mortality rate procedures, evaluation of outcomes becomes more difficult because enormous volumes are needed to calculate reliable mortality rates. In this situation the volume of services provided is often used as a proxy. Although there is a relationship between volume and outcomes for procedures such as CABG surgery, the evidence of such a relationship for other procedures is mixed (47). Thus, there is the danger that selective contracting for such procedures may focus on price simply because there are no readily available measures of quality.

In addition, just as surgical procedures continue to evolve, an individual surgeon's proficiency may continue to improve. Thus, the time frame in which a provider is assessed may be important. Overall improvements in proficiency across settings might require more stringent criteria with time if the purpose is to limit availability. Increased facility with a surgical procedure will often enlarge the patient population considered eligible for the procedure. This may mean the inclusion of sicker patients (in the case of CABG surgery) or healthier patients (in the case of abdominal aortic aneurysm repair). The constantly evolving nature of surgical procedures requires periodic reevaluation of hospital costs (with the development of some economies of scale) and of professional fees (with increased efficiencies) (48).

Some have voiced concern that current payer strategies may squelch surgical innovation, especially if initial costs appear to be high. Blue Shield of California has developed a system of "modified selective contracting" to encourage the development of new procedures, especially those deemed to be potential cost-saving substitutes (46). The institutional and professional fees for such emerging or investigational procedures are based on successful outcome; if the outcome is unsuccessful, the institution agrees to absorb the cost of the procedure. An example is catheter ablation of abnormal cardiac conduction foci. This percutaneous method uses accepted electrophysiologic mapping (EPS) techniques to locate the focus and then ablates it with electroshock to the abnormal area. The older approach to this problem uses EPS to identify the lesion and then surgically destroys the abnormal heart tissue via open-heart surgery (49). The contingent payment approach essentially means that as the success rate approaches 100 percent, providers will be paid in full, but if the rate approaches zero, providers will not be reimbursed at all.

The emphasis on controlling cost can also slow the dissemination of more expensive procedures that might have better outcomes and even potentially lower costs in the long run. Current studies are examining the use of slowly inflatable breast implants with breast reconstruction at the time of mastectomy. Although it increases intraoperative time, this procedure can eliminate the need for a second operation (mastectomy, then reconstruction). Use of the slowly enlarging prosthesis also causes less discomfort and permits better wound healing (50). Changes in practice induced by measures to reduce costs may also affect outcomes negatively. One study of the impact of the PPS on the results in elderly hip fracture patients found that while the mean length of stay fell as expected from 21.9 to 12.6 days, the proportion of patients discharged to nursing homes rose from 38 percent to 60 percent. Unfortunately, the numbers remaining in nursing home care 1 year after hospitalization also rose from 9 percent to 33 percent (51). Although this change is not due to a new surgical procedure, it nonetheless reflects payment effects on surgical outcomes.

## Outpatient Procedures and Payment Incentives

Most of the discussion so far has emphasized hospital costs and hospital-based surgical procedures. In 1980 Medicare changed its reimbursement policies to encourage the growth of ambulatory surgery. The 1980 Omnibus Budget Reconciliation Act waived the Part B deductible and copayment for the facility fee and paid 100 percent of "reasonable" professional charges once a surgeon accepted assignment.[6] Hospitals also received payment on a cost rather than DRG basis for outpatient surgery. With these changes in payment policy, the volume of ambulatory surgery rose explosively; by 1983 over two-thirds of ambulatory surgery for Medicare enrollees was performed in physician offices (52). Although arguments have been made that some specific procedures are cost saving when performed on an outpatient basis (53), those savings have not necessarily been recouped by the payers. Certain procedures, such as ophthalmic intraocular lens implantation, have continued to receive high fees in spite of the volume of services provided and presumed cost decreases (48).

Although there are some efforts to monitor the quality of care in the hospital setting and although it is possible to imagine selective contracting based on rigorous evaluation of the quality of institutional bidders, it is almost impossible to imagine such approaches applied routinely to the outpatient setting. For example, Blue Shield of California has 36,000 individual participating physicians, or 80 percent of the physicians in the state (RW Schaffarzick, personal communication, November 2, 1989). Utilization review and peer group norms linked with quality assessment have been used as evaluation tools in programs such as the Professional Review Organizations; but these efforts are likely to capture only the most extreme outliers among providers. More importantly, routinely collected data from outpatient claims files include little information about diagnoses and are far less reliable than the much-maligned hospital data.

In addition to problems with existing data systems for outpatient procedures, the current system essentially divides the medical care world into inpatient (institutional) claims and outpatient (physician) claims. Although there has been an enormous growth in outpatient procedures, they still comprise only a small fraction of total physician claims, which are dominated by office visits and routine tests. One alternative approach would be to segregate claims for "substantial" procedures and require more data in these cases. Review organizations would then be able to compare the outcomes of all procedures such as herniorrhaphies or lens implants done on an inpatient or outpatient basis. Eligibility for payment could be made conditional on more intensive review of quality and appropriateness.

## OBSERVATIONS, IMPRESSIONS, AND SPECULATIONS

One of the most important observations of our review is that there is very little empirical research on surgical innovation in general, let alone about the influence of payment policies on innovation. Thus, our review must be considered tentative and exploratory, with substantial gaps filled by hypothesis and argument rather than evidence. Given the importance of surgical innovation for both the health of the population and the cost of medical care, this absence of research is unfortunate. Describing an area with so little research is difficult; therefore, predicting the effects of different types of payment on surgical innovation may be foolhardy. Nonetheless, we offer some speculation to encourage further examination, discussion, and, perhaps most important, important research.

The changes in hospital payment in the last few years may have important consequences for surgical innovation. It appears that in the past many innovations were financed internally, through professional fees generated within departments of surgery and by hospitals that were able to pass unreimbursed development costs to other patients and payers. Prospective payment and selective contracts for hospital care have made it far more difficult for hospitals to undertake this type of subsidy. There are already concerns in some teaching hospitals about the sources of financing for new procedures, and it is likely that these concerns will reduce innovation. The revision of physician fees under a resource-based relative value schedule (RBRVS) (48) will likely reduce surgical fees significantly and will certainly eliminate some of the surplus funds used by departments to support innovation.

The adoption of an RBRVS also is likely to have other important effects. First, it will focus much more attention on issues of procedure coding. There may be a formal recognition of experimental or developmental procedures in the coding system, and this could lead to a more formal evaluation of such innovations before their diffusion. While a simpler and more generalized professional fee coding system has been proposed to decrease the rate of miscoding, attention must also be focused on the system's ability to identify new procedures (30).

The change in physician payment is intended to be more than just a coding reform—it is supposed to redistribute payments among providers. Although the effects will vary by specialty, the changes generally will reduce payments for procedures and increase them for evaluation and management services. This may lead to financial disincentives for specializing in surgery (or at least reduce the rewards for the choice of such specialties) and perhaps reduce surgical innovation. Unlike the old cost-based reimbursement system for hospitals, which had no incentives to reduce costs, the old physician payment system did have some incentives for developing cost-saving innovations that could make accepted procedures faster and less expensive. An RBRVS approach would allow payers to recapture some of these savings by lowering standard fees as surgeons became more efficient. However, since fees would be based on average performance, strong incentives for individual surgeons to become more efficient would remain, since they would be able to capture the difference between the fee and their own costs. On the other hand, the new system would make it less attractive for less efficient surgeons to continue to do the procedure since they could not charge above the average fee. The net effect might be a somewhat slower diffusion of new procedures.

The growth of selective contracting for specialized procedures likely will play a stronger role than the RBRVS in affecting innovation and diffusion. Assuming that such contracting is based on quality as well as price and that the price will tend toward an all-inclusive fee, there are several implications. First, there will be strong pressures for cost-reducing innovations to reduce not only operative time but also all other surgery-associated fees, such as hospital costs, laboratory tests, and other physician services. Second, methods of modified selective contracting may help limit the premature diffusion of costly surgical innovations and provide selective support of research in the investigational stage. Third, since there will be more attention to the measurement of quality of care and clinical outcomes, such contracting may also encourage quality-enhancing innovations, particularly if the enhancements are measurable. Fourth, the potential to obtain such contracts means that research institutions might be able to recapture some of their development costs by establishing a reputation for outstanding, state-of-the-art care at volume prices. It probably will be easier for academic centers to do this in fields in which procedures are continuing to develop, while selected community hospital centers may be limited to performing procedures once they become routine.

Furthermore, the conventional division between hospital and professional charges will become less prominent. Payer interest in cost containment and quality assurance will create greater pressure for the development of all-inclusive fees that cover all services related to a surgical procedure. Such package fees will impel providers (both physicians and hospitals) to determine the more cost-effective methods of treatment and the appropriate balance of services required for better patient outcome.

If one looks back to the projections made in 1983 of the likely effects of prospective payment for hospital care, it is apparent that some were correct and others were entirely wrong. Our speculations are based on far less evidence and research. However, it is reasonable to expect future changes in the payment system to have some, and perhaps substantial, effects on the innovation and diffusion of surgical procedures. Better predictions about the nature of those effects and their desirability are important policy questions that should be given careful consideration.

## NOTES

1. Surgical CPT codes are translated directly into the HCFA Common Procedure Coding System (HCPCS).
2. This is similar to the phenomenon of "DRG (diagnosis-related group) creep," described by health policy analysts as a method used by hospitals to maximize revenue by classifying an acute care episode under more generously reimbursed diagnoses.

3. "Unbundling" is the process of individually charging for techniques that comprise a multistep procedure, resulting in a total fee that is greater than the traditional fee for the overall procedure.
4. Selective contracting is a mechanism used by insurers to contract for the provision of certain services with specific providers. By representing large numbers of patients, the insurer can bargain for better prices from providers (both hospitals and physicians). In general, to encourage patients to use contracted services, financial incentives are offered if the contracted provider is chosen.
5. At that time Blue Shield felt that Stanford had shown an adequate "track record" with the procedure, with favorable outcomes and specific eligibility criteria.
6. "Assignment" is the term used to designate provider acceptance of Medicare reimbursement rates as full payment for the services provided. The provider agrees to not "balance bill" the patient for any difference between physician charge and Medicare payment, except for the normal 20 percent copayment, which is waived in this instance of 100 percent coverage.

## REFERENCES


1. Comroe JH, Dripps RD. Scientific basis for the support of biomedical science. Science 1976;192:105-111.
2. Maddrey WC, Van Thiel DH. Liver transplantation: an overview. Hepatology 1988;8:948-959.
3. Garner TI, Dardis R. Cost-effectiveness analysis of end-stage renal disease treatments. Medical Care 1987;25:25-34.
4. Castaneda AR, Mayer JE, Jonas RA, Wernovsky G, Di Donato R. Transposition of the great arteries: the arterial switch operation. Cardiology Clinics 1989;7(2):369-376.
5. Freiherr G, Weiss M. Romancing the market for stones. Healthweek, December 4, 1989;3:18-24.
6. Hoffmann J, Jensen HE, Christiansen J, Olesen A, Loud FB, Hauch O. Prospective controlled vagotomy trial for duodenal ulcer: results after 11-15 years. Annals of Surgery 1989;209:40-45.
7. Cunningham JN, Adams PX, Knopp EA, et al. Preservation of ATP, ultrastructure and ventricular function after aortic cross clamping and reperfusion. Journal of Thoracic and Cardiovascular Surgery 1979;78:708-711.
8. Bunker JP. The Anesthesiologist and the Surgeon: Partners in the Operating Room. Boston: Little Brown, 1972.
9. Bunker JP, Hinkley D, McDermott WV. Surgical innovation and its evaluation. Science 1978;200:937-941.
10. Ruffin JM, Grizzle JE, Hightower NC, McHardy G, Shull H, Kirsner JB. A co-operative double-blind evaluation of gastric "freezing" in the treatment of duodenal ulcer. New England Journal of Medicine 1969;281:16-19.
11. Kramer FM, Stunkard AJ, Spiegel TA, Deren JJ, Velchik MG, Wadden TA, Marshall KA. Limited weight losses with a gastric balloon. Archives of Internal Medicine 1989;149:411-413.
12. Merz B. Neurosurgeons address EC/IC study; question controlled surgical trials. The Journal of the American Medical Association 1986;256:165-167.
13. Sladek JR, Shoulson I. Neural transplantation: a call for patience rather than patients. Science 1988;240:1386-1388.

14. Holoweiko M. Why was the love surgeon allowed to keep cutting? Medical Economics 1989;July 17:125-141.
15. Goldsmith MF. Some new twists to one of most common procedures in US general surgery. Journal of the American Medical Association 1989;262:3248-3249.
16. Rikkers LF, Bland KI, Kinder BK, Lawrence PF, Lynch TG, Modlin IM, et al. Funding of surgical research: the roles of government and industry. Journal of Surgical Research 1985;39:209-215.
17. Ginzberg E, Dutka AB. The Financing of Biomedical Research. Baltimore: The Johns Hopkins University Press, 1989.
18. Bahnson HT. Presidental address: education of a surgical chairman. Annals of Surgery 1988;208(3):247-253.
19. Gleich S, Wolin DA, Herbsman H. A review of percutaneous drainage in splenic abscess. Surgery, Gynecology and Obstetrics 1988;167:211-216.
20. Chaffey MH. The role of percutaneous lung biopsy in the workup of a solitary pulmonary nodule. Western Journal of Medicine 1988;148:176-181.
21. Silvis SE. Current status of endoscopic sphincterotomy. American Journal of Gastroenterology 1984;79:731-733.
22. Jamieson GG. Surgery for peptic ulcer disease in the era of H2 receptor blockers. Digestive Diseases 1989;7:76-85.
23. Health Care Financing Administration. Medicare program: criteria and procedures for making medical services coverage decisions that relate to health care technology. Federal Register, January 30, 1989;54:4302-4318.
24. Ruby G, Banta HD, Burns AK. Medicare coverage, Medicare costs, and medical technology. Journal of Health Politics, Policy and Law 1985;10:141-155.
25. Rettig RA. The politics of organ transplantation: a parable of our time. Journal of Health Politics, Policy and Law 1989;14:191-227.
26. Wagner JL. Reimbursement shapes market for technology. Hospitals 1979:91-94.
27. Bunker J, Fowles J, Schaffarzick R. Evaluation of medical-technology strategies. New England Journal of Medicine 1982;306:620-624.
28. Beahrs OH. Reimbursement in the future: the physician payment review commission. In Rutkow IM (ed). Socioeconomics of Surgery. St. Louis: C.V. Mosby Company, 1989.
29. AMA editorial staff. Physicians' Current Procedural Terminology. Chicago: American Medical Association, 1988.
30. Physician Payment Review Commission. Annual Report to Congress—1989. Washington, D.C.: PPRC, 1989.
31. Kane NM, Manoukian PD. The effect of the Medicare prospective payment system on the adoption of new technology: the case of cochlear implants. New England Journal of Medicine 1989;321:1378-1383.
32. Roe BB. The UCR boondoggle: a death knell for private practice? New England Journal of Medicine 1981;305:41-45.
33. Gay EG, Kronenfeld JJ, Baker SL, Amidon RL. An appraisal of organizational response to fiscally constraining regulation: the case of hospitals and DRGs. Journal of Health and Social Behavior 1989;30:41-55.
34. Schroeder SA, Zones JS, Showstack JA. Academic medicine as a public trust. The Journal of the American Medical Association 1989;262:803-812.
35. Rutkow IM. Surgical operations and manpower: can technical proficiency be

maintained? In Rutkow IM (ed). Socioeconomics of Surgery. St. Louis: C.V. Mosby Company, 1989.
36. Knox RA. Heart transplants: to pay or not to pay. Science 1980;209:570-575.
37. Jones EL. Evolving status of operative versus nonoperative management of coronary arterial obstruction. Cardiovascular Clinics 1987;17:73-89.
38. Showstack JA, Rosenfeld KE, Garnick DW, Luft HS, Schaffarzick RW, Fowles J. Association of volume with outcome of coronary artery bypass graft surgery, scheduled vs. nonscheduled operations. Journal of the American Medical Association 1987;257:785-789.
39. Robinson JC, Garnick DW, McPhee SJ. Market and regulatory influences on the availability of coronary angioplasty and bypass surgery in U.S. hospitals. New England Journal of Medicine 1987;317:85-90.
40. Hannan EL, O'Donnel JF, Kilburn H, et al. Investigation of the relationship between volume and mortality for surgical procedures performed in New York state hospitals. Journal of the American Medical Association 1989;262:503-510, and case abstract data provided by the California Office of Statewide Health Planning and Development.
41. Evans RW. The economics of heart transplantation. Circulation 1987;75:63-76.
42. Renlund DG, Bristow MR, Lybbert MR, O'Connell JB, Gay WA. Medicare-designated centers for cardiac transplantation. New England Journal of Medicine 1987;316(14):873-6.
43. Luft HS. Competition and regulation. Medical Care 1985;23:383-400.
44. Robinson JC, Luft HS. Competition and the cost of hospital care, 1972 to 1982. Journal of the American Medical Association 1987;257:3241-3245.
45. Robinson JC, Luft HS. Competition, regulation, and hospital costs, 1982 to 1986. Journal of the American Medical Association 1988;260:2676-2681.
46. Schaffarzick RW, Bunker JP. Regionalized surgical health care. In Rutkow IM (ed). Socioeconomics of Surgery. St. Louis: The C.V. Mosby Company, 1989.
47. Luft HS, Garnick DW, Mark D, McPhee SJ. Volume of services in hospitals or performed by physicians. In U.S. Congress Office of Technology Assessment, The Quality of Medical Care: Information for Consumers, OTA-H-386, Washington, D.C.: US Government Printing Office, 1988.
48. Hsiao WC, Braun P, Yntema D, Becker ER. Estimating physicians' work for a resource-based relative-value scale. New England Journal of Medicine 1988;319:835-841.
49. Newman D, Evans GT, Scheinman MM. Catheter ablation of cardiac arrhythmias. Current Problems in Cardiology 1989;14:117-164.
50. Artz JS, Dinner MI, Sampliner U. Breast reconstruction with a subcutaneous tissue expander followed with a polyurethane-covered silicone breast implant. Annals of Plastic Surgery 1988;20:517-521.
51. Fitzgerald JF, Moore PS, Dittus RS. The care of elderly patients with hip fracture: changes since implementation of the prospective payment system. New England Journal of Medicine 1988;319:1392-1397.
52. Leader S, Moon M. Medicare trends in ambulatory surgery. Health Affairs 1989; 158-170.
53. Kambouris AA. Ambulatory surgery: its impact on general surgical practice. The American Surgeon 1986;52:347-350.

# 8

# European Policies Influencing Pharmaceutical Innovation

MICHAEL L. BURSTALL

The goals of this chapter are (1) to identify European policies that influence pharmaceutical innovation and (2) to estimate their effect. Every European government is more heavily involved in health care than is the United States government, and the ability of European governments to affect the process of innovation is greater. Most, though not all, European governments have interventionist traditions that make them willing to use their powers. The ways in which they do so, and the degree to which they succeed, is the central theme of this chapter.

How do government policies toward industry affect pharmaceutical innovation? The relationships are illustrated in Figure 8.1. The first step in the process of research and development (R&D) is to discover new medicinal products. This requires a critical mass of capable scientists and a solid scientific and technical infrastructure. Official policies toward the scientific community, past and present, are therefore important. After its initial discovery, a candidate drug must be shown to be safe and effective; the necessary development process is powerfully influenced by national regulations governing the admission of new products to markets.

To remain successful, pharmaceutical companies need to make a suitable return on their investment in R&D. Those that do not will lack the resources to develop more new medicines. The possibility of making a suitable return—and it should be remembered that most drugs fail commercially—will be influenced by the time that it takes to register a product and the effective patent life remaining. What a manufacturer can charge in its major markets will determine its cash flow; most European countries have price controls, and, in practice, drug prices vary widely. In the longer run,

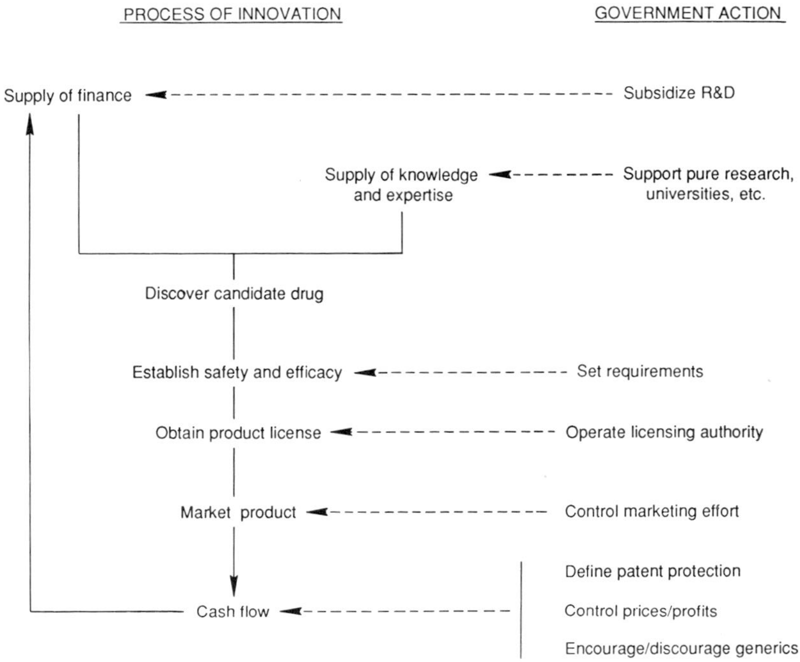


**FIGURE 8.1** How government actions may affect pharmaceutical innovation.

official attitudes toward generic products will also be important. However, what the government takes away with one hand it may give back with the other in the form of preferential pricing and other subsidies for research.

Thus, the effects of government action on pharmaceutical innovation are more extensive and more complex than they might at first appear. This is not all. Europe is fragmented along national lines. The differences in pharmaceutical production and consumption among European countries (as shown in Table 8.2) are quite large. Moreover, under the Treaty of Rome,[1] health care is left to the individual member countries. The European Commission has in practice managed to engineer the convergence of national regulations in some areas, but in others (e.g., pricing policies) large differences between one state and another continue to evolve. Thus, it often makes little sense to talk about "Europe"; rather, one has to talk about the situation in France, West Germany, the United Kingdom, and so on. To overcome this problem, this paper adopts a comparative approach. The salient facts about national markets and industries are summarized in Tables 8.1, 8.2, and 8.3. The following discussion focuses on the major European countries and on current developments.

**TABLE 8.1** Pharmaceutical Production and Consumption in the European Community, 1987

| Country | Pharmaceutical Consumption: Millions of Dollars[a] | Dollars Per Capita[b] | As Percent GNP | As Percent Health Care Spending[b] | Average Price [UK=100][c] | Implied Per Capita Volume [UK=100][d] |
|---|---|---|---|---|---|---|
| Belgium | 1,230 | 125 | 0.86 | 11.7 | 74 | 210 |
| Denmark | 380 | 75 | 0.38 | 6.6 | 103 | 91 |
| France | 7,510 | 136 | 0.84 | 10.0 | 58 | 292 |
| West Germany | 9,350 | 153 | 0.84 | 10.5 | 113 | 168 |
| Greece | 360 | 36 | 0.76 | 16.5 | 61 | 74 |
| Ireland | 200 | 56 | 0.66 | 9.1 | 112 | 62 |
| Italy | 5,940 | 103 | 0.78 | 12.5 | 74 | 174 |
| Netherlands | 960 | 66 | 0.42 | 5.3 | 109 | 75 |
| Portugal | 340 | 34 | 1.11 | 16.9 | 66 | 65 |
| Spain | 2,040 | 52 | 0.85 | 12.5 | 62 | 105 |
| United Kingdom | 4,520 | 80 | 0.67 | 10.8 | 100 | 100 |
| European Community | 33,000 | 102 | 0.78 | 10.9 | 85 | 149 |
| United States | 24,000 | 100 | 0.65 | 5.5 | n/a | n/a |
| Japan | 23,000 | 215 | 0.90 | 18.7 | n/a | n/a |

| Country | Pharmaceutical Production (Millions of Dollars) | Net trade (Millions of Dollars) | Percent Market Held by Local Firms: Home | World | Innovatory Capacity |
|---|---|---|---|---|---|
| Belgium | 1,250 | +160 | 10 | <1 | Moderate |
| Denmark | 920 | +430 | 50 | <1 | Moderate |
| France | 10,520 | +1,310 | 51 | 6 | Moderate |
| West Germany | 11,750 | +2,240 | 54 | 11 | High |
| Greece | 310 | -60 | 16 | <1 | Low |
| Ireland | 400 | +120 | 10 | <1 | Low |
| Italy | 8,450 | -550 | 42 | 3 | Moderate |
| Netherlands | 1,170 | +45 | 12 | 1 | Moderate |
| Portugal | 450 | -60 | 17 | <1 | Low |
| Spain | 3,360 | -80 | 30 | <1 | Low |
| United Kingdom | 8,000 | +1,370 | 37 | 8 | High |
| European Community | 46,500 | +5,100 | 66 | 30 | Mixed |
| Switzerland | 3,360 | +2,030 | 40 | 7 | High |
| United States | 26,500 | +960 | 80 | 37 | High |
| Japan | 22,500 | -1,500 | 80 | 20 | High |

[a]At manufacturers' prices and 1987 average exchange rates
[b]1986
[c]At manufacturers' prices
[d]Per capita consumption/average price

## THE PROCESS OF INNOVATION

### Discovery

The first—and in many ways the crucial—stage in developing a new product is to find new chemical entities (NCEs) with clinical potential. Today, this depends more on advances in scientific knowledge than on serendipity or large-scale screening. In principle, such knowledge is freely available and the discovery stage could be carried out anywhere. In practice, substantial numbers of specialized personnel are needed, together with access to local sources of scientific and technical expertise and the vital infrastructural services, ranging from instrument maintenance to laboratory construction. Accordingly, the size and quality of the local scientific community are central factors. Some qualitative measures of innovative strength and weakness are shown in Tables 8.2 and 8.3. They are of varied nature, those of Table 8.2 referring specifically to the pharmaceutical industry and those of Table 8.3 to national indicators of scientific inputs and outputs. As far as pharmaceutical innovation is concerned, they show that no single European country has the strength of the United States or, less certainly, Japan. The United Kingdom seems to be in the strongest position at the moment, followed by West Germany and, outside the European Community, Switzerland. France has slipped into the second rank, where it is accompanied by Italy. Belgium, Denmark, and the Netherlands have elements of strength

**TABLE 8.2** Measures of the Innovatory Strength in Pharmaceuticals of Various Countries

| Country | NCEs Introduced | | Top 50 Drugs in World by Sales, 1987 | Share of Various Markets, 1987 (Percent) | | | |
|---|---|---|---|---|---|---|---|
| | 1974–1980 | 1981–1987 | | EEC | USA | Japan | World |
| Belgium | 11 | 6 | | 4 | <1 | <1 | <1 |
| Denmark | 1 | 1 | | 1 | <1 | <1 | <1 |
| France | 97 | 26 | | 16 | <1 | <1 | 6 |
| West Germany | 91 | 30 | 5 | 21 | 4 | 3 | 11 |
| Italy | 72 | 28 | 1 | 8 | <1 | <1 | 3 |
| Spain | 15 | 1 | 3 | — | — | <1 | |
| United Kingdom | 29 | 16 | 10 | 10 | 7 | 3 | 8 |
| Switzerland | 45 | 26 | 6 | 10 | 8 | 3 | 7 |
| United States | 153 | 82 | 21 | 22 | 80 | 10 | 37 |
| Japan | 75 | 92 | 7 | <1 | <1 | 80 | 20 |

SOURCE: These estimates are based on data from *Scrip*, various issues, information from IMS Inc., and national government sources.

**TABLE 8.3** Trends in Pure Scientific Spending and Output

| Country | Percent Share of World Scientific Publication, 1984 | | Percent Change, 1975–1984 | | Government Spending (Millions of U.S. Dollars) on Academic Research | |
|---|---|---|---|---|---|---|
| | Papers | Citations | Papers | Citations | 1982 | Percent Change, 1975–1982 |
| France | 5.0 | 4.0 | -14 | — | 2,590 | +49 |
| West Germany | 6.0 | 5.3 | -7 | — | 3,300 | -1 |
| United Kingdom | 8.1 | 9.9 | -15 | -9 | 1,930 | +6 |
| United States | 36.6 | 52.8 | -2 | +2 | 9,370 | +13 |
| Japan | 7.6 | 5.0 | +41 | +22 | 3,170 | +53 |
| All other | 36.7 | 23.0 | +3 | — | n/a | n/a |

SOURCE: Martin BR, Irvine J, Narin F, Sterrin C. The continuing decline of British science. Nature 1987;330:123–126, and Irvine J, Martin BR. Is Britain spending enough on science? Nature 1986;323:591–593

but are handicapped by their small size. Greece, Portugal, and Spain are frankly weak, although Spain is making serious efforts to overcome her problems.

Such measures of scientific vitality, however, reflect to no small extent the strengths and weaknesses of the past. Given the time that it takes to develop a new drug to the point at which it is marketed, currently over 10 years, the products of the 1980s reflect the scientific strengths and weaknesses of the 1970s. What has happened since? Comprehensive data are lacking, but the numbers of Table 8.3 suggest that there was a substantial decline in the relative position of the United Kingdom in the 1970s and 1980s. West Germany, France, and the United States have held their own, while Japan has improved dramatically. These changes are becoming apparent to U.S. pharmaceutical firms operating in Europe.[2]

To no small extent these trends are linked to government spending on academic and related research in the several countries. Funding has grown only slowly in the United Kingdom since the early 1970s and is now well below that in comparable countries. The Thatcher administration chose to stress the applications of science and was less sympathetic to the needs of basic research. It also urged industry to pick up a larger share of the basic science bill, a suggestion firmly rejected by the pharmaceutical companies (2). That said, the United Kingdom is still the first choice as a location for foreign pharmaceutical companies setting up R&D centers in Europe. For the time being it continues to provide good—and relatively cheap—scientific manpower and access to high-quality pure research. Whether this happy situation will continue is doubtful (3).

## Development and Regulation

The impact of government policies on the discovery phase is indirect. That on the development phase is immediate. In all European countries the admission of medicinal products to national markets is controlled by national agencies that provide guidance about the evidence they need to reach a regulatory decision. The requirements of national authorities have converged gradually as a result of directives by the European Commission, and there is a high degree of apparent uniformity within the Community. Common standards for pharmacological and toxicological tests in animals and for the conduct of clinical trials have been adopted, together with common forms of documentation. Products may be rejected only on the grounds of safety, efficacy, and quality. Abbreviated, less rigorous applications are sufficient for products based on known ingredients.

In practice, however, there are still substantial differences between one country and another. Some are minor and essentially residual, but others are more serious. Some reflect variations in administrative arrangements. The United Kingdom, for instance, relies entirely on the employees of the official agency to make the decisions, whereas France depends on nongovernmental assessors. Differences in regulatory policies also reflect national differences in the practice of medicine and in approaches to clinical assessment.[3] Thus, in the United Kingdom and in Scandinavia, the main emphasis is on the large-scale clinical trial. In West Germany it is the pharmacological profile of the product that is most critical. The result is a fragmented European drug approval system. A product has to make its way through 12 national authorities, each of which will apply somewhat different criteria of evaluation (4).

This is expensive and time consuming. How does it affect the process of innovation? Perhaps surprisingly, the answer is "only to a limited extent." Innovative companies are large and by their very nature sell their products worldwide. Accordingly, they carry out the necessary development work with the world market in mind. Most of them work to meet the regulatory standards of the United States, since commercial success in the U.S. market is highly desirable if not essential and since American standards are the most rigorous to be found anywhere. Accordingly, research-oriented firms prepare new drug approval applications with the Food and Drug Administration (FDA) in mind. Thus, pivotal clinical trials will be undertaken in countries whose clinical practices and regulatory procedures most approximate those of the United States. The United Kingdom and Scandinavia are favored for this reason. The former is especially popular because costs are low; hospitals will generally arrange studies free of charge. Some clinical work will be carried out elsewhere, primarily to familiarize local clinical leaders with the new product. A master dossier will then be prepared from which the new drug application for each individual country may be drawn.

The development process is, of course, still prolonged and expensive, currently taking between 6 and 12 years, depending largely on the nature of the drugs.[4] Obtaining a product license can also consume a good deal of time, although generally less than in the United States. Discussions about a unified system of approval have been in progress for some years. Two basic procedures have been suggested: binding mutual recognition and a centralized authority—a European FDA, as its opponents call it. The latest proposals of the European Commission envisage a complex three-tier system. New biotechnology products would be handled by a central agency. For other NCEs companies would be able to choose between this agency and a process of mutual recognition. The central agency would be the arbiter in the case of disagreements between member countries. How this system would work in practice is as yet far from clear.

The regulatory situation in Europe is therefore much like that in the United States. Differences are of degree rather than kind and increasingly marginal. The fragmentation of the European system is an annoyance rather than a major problem; by one estimate a unified approval procedure would produce a saving of no more than 2 percent for the industry (7). This is hardly surprising. The innovative part of the pharmaceutical sector operates on a world basis, and the impact of national peculiarities is reduced correspondingly. But what of the commercial scene?

## RECOVERING THE INVESTMENT

### Patent Protection

Effective patent protection is vitally necessary to the research-based drug industry. Without a period of qualified monopoly to recover its costs, no company could face the expenditure necessary for innovation. Since the late 1970s, a unified system of patents has applied to most European countries. Under the European Patent Convention, pharmaceutical products, processes, and uses are protected for 20 years from the date of application. The patentee makes a single application and receives a bundle of national patents; as yet there is no Europatent. All member states of the Community, with the exceptions of Ireland and Portugal, have signed the convention, as have Austria, Sweden, and Switzerland. Spain, where patent protection formerly was weak, has adhered to the convention and has been granted a transitional period to bring its practices into line.[5]

The main concern, of course, is effective patent life. For good reasons patents normally are taken out toward the end of the discovery phase of a new medicine. Given the length of the development stage, the patent life remaining by the time the product reaches the market typically is between 8 and 12 years, and often less (5,6). The inventor therefore has only a limited time to recover R&D costs and to make a profit before copies appear. This problem was recognized in the United States by the Drug Price Competition and Patent Term Restoration Act (Waxman-Hatch) enacted in 1984 and by similar legislation in Japan. Some progress along these lines has been made in the Community. Under the High Technology Directive of 1987, six member nations—Belgium, France, West Germany, Italy, the Netherlands, and the United Kingdom—have agreed to a 10-year period of marketing exclusivity for all novel pharmaceutical products (8).

In practice this is a rather modest concession. The added patent protection is to start from the date of first marketing within the Community and not the date of authorization in any particular country. Moreover, as mentioned previously, the average period of effective patent life is not far off 10 years already. The commission therefore has proposed a more radical alternative. They envisage the creation of "supplementary protection certificates," which would provide 16 years patent protection from the date of first marketing authorization for pharmaceuticals based on new active substances, with a ceiling of 30 years from the date of filing the original patent. This would go a long way to solving the industry's problem. However, opposition to the measure from consumer groups is building up, and a substantial effort will be needed to get it through the European Parliament. In any case it would not come into force for some time and would be retroactive only to a limited extent.

## Prices

All European countries are heavily involved in the provision and financing of health care, and all are anxious to limit their expenditure. Aging

**TABLE 8.4** General Methods of Controlling Pharmaceutical Expenditure in the European Community, 1989

| Country | Positive List | Negative List | Patient Copayment System | Percent Bill Met by Patient | Generics Promoted |
|---|---|---|---|---|---|
| Belgium | Yes | Yes | 0/25/50/60 percent of price | 35 | Yes but |
| Denmark | Yes | No | 25/50/100 percent of price | 33 | Yes |
| France | Yes | No | 0/30/60/100 percent of price | 30 | Yes but |
| West Germany | No | Yes | Flat rate | 10 | Strongly |
| Greece | Yes | No | 20 percent of price | n/a | Yes |
| Ireland | No | Yes | Varies with patient | n/a | No |
| Italy | Yes | No | 30 or 40 percent of price + flat rate | 19 | Yes but |
| Netherlands | No | Yes | Flat rate | 12 | Strongly |
| Portugal | Yes | No | 0/20/50 percent of price | 25 | Yes |
| Spain | Yes | Yes | 40 percent of price | 14 | Yes |
| United Kingdom | No | Yes | Flat rate | 13 | Strongly |

**TABLE 8.5** Price Control Systems in the European Community, 1989

| Country | Individual Drug Prices Controlled | Basis | Better Price for Local Activities | Average 1988 Drug Prices [UK = 100] | | |
|---|---|---|---|---|---|---|
| | | | | [1] | [2] | [3] |
| Belgium | Yes | Internal comparison | Yes | 74 | 77 | 62 |
| Denmark | Effectively no | | No | 103 | 128 | 86 |
| France | Yes | Internal comparison | Yes | 58 | 62 | 48 |
| West Germany | Some are | Flat rate | No | 113 | 133 | 92 |
| Greece | Yes | Cost plus | Perhaps | 61 | 65 | 83 |
| Ireland | No | Tied to United Kingdom prices | No | 112 | 107 | 93 |
| Italy | Yes | Internal comparison | Yes | 74 | 72 | 63 |
| Netherlands | No | None yet | No | 109 | 119 | 96 |
| Portugal | Yes | External comparison | Perhaps | 66 | 55 | 87 |
| Spain | Yes | External comparison | Yes | 62 | 63 | 70 |
| United Kingdom | No | Profits controlled | Yes | 100 | 100 | 100 |

populations and the advance of medical science make cost containment politically difficult. Economies are sought, and the first and favorite target is the drug bill. Accordingly, all these nations take steps to limit pharmaceutical spending. Such measures are permitted under the Treaty of Rome. The methods used are summarized in Tables 8.4 and 8.5. They include positive lists, which name the drugs that will be paid for, and negative lists, which identify products excluded from reimbursement. Patients everywhere are expected to pick up part of the bill, although exemptions for those in the hospital and the chronically sick are normal. The use of generics may also be encouraged. Over-the-counter medicines are everywhere excluded, although the same products often qualify for reimbursement if they are prescribed. The main emphasis, however, is on direct control of pharmaceutical prices.

The majority of states in the European Community regulate the prices of individual drugs. Cost-plus, in which the permitted price is based on the cost of production, together with allowances for the R&D content and for marketing expenditure, was formerly the favored method for fixing prices. It is, however, cumbersome to apply and has been replaced generally by other approaches. Internal comparison is now used by several countries. Here the price of a new medicine is fixed by reference to existing products in the same therapeutic category; an improved tolerance/efficacy profile or other clinical advantages will result in a better price. Yet other nations rely on external comparison, in which prices are related to those in other European countries.[6]

However, measures of this kind are not universal. Denmark and the

Netherlands do not control prices at all. Until very recently, West Germany also followed a policy of free prices; now, though, it restricts reimbursement under the health insurance scheme for identical multisource drugs to a fixed sum that is related to the generic price. At some future point it intends to extend this scheme to medicines that share a common mode of physiological action. Uniquely, the United Kingdom controls profits on sales to the National Health Service. Companies are allowed to set their own prices, provided that their return on capital does not exceed a certain specified level (9).

The main effect of these controls is that prices differ widely between one country and another. The average price level in Spain, for example, is about half that in West Germany. Nor are low prices necessarily related to low per capita incomes. France is a country appreciably richer than the United Kingdom, yet because of government controls, drugs are much cheaper there. This leads to serious problems for the research-based pharmaceutical companies.

In some countries prices are barely sufficient to support the costs of innovation. France again is an example. During their formative years, French companies were granted an extensive degree of protection from outside competition, which has led to them being abnormally dependent on sales in the French domestic market and the former French colonies. Several of their innovative firms clearly are suffering from low domestic prices (10). Companies with a world wide perspective, such as those of West Germany, Switzerland, and the United Kingdom, are less affected by low prices in any particular country but cannot welcome the example that they set to regulators elsewhere.

A further problem arising from variations in price between one country and another is parallel importing. This is a form of arbitrage. A company in a country where prices are high exports a drug to one where prices are low. A wholesaler buys it there at the local price and exports it back to its country of origin, where it is sold at the normal higher price. The reexporter and the pharmacist divide the profit. Parallel exports are entirely legal within the Community, even when the price differences that make them worthwhile are due to government action. This form of trade is rising and threatens to exert constant downward pressure on drug prices in those countries where they are currently high. The major companies operating in Europe see this as a serious threat.[7]

Uniform pan-European prices are unlikely. Under the Treaty of Rome, such matters are left to individual governments, each of which has its own ideas about the balance between the interests of producers and consumers. Thus, despite continued pressure from the international industry, successive French governments have kept drug prices low, arguing that the French propensity to consume drugs is so great (Table 8.1) and so price inelastic that higher prices would bankrupt the national health insurance scheme.[8] In contrast, the British government generally has tolerated fairly high prices because, by European standards, British consumption of medicines is modest. The possible effects of the recent transparency directive are discussed later.

### Generics

The United States has chosen to promote competition in the out-of-patent drug market by encouraging the use of generic products. This has been successful in that generics now account for a large minority of total sales. It has been less successful in controlling total expenditure, since average price levels have risen sharply in recent years as innovative firms have charged the very highest prices the market will bear for novel products.

Generics have made less impact in Europe. They probably have no more than 5 percent by value of the Community market. In only two major countries—West Germany and the United Kingdom, both of which have high prices—do generics have as much as 10 percent of the market. Elsewhere they are much less important. In part, this is because prices are too low in some countries—Belgium, France, Italy, Spain—to make competition by price commercially attractive. In part, it is because only West Germany permits generic substitution, although that measure is now under discussion in Italy and being mentioned in France, and, in part, it is because governments have preferred to control pharmaceutical expenditure by the means already discussed in the previous section (11).

This situation is likely to change in the not-too-distant future. European governments are keenly interested in each other's cost-containment programs, and if generic substitution were to prove successful in West Germany, it might be widely adopted. Once again, this could have serious consequences for the income of research-based companies, unless concessions such as extended patent lives were to be granted. European firms fear that the use of generics would be combined with price controls and that their combined effect would therefore be larger than in the United States.[9]

## SUBSIDIES FOR R&D

Many European governments have wished to encourage the development of a strong domestic pharmaceutical industry. At first, the objective was import substitution, especially in the remote days of the dollar shortage.[10] Later, a modern, science-based drug industry was seen as desirable in itself, generating a substantial contribution to the national income, the balance of payments, and employment opportunities for skilled and highly educated personnel.

What methods were used to this end? In the early days tariff or nontariff barriers were common; they survived in Spain and Portugal until their accession to the Community in 1986.[11] Ireland used subsidies and tax exemptions as incentives for high-technology, export-oriented industries, such as pharmaceuticals. At present, the main role is played by controls over prices and profits discussed above. An important if latent characteristic of regulations is flexibility—the ability to be relaxed on occasion. For example, a better price for a new wonder drug or a price increase for an existing one may be the reward for increased local investment.

Financial incentives such as preferential pricing have had some effect on the location of R&D facilities. At first, they tended to follow manufacturing investment. Local laboratories were set up for local development work. More recently, major centers undertaking basic research have been set up by foreign companies in several countries, especially in France and the United Kingdom. The French have been particularly aggressive in this respect, offering substantial improvements on product prices determined by the process of internal comparison in return for R&D investment in France. Since French prices are low, such trade-offs can be attractive. Italy and Spain offer similar rewards. The United Kingdom explicitly takes local R&D into account in fixing the permitted profit levels for individual companies. Only West Germany, the Netherlands, and Denmark stand aloof (12).

Such incentives discriminate between companies. They naturally favor indigenous firms above all, since all multinational pharmaceutical enterprises do their most fundamental and sensitive research in their country of origin. They also have a distorting effect on trade. Their legality under the Treaty of Rome therefore is uncertain. Previous Belgian and Italian schemes were struck down by the European Court of Justice,[12] but the French system has so far survived because it is entirely informal in nature. The incentives provided by the United Kingdom appear to be permissible: the concessions offered are not directly connected to any particular investment; they are, in effect, made retrospectively, and they amount to no more than a chance to make a particular level of profit. There is no guarantee that such a profit will be obtained.[13]

The recent Transparency Directive of the European Commission, which came into force on January 1, 1990, will probably have a significant effect on incentives for R&D. Put briefly, it stipulates that member countries must publish full details of the methods they use to classify products for reimbursement, to control pharmaceutical prices and profits, and to operate positive and negative drug lists. A 180-day period for the approval or disapproval of prices or price increases is laid down. If such a price proposal is rejected, the applicant must be given a statement of the reasons based on "objective and verifiable criteria." In the absence of a decision, the company may apply its price forthwith (13).

In principle the directive might expose the use of price concessions as incentives. The initiative would, however, have to be taken by a company or companies that felt unfairly treated. To do so might risk compromising relations with the government in question. To be the first to sue would be to put oneself in an uncomfortably exposed position.

## THOUGHTS

What has been the impact on pharmaceutical R&D in Europe of the various forms of government regulation outlined in this chapter? Specifically, how have they affected the European environment for innovation compared to that in the United States?

### Is the United States a Better Place for Pharmaceutical Innovation?

By and large, the answer is yes. In some areas there is little difference between Europe and the United States. In both the development stage of product innovation is prolonged and expensive. On the whole, it still seems to be rather easier to get a new medicine to the market in Europe. The differences are not large, however, and are tending to become smaller with time. In any case, if drug approval delays in the United States are greater than those in Europe, it is the American consumer who suffers rather than the American pharmaceutical industry. To be denied effective drugs for whatever reason is a loss in welfare. Similarly, differences in patent protection are small. The Drug Price Competition and Patent Term Restoration Act has given the United States a slight edge, but, when implemented, the proposals of the European Commission should shift the advantage back to Europe.

The United States does, however, have a real advantage in two areas. The first is the fundamental resource of basic science. Crude as they are, the data presented in Table 8.3 show the dominance of the United States over all other countries. In terms of both publications and citations, it is clearly much more prolific than the entire European Community. This is equally true when one considers the branches of science that are directly relevant to the pharmaceutical industry, such as cell biology, genetics, immunology, and computer modeling. In a science-driven industry like pharmaceuticals, this gives the United States a substantial lead over others when radically new approaches and techniques are required. In this light the continued American dominance of pharmaceutical innovation is hardly surprising.

The other advantage of the United States lies in free and relatively high drug prices. Innovation is expensive and, as previously shown, price levels in some European countries are too low to provide adequate support. Does this matter? After all, new medicines have to sell worldwide, and the income from any one country is only a minor part of the whole. In practice, however, all companies depend to a quite disproportionate degree on their own local markets or regions (Table 8.2). If local prices are low, profits and return on investment will be low. Once again, the position of the French companies illustrates this problem.

The R&D incentives provided by several European countries are significant but do not provide a sufficient stimulus for innovation. Their impact is relatively small. In a recent inquiry American firms operating in Europe rated these incentives as not very important. They have had only a modest effect on the location of R&D facilities. As has been seen, the future of such schemes is in any case problematic. From the standpoint of the European pharmaceutical industry as a whole, this is all to the good. Incentives in the form of better prices for local investment discriminate between companies and may distort policies concerning the location of R&D facilities. Opportunities to exploit economies of scale and scientific critical mass may be lost. In addition, companies may be led to neglect scientific opportunities outside their own countries or outside the community.

## Are There Lessons for the United States from the European Experience?

One can look on the European experience of pharmaceutical regulation as a series of large-scale natural experiments. What lessons could the United States learn from them that might improve the efficiency of the innovatory process? As the previous section has suggested, most of these policies inhibit innovation. Where European regulatory practice has differed from that of the United States, it has usually been for the worse. Nevertheless, it is worth considering whether there are any exceptions to this gloomy conclusion.

One area that has already been mentioned is marketing authorization for new products. The procedures used in the various European countries appear to be rather more rapid and appreciably more flexible than those of the FDA. This owes something to differences in the position of the regulators. Despite considerable variations between one European country and another, the senior decision makers are always independent, high-status professionals rather than career bureaucrats. Unlike their American colleagues, they are generally sheltered from the blasts of political controversy and are freer to exercise their judgment.

Moreover, the legal situation is probably more favorable in Europe. Europeans seem to be less litigious than Americans. Class action suits generally are illegal, as are contingency fees. Although strict liability for manufacturers has now been agreed upon by the Community, most member countries have introduced or are expected to introduce a development risk proviso, which will exclude damages from causes that could not have been foreseen at the time a drug was introduced. Several countries— most notably Sweden— have experimented with no-fault compensation schemes, with encouraging results in relations between the industry and the public.

Finally, there are promising developments in the field of post-marketing surveillance of drugs in Europe. For instance, new computer-based systems being introduced in the United Kingdom will make it possible to track indefinitely the effects of particular drugs on particular patients. An effective system of surveillance is at hand and, in principle, could even replace to some extent the lengthy pre-marketing clinical trials now required.[14]

Such developments could have an appreciable effect on the time it takes to bring a new drug to the market. There is a reasonable chance that such practices will be adopted widely in Europe during the next few years. Whether they could be transferred to the United States is more doubtful. As already suggested, the advantages the European countries enjoy are the result of cultural factors as much as anything. Ambulance-chasing lawyers and acrimonious congressional hearings are as permanent a feature of American life as obsessional anxiety about health. All would make a general relaxation of drug regulation difficult.

## 1992 and After

During 1992, the member countries of the European Community will form a single unified market, with all that implies. As far as the European pharmaceutical industry is concerned, this will initiate yet another stage in a process of changing economic dynamics. Many issues, notably prices, remain unresolved. At the same time the trend toward ultimate unification is both clear and unstoppable. What are the implications for pharmaceutical R&D?

A unified system of marketing authorization is likely to be in place by 1993. It could reduce approval times or lengthen them, depending on the policies followed. In the long run prices might be harmonized, but would the revision be upwards or downwards and where would it be felt? Longer effective patent lives and the phasing out of local incentives for R&D seem both probable and beneficial. If the European Commission were to play a larger part in health policy—and this cannot be ruled out if there is further progress toward a federal Europe—this might mean either more or less regulation. Much remains to be determined.

Who is likely to benefit? Increased competition will impact adversely on the smaller and more marginal research-based firms, to the benefit of the larger and stronger ones. Unified marketing authorization and longer patent lives will benefit those who have new products to introduce. The decline of incentives will benefit those who can stand on their own. It will also help those firms that have been forced in the past to fragment their European activities. Concentration will be the policy of the future. The strong will become stronger and the weak weaker.

American companies stand to benefit from 1992. By international standards they are large and innovative. Their competitive position is already very strong. They are firmly entrenched in Europe, where they have more than 20 percent of the market by value; virtually all they sell is produced locally. They will gain considerably from the opportunity to concentrate their European activities. They are well placed to exploit their existing contacts with the European scientific community.

It is difficult to be as optimistic about the competitive position of the European drug companies. In terms of innovative capacity, the French companies are now in the second rank; the Italian ones have always been there. There are signs that the Swiss and German firms are losing their edge. The British companies are still riding high, but it is distinctly possible that the foundation of their success is being eroded. As the nature of innovation changes, all will have to adapt or vanish. Whether they will be able to do so remains to be seen.

## NOTES

1. The Treaty of Rome is the basic law creating and governing the European Community. The provisions particularly affecting the pharmaceutical industry are articles 30, forbidding quantitative restrictions on imports; 85, prohibiting restrictions on competition; 86, relating to abuse of a dominant market position; and 92, governing the provision of state aid to industry. The European Court of Justice is the Supreme Court of the Community. Its decisions are binding on member nations. It has been very active and has consistently interpreted article 30 in particular in the broadest way.
2. In the case of the United Kingdom the decline between 1973 and 1982 was especially marked in the case of chemistry but less so in biomedical research and clinical medicine. This trend seems to have continued in the 1980s but at a slower pace (2).
3. These differences appear to be related to the way in which physicians are trained. There are basically three medical cultures in Europe—one common to the United Kingdom, Ireland, the Netherlands, and Scandinavia, one common to Belgium, France, Italy, and Spain, and one unique to Germany and Switzerland. Both the volume of drugs consumed and their nature vary markedly between the three areas.
4. In the United Kingdom drug development time peaked at 13 years in 1984, subsequently falling to 10 years in 1987. The largest element was clinical testing, which accounted for two-thirds of the total. Central nervous system drugs spent twice as long in the development phase as anti-infective products (6). An earlier estimate (7) suggested 1982 figures of seven years for France, nine for Switzerland, 11 for Italy, and 12 for the United Kingdom (3).
5. Ireland has adhered to the Convention but has failed to give it effect by national legislation. Both Portugal and Spain were obliged to adhere to the Convention before 1992 as a condition of entering the Community in 1986. While Spain has done so, Portugal has not and continues to offer only process patents with a life of 15 years from the date of grant.
6. Countries such as Spain which use external comparison to fix prices naturally tend to use the countries where drugs are cheapest—usually France or Greece—as their point of reference.
7. Pharmaceutical companies market their products themselves but do not distribute them, since the number of outlets to be supplied is very large. Instead, they sell to specialist wholesalers who in turn supply retail pharmacies. National health services and insurance schemes normally reimburse retailers at prices based on manufacturers' list prices for the prescription drugs that they dispense. Clearly, the lower the price at which the distributor can obtain a drug, the greater his or her profit margin.

8. The elasticity of demand with price is the ratio of the proportionate increase in volume sold to the proportionate decrease in price. Thus, if a 1 percent decrease in price produces a 2 percent increase in sales, the elasticity is 2. A little calculus shows that if the elasticity of demand is less than 1, expenditure (i.e., price x volume) will increase when the price is increased. In so far as it can be measured the elasticity of demand for drugs is well below one in all countries.
9. Under the Drug Price Competition and Patent Term Restoration Act research-based United States companies received a qualified extension of patent life; in return they had to allow the information in their original new drug applications to be available to generic companies when the latter applied for marketing authorization. This meant that the generic firms only had to demonstrate to the FDA that their copies were of satisfactory quality and had the requisite bioequivalence and bioavailability. Formerly they had to undertake a full program of testing if the product they wished to copy had been introduced after 1962. This information has always been available to would-be generic copiers in European countries; accordingly some other, and less welcome, quid pro quo for patent life extension may well be sought.
10. Between 1945 and 1955 all European nations suffered from an acute lack of dollars as they underwent reconstruction after World War II. In order to conserve foreign exchange many of them encouraged United States firms to set up local subsidiaries; this was a major stimulus to the multinational system of operation in the pharmaceutical industry.
11. Tariff barriers were widely used to encourage local investment in the 1950s and early 1960s. Illegal under the Treaty of Rome, they have now been eliminated within the Community. Non-tariff barriers comprise measures such as unusual safety or packaging requirements which have the effect of restricting imports. An example is the Japanese demand that all safety testing of drugs be carried out on Japanese subjects. They too have largely disappeared within the Community.
12. In both cases the Court struck down the schemes as contrary to article 30 of the Treaty of Rome because they laid down different criteria for imported and domestically produced drugs, thereby explicitly discriminating in favor of domestic products.
13. I am grateful to a senior official of the United Kingdom Department of Health for clarifying the legal status of the United Kingdom scheme and to spokesmen of the Société Nationale de l'Industrie Pharmaceutique for discussions on how the French pricing system works.
14. Two commercial systems are already in existence. That of VAMP Ltd. covers about 20 percent of all United Kingdom medical practices. The information obtained is collected regularly, analyzed, and sold to pharmaceutical firms.

## REFERENCES

1. Martin BR, Irvine J, Narin F, Sterrin C. The continuing decline of British science. Nature 1987;330:123-126.
2. Irvine J, Martin BR. Is Britain spending enough on science? Nature 1986;323:591-593.

3. Burstall ML, Wallerstein K. American Pharmaceutical Companies in Britain and Europe, unpublished.
4. Burstall ML, Reuben BG. The Cost of Fragmentation in the European Community's Pharmaceutical Industry and Market. Brussels: European Community 1988: 52-67.
5. Lis Y, Walker SR. Novel medicines marketed in the United Kingdom 1960-1987. British Journal of Clinical Pharmacology 1989;28:333-343.
6. Chew R, Teeling-Smith G, Wells N. Pharmaceuticals in Seven Nations, London: Office of Health Economics, 1985, Table 26, p. 39.
7. Burstall ML, Reuben BG. The Cost of Fragmentation in the European Community's Pharmaceutical Industry and Market. Brussels: European Community 1988: 90-99.
8. European Commission. Report from the Commission on the Activities of the Committee for Proprietary Medicines [COM (88) 143 Final].
9. Association of the British Pharmaceutical Industry (ABPI) and the United Kingdom Department of Health and Social Services (DHSS): The Pharmaceutical Price Regulation Scheme, 1986.
10. See the company-by-company information given in the annual issues of Scrip's Pharmaceutical League Tables, 1981/2 to date. Richmond-on-Thames: PJB Publications.
11. Burstall ML. Generic Pharmaceuticals in Europe—Blessing or Threat? London: Economists Advisory Group Ltd., 1986, pp. 16-32, 47-55.
12. Burstall ML, Wallerstein K. American Pharmaceutical Companies in Britain and Europe, unpublished.
13. Council Directive relating to the Transparency of Measures Regulating the Pricing of Medicinal Products for Human Use and Their Inclusion Within the Scope of National Health Insurance Systems [COM (88) 231. OJ C 129, 18/5/1988].

# 9

# Medical Device Innovation and Public Policy in the European Economic Community

JOHN HUTTON

The general theme of this volume is "improving the translation of research findings into clinical practice." This is often taken to mean speeding up the process by which research findings can be developed into pharmaceutical products or medical devices—that is, turning inventions into innovations in the economic sense. In such circumstances public policy would be directed toward stimulating clinical research and smoothing the passage of new products into the marketplace, on the assumption that all advances in medical technology must be regarded as beneficial. This concept would be more readily accepted if the current diffusion and use of medical technology were considered appropriate universally.

In fact, the interpretation of improving the translation of research findings into clinical practice can be broadened in at least two directions. The relevant research findings could be taken to include studies of the effectiveness and cost of existing technologies, as well as the development of new ones, and the idea of improvement could be taken to mean better selection of socially desirable innovations. The broader interpretation opens the scope of public policy to include technology assessment, both in identifying deficiencies in existing technologies and in identifying the potential benefits and costs of new developments. This is the perspective from which the first two sections of this paper review the public policy in this area, the interested parties in policy formulation, and their reactions in different circumstances. The third section reviews the characteristics of European health care systems and the nature of the European medical devices market, and the fourth section examines the potential influences on policy in the European context, using illustrations from different countries. The final section deals with developments in policy at the European Community level and how they may influence the actions of national governments.

## PUBLIC POLICY AND INNOVATION: A MODEL

### Social Objectives

Defined in the most general terms, the objective of most societies is to improve the quality of life of its members. Quality of life has many dimensions, but it is increasingly recognized that health is an important one because of its influence on an individual's ability to enjoy the other aspects of life. The links between health and quality of life have been developed to the point where the benefits of health programs are now generally assessed in terms of their impact on patients' quality of life. A variety of instruments and methods have been used (1,2). Figure 9.1 sets out the relationships among health, quality of life, and economic growth that are relevant to the discussion of the benefits of medical device innovation.

The left-hand column describes the assumed relationship by which more medical technology leads to better health care, which in turn leads to better health and improved quality of life. The right-hand column describes, in equally simplistic terms, a series of economic relationships. Increased research generates more innovation, which increases industrial output thus leading to higher incomes. The improvement in standard of living will have an impact on quality of life for society in general, although the benefits may be spread unevenly.

In fact, the economic and health elements are inextricably linked by cross-relationships at different levels. For example, higher national income levels can improve health through the provision of better housing, education, and nutrition and therefore can influence the health-related aspects of quality of life. Increased industrial output may improve the capability to provide health care, but it may also increase the demand for health services because of industrially related injury and illness. The links between research and industrial innovation are essential for the production of new medical devices that cannot be taken beyond the prototype stage within the laboratory or hospital research environment.

Accept for the moment that the relationships outlined in Figure 9.1 hold. Before we can say that efforts to increase medical device innovation are desirable, we must look at the alternatives. If resources are drawn into the health sector to develop more medical technology, this may simply switch resources from other sectors of the economy, resulting in transfers of benefit without necessarily producing a net gain (Figure 9.2). To produce a net gain in social value, medical device innovation must either improve the cost effectiveness of health care by providing increased changes in quality of life per dollar spent or produce equally effective technology at lower cost.

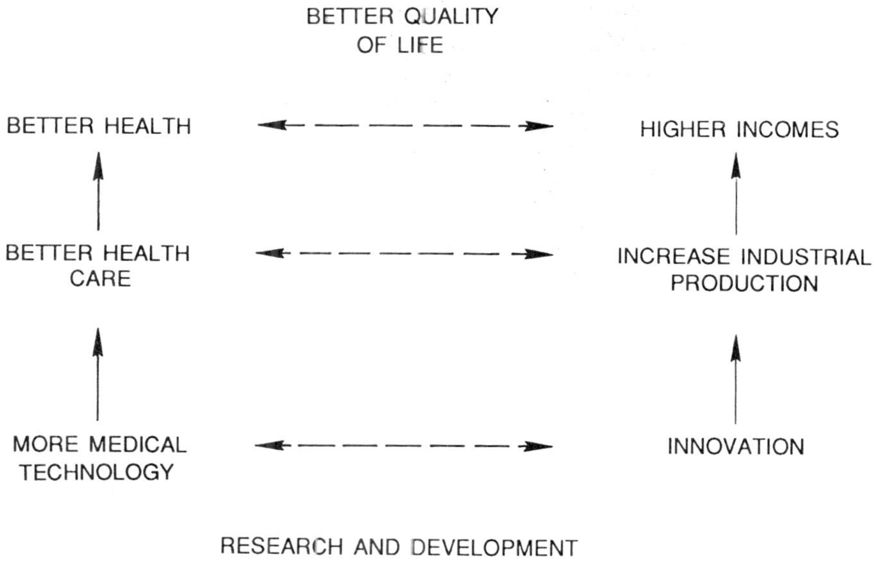


**FIGURE 9.1** Social objectives.

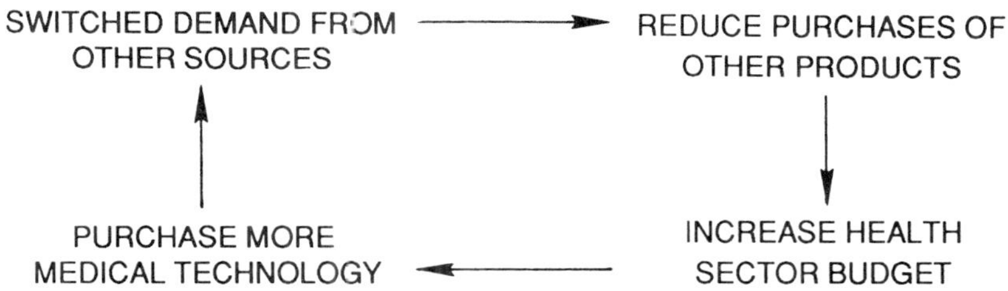


**FIGURE 9.2** Transfers of benefit.

Also, it must be shown that innovation in the medical device industry is a more effective way of increasing quality of life and productive efficiency than innovation in other sectors of the economy.

## Parties of Interest

The interest groups involved in medical device innovation can be grouped into three categories: manufacturers, health care providers, and government policy makers. Within each of these broad groups there may exist conflicts of interest between subgroups that make unambiguous identification of the objectives of the groups more difficult. For example, the attitude of established firms toward complicated and costly regulatory procedures may be different from that of small companies trying to enter a market. Equally, the attitude of providers of health care toward new technology may be rather different from that of the health care financing bodies. Even within a hospital there will be a difference of attitude among managers, doctors, and boards of governors (3). At the government level overall objectives may be less easily determined because of the many policy concerns relating to health. For example, for reasons of macroeconomic policy, the government may wish to restrict public expenditure, including that on health care, while at the same time wishing to promote better quality of care and the development and diffusion of new technologies. Similarly, a desire to improve access to care by disadvantaged groups may not be compatible with policies to increase the cost effectiveness of service provision (4).

Because of the disparate objectives of subgroups within the main parties of interest, generalizations about policy responses are unwise. However, in the following section an attempt is made to characterize the different perspectives of public policy and the response to it by industry.

## Policy Responses

Analysis of public policy responses to new technology generally takes place in the framework of a technology assessment model. In Figure 9.3 three key elements of technology assessment are represented: technical feasibility, social acceptability, and cost effectiveness.[1] Technologies that exhibit all three characteristics, represented by the shaded area, are considered appropriate for implementation. Where technologies meet only two of these conditions, policy may be directed toward meeting the third. For example, in Figure 9.3, area (b), if a technology is socially acceptable and potentially cost effective, an effort to achieve technical feasibility could be supported by public policies aimed at increasing targeted research and development (R&D) expenditures.

The development of a drug therapy for acquired immune deficiency syndrome (AIDS) might fall into this category. On the other hand, in area (c) an existing technology that is considered cost effective may not be accepted by the section of the population that would benefit. In this circumstance investment in health education programs might be the appropriate policy response. A media campaign to promote cancer screening in groups most at risk would be one example. Technically feasible interventions that are publicly accepted or even in demand, area (a), pose problems for public health funding agencies if they are not cost effective. The overuse of expensive diagnostic testing procedures is an example. The policy response might be to fix reimbursement rates below the cost of using inappropriate technology in an attempt to delay diffusion of the more expensive methods. The reimbursement system needs to be quite complex in order to permit the use of the more expensive technology in cases where it is appropriate.

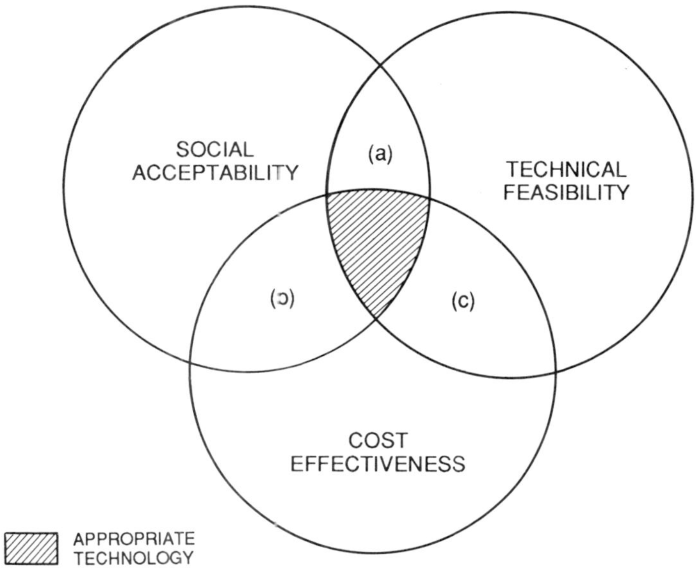


**FIGURE 9.3** Technology assessment model.

Equally important are the responses of the manufacturers of the technology to the system of economic and bureaucratic incentives and disincentives. These can be analyzed in a similar way, but as Figure 9.4 shows, the industry is more likely to be concerned with the economic viability of technology, that is, marketability and profit, rather than its cost effectiveness and social value.

Thus, the third factor in Figure 9.4 is economic viability, and the coincidence of the three factors indicates marketable technology. In area (b) a socially acceptable innovation that appears to be economically viable but is not yet technically feasible is likely to be encouraged by public and private organizations. Both government and industry will have an incentive to invest in further R&D, as is evident in the case of AIDS drugs. Where industry feels that a developed product is economically viable but not yet socially acceptable, area (c), the solution is more difficult. A public education campaign and promotion to health care providers who might influence public opinion may be one option. A recent example of this is the resistance from large sections of society to the application of advances in genetic engineering, even though they would probably not be the group affected, nor would they necessarily benefit from the new techniques. The third case involves a technically feasible and socially acceptable technology, area (a), for the use of which public health care funders are reluctant to reimburse and private demand is insufficient to produce economic viability. One possible response by the industry would be to undertake further development to reduce the

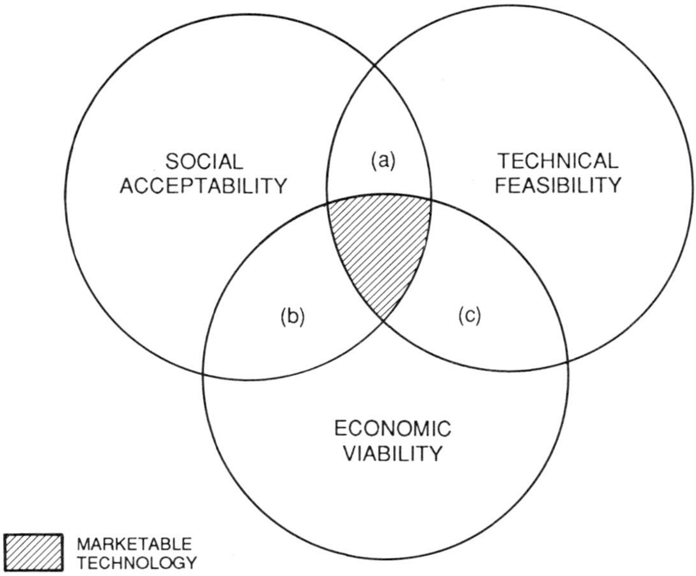


**FIGURE 9.4** Diffusion model.

costs of the innovation. Alternatively, industry might lobby funding authorities for better reimbursement, with the support of patient groups and clinicians wishing to obtain the best, most modern medical care. The diffusion of whole-body computerized tomography (CT) scanning in the United Kingdom initially was funded extensively from private and charitable sources. The large amount of private funds ultimately drew in public funds, making the market viable. This was not the case for magnetic resonance imaging (MRI) in the United Kingdom, where tighter restrictions on public funds available for acquisition of the new technology severely affected its marketability and the apparently less dramatic nature of the innovation reduced public interest in raising charitable funds for its purchase.

Whereas the responses of government and industry to the existing situation will focus on increasing the marketability and cost effectiveness of technology, both parties will be pursuing long-term policies to alter the domains of Figure 9.4. R&D activities will expand the area of technical feasibility, and general economic growth will increase the economic viability of innovations through the consequent increase in purchasing power. These two elements clearly are closely linked. The pace of technological change has a strong influence on the rate of economic growth and richer societies adopt innovations more readily. Thus, the area of triple intersection in Figure 9.4 might increase over time, indicating marketable technology will increase not through convergence of the domains but through expansion of the domains.

## THE EUROPEAN HEALTH CARE ENVIRONMENT

Europe has a wide variety of systems of health care organization and provision. In each country there is a mixture of public and private provision and public and private finance. This distinction is important because in many countries care is delivered in private hospitals but funded from public sources. The following framework is useful in classifying the different elements in the systems (6).

### Public Health Care Systems

In these the whole system is owned, planned, managed, and financed by public authorities. Examples of such systems are the United Kingdom, Sweden, Denmark, Ireland, and Italy. The essential feature of the organization of these systems is that payment to individual health care institutions, such as hospitals and individual doctors, is not related directly to the number of patients treated.[2] In the United Kingdom and Ireland a small proportion of funding comes from user charges, but the bulk comes from national taxation. Although the administration of the system is decentralized through regional and district structures, the national budgetary system gives the central government very strong control over total spending on health care.

In Denmark and Sweden national tax finance is supplemented by local taxation, and the service is managed by the counties. The budgetary system is similar for hospitals. They have local control over the use of funds, but the overall size of the budget is controlled centrally.

### Social Security Health Care Systems

These systems are planned by public authorities, but funding comes from insurance agencies belonging to the social security system, from private insurance, and, directly, from patients. Health care is provided by institutions in public and private ownership. The health care systems of Germany, France, Belgium, the Netherlands, Spain, Portugal, and Greece come into this category.

Insurance contributions to the sick funds come from employees and employers and may be subsidized from general taxation. Membership of an insurance scheme is generally compulsory, although the scheme may be private rather than public. Reimbursement systems vary among countries. In France patients must pay for services and claim back the proportion of cost covered by the insurance More generally, the sick funds are billed directly by the hospital or doctor providing the service. Because the income of service providers is linked directly to service provision, concern has been expressed over the tendency for expenditures to rise. As a consequence, extra controls over the overall budgets of hospitals have been introduced in France and the Netherlands (8).

### Private Health Care Systems

Where the hospital service is publicly owned and funded from taxation, as in the United Kingdom and Denmark, the private sector is relatively small, as very few people carry private health insurance. In countries where provision of services by the private sector is much higher, as in Spain, Germany, and France, the main source of funding is still the public sector, through the social security system. Although there is less government control over the operation of privately owned hospitals, the reimbursement system can be used to control service provision. Purely private medicine, in the sense of services provided by independent physicians in privately owned facilities and paid for directly by patients (out-of-pocket or through private insurance), is not a major feature of any European system.

## THE EUROPEAN MEDICAL DEVICE MARKET

The European market for medical devices is characterized by a high level of intercountry trade; a strong overseas presence, particularly by United States companies; and a concentration of production in many submarkets with a small number of large multinational companies producing a large proportion of the output.

It was estimated in 1985 that Europe represented 25 percent of the world market for medical devices, which was worth around 30 billion dollars. The U.S. share was 53 percent (9). An analysis of the United Kingdom trade position for 1985 gives a good illustration of the complicated patterns of trade flows. The United Kingdom imported £470 million in medical devices and exported £560 million. Over 60 percent of the imports came from other European countries, whereas 42 percent of U.K. exports went to Europe. Direct trade with the United States represented 26 percent of U.K. imports and 17 percent of U.K. exports (9). This is only a partial indicator of U.S. involvement in the U.K. and European market, since much of the intra-European trade involves products manufactured in Europe by subsidiaries of U.S. companies.

The major European countries generally have a small number of major international medical device companies and a large number of small specialist companies. There is a considerable amount of merger activity. Smaller companies with innovative products often are absorbed by larger companies with the resources to market products on an international basis. Although the major companies have extensive research laboratories, many innovations come initially from universities and research institutes or nonspecialist companies. For example, the CT scanner was developed by EMI, a U.K. electrical goods company with no previous medical products. The same firm developed the earliest clinical MRI system in the United Kingdom in collaboration with university researchers.

The largest European companies in the medical device market are Siemens of West Germany and Philips of the Netherlands, although both companies have significant production facilities in several other European countries. U.S. companies such as IGE of New York, Hewlett-Packard, and Baxter International also have a strong presence in Europe. The relative importance of individual country markets varies with the size of their overall economies but is also related to the characteristics of the health systems. For example, a recent survey of the imaging systems market in Europe found that West Germany had the largest share (42 percent), followed by France (20 percent), Italy (15 percent), and the United Kingdom (10 percent) (10).

## FACTORS INFLUENCING MEDICAL DEVICE INNOVATION

### Research and Development

Research activity is spread throughout the private and public sectors in European countries. A large amount of basic research is funded from public sources, by either direct government funding for national research organizations such as the Dutch Organization for Applied Scientific Research, or grants to other bodies. A great deal of research is undertaken by university institutes with government funding, often through academic commissioning bodies such as the U.K.'s Research Councils, as well as contracts with industrial companies (9,11). The proportion of public and private funding for research varies between sectors and between countries. In the United Kingdom, public funding has traditionally been high compared with the contribution of private industry. In other countries, such as West Germany, the industrial contribution has been much stronger, particularly in basic research, and the whole activity is seen much more as a partnership between government and industry to achieve longer-term economic objectives.

Generally, European countries see the funding of basic research as a government responsibility, with much of the health-related work being funded from the education budget, which supports universities and equivalent institutions, rather than from Ministry of Health budgets (9,11). Applied R&D of innovations is seen much more as the responsibility of industry. Although industry may receive some support from government, public sector organizations generally are not involved. In the development of the lithotripter in West Germany, the Dornier Company received research grants totaling 8.9 million German marks over an 8-year period from the Ministry for Research and Technology. Because of the expected cost effectiveness of the equipment in comparison with surgical techniques for the treatment of kidney stones, the health insurance organizations promoted the rapid diffusion of the technology, aided by the political support given to a German innovation (12). The advantages of a strong domestic market, such as that enjoyed by the West German manufacturers, are illustrated by the much slower diffusion of the Dornier lithotripter in France, partly because of the potential development of a competing French product (13).

## Regulation

Direct regulation of the marketing of medical devices exists in all European countries, but in no case does the system approach the strictness and detail of the U.S. system (14). Because the United States is still the world's most important market for medical devices, European manufacturers ensure that their products comply with U.S. standards, and, by doing so, they will also meet European requirements. The problem for manufacturers is that a separate process of approval has to be undertaken in each country, leading to an excessive administrative burden. This may well deter innovation by smaller companies without the resources to meet bureaucratic requirements (15).

Regulation may be product specific, as in France, or manufacturer specific, as in the United Kingdom (14). In the former system each product has to meet a range of safety and technical performance criteria. In the United Kingdom the system of Good Manufacturing Practice assessment has been established. Companies registering under the scheme must get approval of the organization and quality of their production processes. Products from approved companies can then be marketed to the U.K. Health Service (provided they meet conventional international electrical safety standards).

Although time consuming and sometimes expensive to meet, the regulatory systems for devices have not been a major impediment to the diffusion of new technology. This has partly been the result of the lack of requirements for demonstration of clinical effectiveness or economic efficiency in the approval process, which is essentially a technical exercise. A more important influence on innovation has been the regulation of technology in clinical use (16,17). This is achieved primarily through adjustment of the reimbursement system.

## Reimbursement

Public health systems, such as the United Kingdom, Sweden, and Denmark, have controlled the diffusion of technology through the size of the overall budget given to each hospital. No formal barriers are raised against particular technologies, but budget constraints limit the freedom of individual units to acquire expensive items of equipment. In some cases positive moves have been taken to encourage the diffusion of some technologies and their related equipment, through the provision of extra central government funds. For example, the promotion of the U.K. heart transplantation program and the expansion of renal dialysis services in Denmark and the United Kingdom followed this pattern (6,16,17).

Since 1986, public hospitals in France have been given fixed annual budgets to cover expenses for the treatment of social security members in their area. They are still able to charge fees for service for patients coming from outside their area. The system does not, however, apply to private hospitals. For certain expensive medical technologies specific approval is required from the Ministry of Health, which attempts to achieve a sensible diffusion of such technologies, geographically and between private and public sector hospitals. The Carte Sanitaire (or health map) is based on predetermined criteria relating to population and other characteristics of each region. The technologies regulated in this way include linear accelerators, CT and MRI scanners, dialysis machines, and lithotripters (8). Once approval has been given for acquisition of a technology, public hospitals can receive financial assistance for its purchase and are eligible for reimbursement for its use. Proposals have been put forward to extend these controls to private hospitals (10).

Similar controls have been instituted in other social security-funded systems, such as the Dutch Article 18 of the Hospital Provisions Act. It requires the government to produce a national plan for certain expensive technologies that cannot be used without a license. The technologies to which this provision applies are similar to those controlled under the French system. An additional provision allows the government and the Sick Funds Council to fund procedures on an experimental basis while they are being evaluated and before they come under Article 18. This was done initially with heart and liver transplantation (11).

More generally in social security systems, control over the diffusion and use of medical devices is exercised through the reimbursement rate. This has the advantage of applying to all users of the devices in both private and public sectors. Even in West Germany the continued rise in health care costs has led to restrictions on the approved applications of techniques such as MRI and more careful consideration of the level of reimbursement (18).

## THE ROLE OF THE EUROPEAN COMMUNITY

Given the background of different systems of technical assessment of equipment for safety, design, and performance and the variable planning controls on the diffusion and use of devices in health care, what hope is there of any standardization? The most likely vehicle is the European Community, which has for many years been trying to coordinate the activities of its member states in this field (19). The Community has no official role in health care—this is regarded as a national government responsibility—

but it has a direct interest in industrial matters. Its interest is centered on opening access to markets and ensuring fair competition.

The development of the Community's role in industrial policy carries further implications for the medical device industry, which is dominated by multinational companies. The ability of national governments to control such companies is declining, but an active community anti-trust policy could have a stronger influence. Through its industrial policy role the Community has devoted resources to R&D in industries related to health care. Two of the most important justifications for funding one such program were "national interest" and "European cooperation" (20). To justify further R&D programs in the field of medical informatics, the need to improve "European competitiveness" features strongly (5,6). The European Commission is much more involved in funding applied research in industry because of its limited powers in the field of heath care, although it does have a medical and health-related research program (17). In the area of regulation, the European Community is encouraging the standardization of testing procedures for medical devices by member states in preparation for the "single market" in 1992. In spite of earlier delays and pessimism, significant progress is being made (14,19,21). Directives eventually will be introduced for different types of device, introducing stricter requirements, particularly with regard to clinical evidence on safety and performance.

## CONCLUSIONS

Several trends that emerge from this overview of the European scene are significant from the U.S. perspective. All European governments are concerned about the cost and efficiency of their health care systems and are taking a more active interest in medical technologies as a potential cause of increased costs. As a consequence, there is increased emphasis on the cost effectiveness of innovations rather than just technical and clinical matters. How far this will influence the industry in terms of the quantity and nature of the devices that are selected for development remains to be seen.

The influence of the European Community is increasing, particularly through its encouragement of harmonization and standardization of regulations among member states. This will greatly ease the burden on manufacturers selling from within the Community, but its effect on those outside is less easy to predict. As the Community's standards are unlikely to be stricter than U.S. regulations, it seems plausible that U.S. companies not located in Europe would also benefit from a system requiring approval of products in only one member state in order to market throughout the Community.

In terms of competitive R&D the Community is keen to support the activities of European manufacturers through programs administered by the Commission. This compensates for the restrictions placed on national governments by Community competition laws. Although encouraging complete freedom of competition within its boundaries, the Community may take on a more protective attitude toward the outside world. However, the truly global nature of the market, the dominance of multinational companies, and the dependence of many European companies on U.S. markets make it unlikely that the medical device market would be chosen for a confrontation with the United States on trade policy.

## NOTES

1. This form of presentation was first used by the author at the Workshop on Technology Assessment and Industry at the 1989 Conference of the International Society for Technology Assessment in Health Care, held in London. It was subsequently used in a report produced for the European Commission to which the author contributed (5). He is grateful to Dr. Anne-Marie Warning of WHO, Copenhagen, for her contribution to the development of the approach.
2. The current reforms of the U.K. National Health Service (7) will change this, but the new system will not come into operation until April 1991. Under the new arrangements a proportion of hospital budgets will be dependent directly on the number of patients treated. Similar changes also are under consideration in Sweden.

## REFERENCES


1. Torrance GL. Measurement of health state utilities for economic appraisal. Journal of Health Economics 1986;6:1-30.
2. Kind P. The Design and Construction of Quality of Life Measures. Discussion Paper No. 43. Centre for Health Economics, University of York, 1988.
3. Greer AL. Adoption of medical technology: the hospital's three decision systems. International Journal of Technology Assessment in Health Care 1985;1:669-680.
4. Hutton J. The conflict between industrial policy and health policy in the UK medical equipment market. In Hutton S, Hutton J, Pinch T and Shiell A (eds). Dependency to Enterprise. London: Routledge, 1991.
5. Commission of the European Communities. Research, Development and Technology in Medical and Bio-Informatics: Specification of Priority Tasks in Research, Development and Technology. Commission of the European Communities, Directorate General XIII, Brussels, 1989.
6. Groot L. An overview of the systems and regulations concerning medical technology and the diffusion of six technologies. In Stocking B (ed). Expensive Health Technologies. Oxford: Oxford University Press 1988;op.cit.:3-18.
7. Department of Health. Working for patients. London: Her Majesty's Stationery Office, 1989.
8. Lacronique JF. Technology in France. International Journal of Technology Assessment in Health Care 1988;4:385-394.
9. Advisory Council on Applied Research and Development. Medical Equipment. London: Her Majesty's Stationery Office, 1986.

10. Editorial. West Germany leads EC imaging market. Clinica 1990;383:10.
11. Banta HD, Gelijns AC. Steering Committee on Future Health Scenarios. Anticipating and Assessing Health Care Technology. Volume I. Dordrecht: Martinus Nijhoff, 1987.
12. Kirchberger S. The process of diffusion of the lithotripter in the Federal Republic of Germany. In Stocking B (ed). Expensive Health Technologies. Oxford: Oxford University Press, 1988;54-59.
13. Dirieux P, Blum C, Jolly D. The Introduction of the First Lithotripter in France. In Stocking B (ed). Expensive Health Technologies. Oxford: Oxford University Press, 1988;46-53.
14. Sargentini A, Mariani L. Regulations governing medical devices. In Rapparini, R (ed). The Health Service Market in Europe. Brussels: Elsevier 1984;46-83.
15. Johnson P. Problems Facing Manufacture of Electromedical Devices. In Rapparini R (ed). op.cit.:99-108.
16. Stocking B (ed). Expensive Health Technologies. Oxford: Oxford University Press, 1988.
17. Drummond MF (ed). Economic Appraisal of Health Technology in the European Community. Oxford: Oxford University Press, 1987.
18. Krebs KH, John J. Federal Republic of Germany. In Drummond MF (ed). Economic Approval of Health Technology in the European Community. Oxford: Oxford University Press, 1987;170-188.
19. Rapparini R (ed). The Health Service Market in Europe. Brussels: Elsevier, 1984.
20. Lavelle SM, Morucci JP, Dawids S. Committee in Bio-Medical Engineering Report on Technology Transfer and Assessment. In Drummond MF (ed). Economic Appraisal of Health Technology in the European Community. Oxford: Oxford University Press, 1987;85-88.
21. Higson G. 1989—Year for big decisions in the active implantable medical devices directive. Clinica 1988;383:12.

# 10

# Japan's Pharmaceutical Industry Postwar Evolution

ROBERT NEIMETH

Since World War II, the emergent pharmaceutical industry in Japan has transformed and retransformed itself in response to four factors that have shaped the business environment. Broadly defined, these factors are government policy, business capacity, national economic development, and societal trends that today are driving the Japanese pharmaceutical industry at home and in external markets. By identifying opportunities and limitations within particular time phases, these factors have, in effect, provided a map of the commercial direction Japanese and non-Japanese companies have taken over the past 45 years. This "environment-to-industry" analysis provides the framework for a review of the three distinctive historical phases of pharmaceutical industry development since World War II and the evolution of a likely fourth phase in the 1990s.

## PHASE I: EMERGENCE (MID 1940s TO MID 1960s)

Immediately after the war, Japan began rebuilding its shattered economic base amid widespread skepticism about its ability to recover. Edwin O. Reischauer, a member of the U.S. Occupation Administration and later Ambassador to Japan, echoed the sentiments of both nations when he observed that postwar Japan's economy "may be fundamentally so unsound that no policies . . . can save her from slow starvation."

Mirroring this bleak business landscape was a domestic drug industry whose manufacturing facilities were virtually destroyed but whose human infrastructure—labor, management, and scientists experienced in sulpha drugs and penicillin—remained largely intact. The industry's revival would hinge on policies aimed at resurrecting the nation as a whole.

As a first step toward recovery, the Occupation Administration and the Japanese government embraced a series of rigid economic measures, including strict curbs on imports and investment designed to revitalize domestic manufacturing and employment. At the time, early forms of protectionism were viewed not as an evil but as necessary for national survival.

Other measures soon emerged that were even more directly protective of Japan's pharmaceutical industry. Imports were subjected to strict quotas, pharmaceutical licenses could not be obtained without government registration, and ceilings were clamped on royalty rates. Foreign investment was allowed only under narrowly defined conditions that normally took the form of 50-50 joint ventures. Moreover, a joint venture had to manufacture all products locally within 2 years of formation. And, finally, only manufacturing ventures were permitted to invest in Japan.

Paralleling these restraints against foreign entry was a mix of regulatory and legal rules that facilitated the reemergence of a domestic pharmaceutical industry. As in most countries, Japan's system of drug regulations and controls was relatively primitive. Until 1967, when complex changes were introduced, virtually no preclinical studies were required, and only basic clinical studies were mandated. The result was an uncomplicated process biased toward quick regulatory review and approval. Pfizer's own experience in Japan underscores this point. In 1965 the company's submission for hydroxyzine injectable contained only 88 pages, whereas Pfizer's most recent post-1967 filing for doxazosin consisted of 2,430 summary pages.

A related feature of the regulatory/legal universe was the absence of effective patent protection for pharmaceutical products. Without a patent law (one was in fact enacted in 1976) the Japanese could make and sell "copycat" versions of brand name medicines without permission of the proprietor company. Although a patent law protecting pharmaceutical processes existed, it simply meant that Japanese companies could use a different, unprotected process or path to reproduce the end-product medicine. Without a law protecting the drug itself, Japanese industry was legally free to exploit the inventions of American and European industry.

In addition to these procedurally oriented mechanisms of patent law, regulatory control, and trade protection, the Japanese government proceeded to institute measures that gave its drug industry what it needed most: domestic supply and production capability.

Immediately following the war, the Occupation Administration had established a semigovernmental organization charged with procuring and supplying raw materials to pharmaceutical producers at frozen prices on a carefully rationed basis. Moreover, the Occupation Administration encouraged the government to expedite imports of manufacturing technology for key drugs such as penicillin, thus enabling production to begin in 1946.

Enhancing these early interventions was the development in 1961 of yet another substantive element in Japan's policy toward the pharmaceutical industry: government underwriting of domestic demand.

In 1947 the Allied Administration had urged the government to reorganize and expand the health insurance scheme as a key welfare program. The overall weakness of the Japanese economy, however, prevented its adoption and full application. Instead, the government concentrated on policies for incremental liberalization of the pharmaceutical industry. Controls on drug prices and distribution were relaxed in 1952. This was followed in 1955 by the first of numerous in-market surveys of National Health Insurance (NHI) drug prices and, in 1960, by another round of liberalized controls on pharmaceutical imports.

With the economy now stabilized, the government in 1961 delivered what was asked of it in 1947. Via legislation the government required all Japanese to become members of an insurance scheme in exchange for essentially free, high-quality medical care. One result was to escalate health care spending and, with it, the size of the pharmaceutical market.

Another consequence was the creation of a new, more complex network of relationships that all but assured continued government underwriting of domestic demand. In Japan physicians play a larger role than in the United States. Influenced in part by a Chinese heritage, they have traditionally dispensed—as well as prescribed—medicines. What naturally came about over time was their ability to earn profits on the medicines they dispensed. After 1961 this took the form of pharmaceutical companies selling medicines at discounted prices to physicians who would resell them to patients—and thus to the government—at the NHI list price. The appropriateness of this practice notwithstanding, a state-sponsored "demand side" pharmaceutical market became a fixture of Japanese health care and political life.

This early mix of environmental factors effectively created a two-tier pharmaceutical industry in Japan: one Japanese and the other foreign. On one level were the Japanese companies that had rapidly rebuilt their manufacturing capabilities. By 1950 Kyowa, Meiji, Toyo Jozo, Taito, and others had established new antibiotics facilities. A measure of this quick turnaround was the government's decision to abolish pharmaceuticals rationing in 1952, a mere 7 years after the end of World War II.

Nevertheless, a fundamental weakness affected the Japanese drug industry. In an environment that encouraged basic rebuilding and more open regulation, the Japanese continued to rely on the licensing of offshore technology and on acquiring rights to manufacture and sell the discoveries of other companies. The emphasis on manufacturing remained and, as a result, few laboratories existed. Those that did stressed development rather than discovery—this in stark contrast to the United States and Europe, which were entering the "golden age" of drug discovery in the 1950s and 1960s.

Although the Japanese missed this discovery period, they were still able to benefit because of American and European business decisions at the time. Faced with an uncertain economy and increasingly protectionist trade policies, U.S. and European firms happily licensed their drugs to the Japanese. This made available to Japan a range of important licensed products from overseas laboratories whose parent companies were underrepresented in Japan.

Several foreign firms did form joint ventures with local Japanese partners in the 1950s. Among them were Schering AG, Ciba-Geigy, Lederle, Pfizer, and Roussel. In the 1960s Sandoz, Bristol Myers, Hoechst, and Merck entered Japan. Still, most American and European companies were content to remain second-tier players via licensing agreements in a country whose investment laws and economic prospects neither pleased nor welcomed them.

## PHASE II: TRANSFORMATION (MID 1960s TO LATE 1970s)

During the first phase of the pharmaceutical industry's emergence, production rose slowly, with sales reaching only 500 billion yen in 1965. Even so, that period was significant, for it consolidated the base for an industry takeoff. Under a shell of protectionist trade policies, Japanese companies acquired manufacturing facilities, raw materials, pharmaceutical products, government-guaranteed demand, and other critical elements that positioned them for dramatic growth.

The growth that followed occurred not simply in terms of linear expansion but in the shape of pulls and pushes exerted by a new set of environmental demands. The starting point for this transformation was the thalidomide tragedy of 1961, an event that radically altered the regulatory/governmental policy landscape. As a result, Japan, as well as many other nations, enacted an array of regulations governing pharmaceutical approvals. In 1965 new requirements on animal teratogenicity, double-blind clinical studies, and pharmacokinetic tests were mandated. Two years later, a monitoring system for side effects was started and, more importantly, a landmark drug development and registration guideline was implemented, "The Basic Policies for Drug Manufacturing Approval."

Abandoning what had been an open regulatory system, the government, with the adoption of the 1967 act, installed a system whose preclinical and clinical standards not only differed from those of the West but also required locally generated supporting data.

Clinical trials in Japanese subjects, for example, were only one of the new requirements of the extensively revised 1967 act. This particular change may have been justified, given the problems of diiodohydroxyquinolin, a side effect disaster that appeared to affect only Japanese patients, possibly because of the way the product was used. Nevertheless, the aggregate impact of all new requirements was to erect another protectionist edifice.

Whether intended or not, this new demand that lengthy and costly preclinical and clinical trials be repeated according to unfamiliar Japanese standards combined with the additional complexities of drug approval to delay the entry of foreign innovators. In truth, the 1967 act imposed a comparatively lighter burden on companies with a subsidiary presence and laboratories already in Japan. Firms so situated flourished during this period. But for the greater majority of U.S. and Europe-based companies, the 1967 act constituted a new and major impediment to entering the Japanese market. Conversely, it added another layer of insulation for the Japanese.

The 1967 act contained another element that helped shape the conduct of Japanese research and development (R&D). After 1967 the regulatory system in Japan was predicated on demonstrating merit for a new chemical entity (NCE) as necessary for approval. Merit could be shown in a variety of relatively modest ways—for example, improved pharmacokinetics leading to a simplified dosage, higher potency, and the like. As a result of this low-threshold requirement, a drug discovery process emerged that remained essentially low risk and incremental in its approach. Rather than pursuing high-risk/high-cost pharmaceutical breakthroughs, the Japanese opted for modest advances on existing agents whose development was relatively quick, simple, inexpensive, and risk free—and whose registration virtually was guaranteed.

Two other environmental factors reinforced this trend. First, the NHI pricing policy rewarded modest innovations on existing "me too" compounds with virtually the same level of premium as that of true breakthrough products. There was little incentive to assume the greater costs and greater risks of *bona fide* discovery-focused research. Second, the social phenomenon of physician dispensing ensured a market that was receptive to "me toos." Earning only low, government-set technical fees from their professional services, Japanese doctors depended increasingly on pharmaceutical sales to supplement their incomes.

This contributed to a transformation within the pharmaceutical industry that benefitted the Japanese a great deal but did very little for the foreign sector. A steady stream of new products derived from domestic higher priced "me toos" and licensed-in new agents from abroad, intertwined with physician dispensing, government-sponsored demand via the NHI system, and expanded R&D capability created an increasingly profitable and increasingly research-competent Japanese drug industry.

The 1970s saw a sustained boom in the overall health care market and a dramatic rise in pharmaceutical production and consumption. By 1970, for example, pharmaceutical sales were one trillion yen, double the 1965 figure, and by 1980 drug sales were four trillion yen, four times the 1970 total. Clearly, the leading Japanese firms had benefitted from an environment that, in just 15 years, had transformed them into large, highly successful ventures.

Even more important than volume growth was the transformation in Japanese

R&D. In the prior phase almost nothing new was discovered in Japan, but by 1973 Japanese R&D accounted for 10 percent of the world's research spending. Moreover, Japanese companies were credited with 10 percent of the NCE discoveries made in the decade. Although the overall quality of these discoveries can be debated, the Japanese were outstanding in one area of scientific inquiry that commanded their special attention. In 1971 Fujisawa discovered and licensed out to Lilly and others the country's initial pharmaceutical innovation, cefazolin, the first injectable cephem that became the leading cephem worldwide in the 1970s. Made possible by the isolation of the 7-ACA nucleus at Oxford and combined with Beecham's isolation of 6-APA, this breakthrough triggered Japanese antibacterial programs in the 1970s. Success was swift and spectacular as Japan delivered a flow of important antibacterial innovations that they proceeded to commercialize at home and to license throughout the world.

From a discovery research perspective, Japan had achieved world-class status in antibacterials by the end of the 1970s, and was poised for greater advances in the 1980s under a new law enacted in 1976 that granted product patent protection for pharmaceuticals. This legislation was timely, for Japanese companies had acquired by 1976 the basic technology, R&D capability, and financial strength to generate major discoveries needing protection from infringement. The fact that the Japanese were then the beneficiaries of a product patent law suggests that its timing was not accidental.

Despite these generally positive changes for Japanese industry, foreign-based firms continued to reside on a much lower commercial level. As mentioned earlier, there was the institutional barrier of revised regulations governing the approval process. There was also an equally restrictive pattern of business practice that was uniquely Japanese and out of step with the West.

In responding to regulatory and pricing pressures, the Japanese had consciously chosen a business strategy aimed at developing numerous products requiring modest levels of innovation. By contrast, U.S. and European firms elected to discover high-impact innovative products on a limited basis. This divergent orientation, coupled with regulatory impediments, yielded a Japanese market in which products of foreign origin—which held a 38 percent market share elsewhere in the world—were underrepresented in Japan.

## PHASE III: RETRANSFORMATION (THE 1980s)

Against a backdrop of increased scientific competence and sales growth in a protected market, Japan's pharmaceutical industry confronted in the 1980s a new alignment of forces that retransformed its business and research strategies. Exerting new and different forms of pressure, these external factors triggered a process of change that continues into the 1990s.

The starting point was a regulatory shift that changed the ground rules for operating in Japan. Caught between the political pledge to provide universal, high-quality health care and the budgetary need to contain health care costs, the government tried to "fine tune" the NHI system in a way that would accomplish both. For pharmaceuticals this led to a significant adjustment of product pricing. Under the NHI system, only products on the NHI price list are reimbursable. Prior to the 1990s, the government had routinely reduced the price of NHI-listed medicines. What separated the 1980s from the earlier two periods was the aggressiveness with which the government pursued that objective. More than a matter of degree, Japan clearly sought to squeeze pharmaceutical expenditures down to what, in its view, was an acceptable percentage of the health care budget.

In 1981 the government regularized reductions of the NHI price of pharmaceuticals based on the difference between the official reimbursed price and the discounted selling price to physicians and institutions. Without detailing the complexities and, from industry's perspective, the iniquities of this system, suffice it to say that the government achieved its objective in spectacular fashion. Under this system, pharmaceutical prices set at a base of 100 in 1980 fell to 53 in 1989, with an additional 8 to 10 percent reduction, depending on therapeutic class, that occurred earlier this year. In terms of the pharmaceutical portion of the total health care budget, this translated into a decline from 40 percent in 1981 to 30 percent in 1987.

Two other factors compounded this difficulty. The first was the influx of new foreign pharmaceutical companies. During this period, the government dismantled numerous regulations that favored Japanese industry. Although aimed at harmonizing pharmaceutical regulations with international standards, these changes significantly eased earlier difficulties of doing business in Japan. In 1980, for example, there was a general revision of the Pharmaceutical Affairs Law to realign Japanese regulations with commonly accepted global standards. Also, in 1985 new guidelines were issued on Good Manufacturing Practices, Good Licensing Practices, and preclinical data, and action was taken to facilitate the transfer of registration approvals to foreign companies. Although many earlier problems persist, they will be addressed and possibly resolved in ongoing, bilateral, and multilateral discussions involving the United States, the European Economic Community (EEC), and Japan. With this lowering of regulatory barriers and the likelihood of continued progress, many of the leading foreign-based companies either entered the market directly or dramatically increased their presence in Japan to tap a pharmaceutical market whose size was second only to that of the United States. Included among them were Merck, Glaxo, Ciba-Geigy, and Hoffmann-La Roche.

Adding to this new competitive pressure was a third factor: the entry of nonpharmaceutical Japanese companies into the domestic market. In the 1980s major breweries and textile and chemical companies diversified into pharmaceuticals for a variety of reasons. First, they judged biotechnology to be an important product source for food, nutrition, and pharmaceuticals.

**TABLE 10.1** Pharmaceutical R&D Spending, 1985

| Country | Total Spent (Billions of Dollars) | Number of Researchers | Per Researcher (Thousands of Dollars) | Percent Sales | New Products Approved |
|---|---|---|---|---|---|
| United States | 3.4 | 28,010 | 121.3 | 14.80 | 30 |
| Japan | 1.4 | 11,325 | 123.6 | 7.04 | 53 |

Second, many of them felt internally pressured to shift from increasingly expensive and inefficient smokestack industries to more profitable, technology-intensive ventures. Third, they calculated that the demographic patterns of Japan would make health care and pharmaceuticals a long-term growth industry.

With this emergence of new Japanese and non-Japanese pharmaceutical players, and with policy changes that rapidly eroded prices, Japanese industry reacted with two sets of responses. One emanated from the perception that increased new-product flow and increased R&D were the only way to survive in a more crowded, less profitable domestic market. By 1985 Japanese industry was spending as much on research per employee as American industry (Table 10.1). It was filing as many drug patents per year as Germany by 1984 (Table 10.2). During the 1980s, the top 17 Japanese companies had built more new laboratories than in the 30-year span from 1950 to 1980.

Between 1983 and 1987, Japan equaled the United States in the total number of NCEs discovered. Interestingly enough, because Japan was generally considered a slow and difficult drug development and registration market, the government responded to industry's predicament with 72 NCE approvals: double the NCE approvals of Italy (the second-ranked country) and nearly quintuple those of the United States.

None of these statistics addresses the quality of NCEs—that is, the extent to which these NCEs were imitative products or world-class discoveries. Nevertheless, Japan has clearly diversified from imitative and antibacterial research, although both remain important. Some examples of Japan's world-class innovations include the discovery of quinolones, the first cholesterol reducers, Fujisawa's work on immunostimulants, and other companies' work on renin inhibitors and platelet activating factor antagonists.

While much of this new research focus flows from Japan's aging society and the growing need for chronic therapy products, it also reflects the requirement for world-class products that will penetrate and compete effectively in overseas markets. Given the increased capital investment in new discovery facilities made by domestic companies in the 1980s as well as the fundamental shift to discovery itself, it is natural to expect leading Japanese companies to generate excellent product portfolios in the 1990s.

**TABLE 10.2** Number of Patents Related to Drugs, 1984

| Country | Total Patents | Patents Related to Drugs | Percent Related to Drugs |
|---|---|---|---|
| United States | 43,692 | 2,510 | 5.7 |
| West Germany | 24,870 | 739 | 3.0 |
| Japan | 54,040 | 797 | 1.5 |

The second Japanese response to increased domestic competition and decreased profitability was the buildup of business activities in global markets, particularly in the United States and Europe. These included joint ventures on a country and/or regional basis, self-development, strategic alliances, and minority shareholdings, as well as complete acquisitions. Currently, there are 26 companies with 140 international units. While that may seem a lot, consider that one U.S.-based company, Pfizer, has more than 100 international units. A pattern to these business activities clearly emerged in the 1980s. The leading expansionist Japanese companies focused first on drug development and on obtaining regulatory approval abroad. Then they moved downstream into marketing, sales, and production. As a result, leading Japanese companies are well positioned to compete in the United States and the European Economic Community.

## PHASE IV: THE 1990s AND BEYOND

The future is, to a certain degree, wedded to present trends. Most important among external forces will be the rapid demographic shift to an increasingly aged population that, by 2020, is expected to comprise 24 percent of the total Japanese population. There will also be a shrinking pool of active workers resulting from steadily declining birth rates. These two factors will slowly erode the actuarial foundation of the present NHI system. By 2020 there will be only 2.5 workers to support one retiree versus the 6.2 workers per retiree in 1988.

Over time the government will be caught between two objectives that, from its viewpoint, will be difficult to meet: the need to continue paying for universal, high-quality health care while sustaining and nurturing a profitable health care industry. The 1990s will be riddled with disagreement and debate on the wisdom and methods of achieving one or both objectives. At a minimum, there will in all likelihood be increasing copayment requirements, rising from a flat 20 percent rate for policy holders and dependents alike in the early 1990s to possibly 50 percent much later in the decade. In addition, there may be partial privatization of the health care system as well as delisting from NHI reimbursement of those products or services that the government perceives to be nonessential. How demographic change will affect pharmaceutical reimbursement is difficult to say. It is clear, however, that in an atmosphere of greater individual responsibility and decreasing government support, neither government nor private citizens will be willing to pay more and, indeed, may look for ways to pay less.

In contrast to this will be a second factor that may ease the task of operating in Japan: simplification of the regulatory review system to speed drug approval. When coupled with the more rapid development of new drugs, this will cement Japan's position as a "first launch" market. A more simplified system will in all likelihood result from various bilateral discussions involving Japan, the United States, and the European Economic Community as well as from the global "harmonization" exercise that seeks, in part, to standardize the various regulatory drug approval systems. To a lesser extent the Uruguay Round will also help by reaffirming major trilateral (Japan, EEC, United States) commitment to strong intellectual property standards. One result will be to decrease the chances of government retrenchment on patent protection (via compulsory licensing) should there be future budgetary pressure on Japan to reduce its pricing-reimbursement obligations under the NHI system.

The final projected factor will be the full emergence of competitors against Japan's pharmaceutical industry. U.S. and EEC-based companies can be expected to go it alone in Japan—either splitting away from existing joint ventures (Eli Lilly-Shionogi) or acquiring a complete equity stake in their joint venture partners (Merck-Banyu). The need to maximize control and hence profit in this high-risk/high-payoff market will trigger a move to operational autonomy. The second competitor group will be the nontraditional pharmaceutical firms mentioned earlier—the major breweries, for example—that will gradually begin to enter the market based on their R&D commitment in the 1980s and the formation of strategic alliances with respect to production, marketing, sales, and distribution.

Within this sphere of heightened competition, a third and largely overlooked player may emerge. In Japan small and medium-size pharmaceutical companies that cannot afford major drug discovery operations will be squeezed by the interrelated dynamics of health care cost containment and new products from the leading research-based companies. Whether induced by government administrative guidance or by marketplace reality, these small and medium-size pharmaceutical companies might initiate merger activities, Japanese style, to gain the capital base required for survival.

How these various environmental factors will affect Japanese industry can only be surmised. Nevertheless, what occurred during the 1980s serves as a partial guide. One response would appear to be continuation of the massive buildup in discovery research by Japanese and foreign companies. Not only will Japanese companies continue to discover, develop, and commercialize some 20 to 25 NCEs per year—with a similar number from

**TABLE 10.3** Leading Countries by New Product Launch

| Country | 1983 | 1984 | 1985 | 1986 | 1987 | 1983-1987 |
|---|---|---|---|---|---|---|
| Japan | 8 | 14 | 11 | 20 | 19 | 72 |
| Italy | 4 | 6 | 10 | 6 | 7 | 33 |
| West Germany | 7 | 4 | 12 | 5 | 1 | 29 |
| United States | 2 | 3 | 1 | 5 | 4 | 15 |
| Total | 44 | 39 | 64 | 52 | 55 | 254 |

foreign firms—but there will be several qualitative changes regarding these NCEs themselves (Tables 10.3 and 10.4).

First, Japanese NCEs will come increasingly from Japanese discovery research occurring in the United States and Europe via diversification into offshore facilities. Second, Japanese NCEs will remain increasingly in the hands of Japanese companies. Except for strategic reasons, in-and-out licensing will evaporate as Japanese companies decide to retain their important discoveries for new overseas subsidiaries. Third, the specific direction of NCE research will aim increasingly at establishing world-class positions in biotechnology and diseases of the elderly, where market demand will accelerate.

Intertwined with this research response will be an operational reorientation. The leading Japanese companies gradually will step up their globalization efforts, primarily in the United States and Europe, initially by learning how to prosecute a drug development and registration program and later through integrated manufacturing, marketing, and sales operations. Even while continuing to form strategic alliances with foreign companies, Japanese industry will, in the long term, seek to establish fully owned subsidiary operations in major pharmaceutical markets overseas.

As its possibly final response, Japanese industry will use public policy as a mechanism to protect its globalization objectives. Already allied with U.S. and European industry in seeking stronger patent protection under the Uruguay Round, Japanese industry will work with its own government as well as with United States and EEC industry on other major issues. Among them are the patentability of plant varieties derived from biotechnology in the EEC; adoption of the "first-to-file" criteria in U.S. patent law; and modifications in European Community directives on registration, promotion, pricing, and the like that would negatively affect the interests of the pharmaceutical industry. This more active advocacy role will flow as much from growing self-confidence as from increased presence and exposure overseas.

## A FINAL WORD

Japan's pharmaceutical industry can be characterized as one that has been highly successful domestically but remarkably unsuccessful overseas. By the 1980s, however, Japan emerged as a powerful domestic competitor based on newly acquired innovative skills. In the 1990s Japan may become a formidable player in the global marketplace as well.

What the past suggests is that these levels of actual and potential success were achieved without an explicit industrial policy for the pharmaceutical sector. The stimulus was *not* provided through an open market but rather by an array of factors that protected and promoted the industry through a highly regulated market with government controlled and supported prices. Clearly, these factors created a pharmaceutical industry in Japan that can deal from a position of strength based on its considerable financial resources and research capabilities. But at the same time, it can be argued that Japan's innovative capacity would have developed sooner if governmental policies had made the domestic market more open to competition from foreign research-based companies and if adequate product patent protection had been in place earlier. Most research in Japan until the mid 1970s was aimed at exploiting a system that rewarded copiers rather than creators. Japan now, perhaps belatedly, takes its rightful place alongside the traditional four highly inventive nations: the United States, West Germany, the United Kingdom, and Switzerland. Within Japan's pharmaceutical industry, at least the top 5 or 10 companies are poised for globalization.

The challenge ahead is not discovery, for that capability has already been demonstrated and put in place. The real challenge is how to build and exploit a global clinical development and registration capability and how to establish a global network of subsidiaries to commercialize their inventions. The Japanese doubtlessly have the ability to accomplish this. But it could have happened much earlier had Japanese industry not suffered from the insularity and lack of confidence in its ability to compete that were a product of the environmental factors reviewed in this paper.

## SELECTED BIBLIOGRAPHY

### English Language

1. Broida JH, Maeda N. Japan's high-cost illness insurance program, a study of its first three years, 1974-76. Public Health Reports 1978;93:153-160.
2. Dibner MD. Biotechnology in pharmaceuticals: the Japanese challenge. Science 1985;229:1230-1235.
3. Fujii M, Reich MR. Rising medical costs and the reform of Japan's health insurance system. Health Policy 1988;9:9-21.
4. Maurer P. Competing in Japan (Tokyo: The Japan Times, 1989) and Yano Keizai Kenkyujo (Yano Research Institute). Cited in Nihon Seiyaku Kogyo Kyokai (Japan Pharmaceutical Manufacturers Association), Data Book 1987, Tokyo: JPMA, 1967.
5. Reich MR. Why the Japanese don't export more pharmaceuticals. California Management Review 1990;32:124-150.
6. Relman AS. Doctors and the dispensing of drugs. New England Journal of Medicine 1987;317:311-312.

7. Shah HK, Hasebe M, Kondo K, Moroe Y, Kitagawa T, Nomura Y. Globalization of the Japanese Pharmaceutical Industry. New York: Nomura Research Institute.
8. Yoshikawa A. The other drug war: U.S.-Japan trade in pharmaceuticals. California Management Review 1989;31:76-90.

## Japanese Language

1. Hasegawa H. "Iyakuhin, Sangyo no Showa Shakaishi (Pharmaceuticals: Industry's Social History). Tokyo: Nihon Keizai Hyoronsha, 1986.
2. Seo T. Iyakuhin (Pharmaceuticals) Tokyo, Nihon Keizai Shinbunsha, 1986.
3. Suguro T. Iyakuhin Sangyo (Pharmaceutical Industry). Tokyo: Kyoikusha Shuppan, 1987.
4. Yakuji Handobukku '89 (Pharmaceuticals Handbook '89). Tokyo: Yakugyo Jihosha, various years.

# Appendix A

# The Impact of Regulation and Reimbursement on Pharmaceutical Innovation

Commentary by
PETER BARTON HUTT

The purpose of this commentary is to identify and evaluate the major U.S. public policies that affect pharmaceutical development. Unfortunately, there are no good data with which to evaluate the impact of public policy on pharmaceutical innovation. I will rely more on qualitative evidence and observations, and I will especially consider regulatory and reimbursement policies, because in my judgment they have great impact on the industry. Finally, I will discuss the desirability and feasibility of some options for policy change.

## REGULATION AND PHARMACEUTICAL INNOVATION

There are two sources of regulation of the pharmaceutical industry. The first is the statute itself, the Federal Food, Drug and Cosmetic Act of 1938, as amended by the Drug Amendments of 1962. The statute establishes a structure; that is, it establishes the most stringent form of regulation, pre-marketing approval, from among a wide variety of regulatory mechanisms (such as pre-marketing notification, pre-marketing testing, or standard-marketing) that could have been selected.

Although the statute mandates the general structure of the regulatory system, the Food and Drug Administration (FDA) is given wide latitude to do, in effect, anything it wants within that extraordinarily broad concept of pre-market approval. All daily administrative practice and procedure at the FDA (e.g., deciding whether a manufacturer needs to perform another study or whether to approve a product for marketing now or 10 years from now) is within the agency's discretion. This has resulted in large variations in the form and content of FDA requirements. Sometimes they are written down; most typically they are not. Some procedures are uniform throughout the organization; most are not. Administrative policies vary widely within the FDA because it is not monolithic. The FDA, like every organization, is a lot of little principalities with their own rulers, each dictating policy according to what he or she thinks is the way the world ought to work. Significant differences can be observed between the various centers at the agency[1] as well as at the level of individual reviewers. To say there is a single FDA policy that needs to be changed does not recognize the way it or any other government agency, particularly a regulatory agency, works.

Finally, one omnipresence must never be forgotten: the United States Congress, which has what is known as oversight jurisdiction over the FDA. It influences the FDA through the congressional hearing. The sword of Damocles hanging over the head of the FDA is the threat of testifying at nationally televised congressional investigations on why its practices resulted in fraud, injury, and loss of life.

This tends to reduce somewhat the regulatory discretion that is inherent in the statute. For the past 30 years there has been unrelenting pressure on the FDA to be very conservative and to avoid risk. The price of making a wrong decision is high, whereas the reward for making a correct decision is nonexistent. There are no rewards in the system for being expeditious, and there are enormous incentives to delay.

With that prelude, I will examine the dynamics and difficulties of the regulatory process. I have divided the process into five phases: the preclinical phase; the clinical investigation or investigational new drug (IND) phase; the FDA approval or new drug application (NDA) phase; the post-marketing approval phase; and a fifth one I would not have considered 10 years ago, the post-marketing approval generic competition phase. I will consider these five segments individually and then as a whole.

## Preclinical Testing

The preclinical testing phase is composed of laboratory and animal studies designed to show biologic activity against the target disease and to evaluate the short-term safety of compounds in animals. Long-term animal studies are initiated to detect possible mutagenicity, carcinogenicity, and teratogenicity. These often continue for several years, concurrent with early human trials. The FDA has laboratory practice regulations that dictate the way in which animal studies must be conducted if they are to be considered for product approval, but these probably add very little to the length and cost of the overall drug development process.

Beyond this is the much more fundamental issue of how much and what kind of animal studies need to be done before an investigator can begin testing in humans and how much animal work needs to be done to receive

FDA approval. Some 12 to 15 years ago a citizen advocacy group urged the FDA to require that all animal toxicity studies be completed before any drug be given to any human, including full chronic carcinogenicity studies in two species. Fortunately, the FDA did not adopt this overly stringent strategy.

The issue of animal testing in the preclinical stage remains important. Until 1982, the FDA had no rule requiring a full carcinogenicity bioassay in two species prior to NDA approval. It requires it now. This rule came into effect because Congress said, in no uncertain terms, "either you adopt the rule or we will criticize you publicly." The FDA adopted the rule. Now, any drug to be used chronically in humans must have full carcinogenicity bioassays in two species to be considered for FDA approval.

I mention this example to make us more mindful of the potential impact of regulations regarding preclinical testing. Grabowski's calculations show that 1 year added to the NDA approval process costs a lot of money. If a manufacturer had to add 1 to 3 years for comprehensive animal toxicity studies before initiating Phase I human testing, the financial impact would be tremendous.

## Clinical Investigation: The IND Phase

Let me now turn to the clinical investigation or IND stage. After completing preclinical testing, a manufacturer files an IND with the FDA to receive permission to begin testing in humans. The IND contains all the information known about the compound, including its chemical structure, proposed mechanism of action, stability and manufacturing information, the methods and results of preclinical laboratory and animal studies, and the proposed plans, methods, and investigators for clinical trials. The IND must also be reviewed and approved by the Institutional Review Board where the proposed clinical studies will be conducted.

There is no statutory requirement that there be an IND, and there is no statutory requirement that the FDA be notified about clinical investigations with new compounds. The elaborate protocol that the FDA has constructed is based upon what it, not Congress, regards as good public policy. As a result of the thalidomide incident, the FDA promulgated regulations requiring that a sponsor, commercial or noncommercial, submit an IND plan to the FDA and wait 30 days for the agency to review and approve it.

Technically, if you do not hear from the FDA by the end of 30 days, you can start your clinical study. This almost never occurs. Who would take the risk that the FDA would later disapprove an IND? Informal methods have been developed to deal with this problem. If you do not hear from the FDA, you call them; within the next 30 to 90 days, you will get an answer. Sometimes the FDA will respond with, "We have not reviewed it yet; would you mind waiting another two months?" Sometimes it will call and say,

"We have some real questions about your IND," and you say, "Is this a clinical hold?" They reply, "No, we are not telling you not to start the study, it is just that we think it is a problem." Sometimes they will call and say, "We not only have questions, we have deep concerns." The meaning of "deep concerns" can vary widely, depending on the individual reviewer making the comments.

In 10 percent of the cases, there will be a formal clinical hold on an IND. What happens in the other 90 percent of cases? National Cancer Institute (NCI) representatives, before the National Committee to Review Current Procedures for Approval of New Drugs for Cancer and AIDS (the so-called Lasagna Committee), testified that they would not consider going ahead with a clinical study if they did not have absolute FDA approval. The pharmaceutical industry behaves similarly. Thus, months can go by where nothing occurs because of concern about the FDA assessment of the IND.

Once an IND is approved, technically you can tell the FDA you are changing the protocol and proceed at will. There is no requirement to seek its views or approval of the study changes. Not many investigators do that. Researchers at the NCI said they would never go ahead with changes without getting FDA agreement, and many in the pharmaceutical industry do the same thing.

When an investigator goes from a Phase I to a Phase II clinical trial, it may take 6 months to a year to get agreement from the FDA on the protocol. Yet academics and industry researchers alike are unwilling to continue with the next phases of trials without informal approval of the design from FDA officials. If they disagree with the protocol 3 years later, you do not get approval of the NDA.

This clearly puts the FDA in a difficult position. If it does not give the investigator feedback on the study and it turns out to be the wrong type of study, the FDA must turn down the drug and face the criticism of the manufacturer and other advocates. If it does tell the investigator what is wrong with the study, it is accused of "micromanagement," "fussing over minor details," or "telling researchers how to run good science." It is a catch-22 for the agency.

The industry itself is ambivalent about the involvement of the FDA in overseeing research protocols. The industry wants FDA feedback, and the resulting implied approval, as long as the agency agrees with its trial design. It does not want oversight if the feedback is critical, and it does not want FDA micromanaging a project the manufacturer feels it knows more about. NCI says the same thing.

Two proposals for reform have been suggested to help resolve the conflict between feedback and micromanagement. One is to use the advisory committees within the FDA to resolve some of these protocol disputes. The advisory committees would be able to give quick scientific advice and possibly provide an appeals mechanism to adjudicate disputes between companies and the FDA. Reformers suggest that this would remove delays in the process, be more objective, and diminish the amount of micromanagement.

Another, and more radical, proposal is to deregulate at least Phase I of clinical testing.[2] The proposal would do for drugs what is done for many medical devices. An investigator would obtain approval of an IND by an Institutional Review Board (IRB)[3] and not go to the FDA until a later point in drug testing. The rationale is that Phase I involves basic pharmacology and toxicology research that poses little risk. Much of it is done in universities. The IRB can do as good a job as the FDA in evaluating the protocols. In addition, since 30 percent of drugs in Phase I testing never go on to Phase II, unburdening the FDA from regulation of this early step would lead to a substantial decrease in its administrative workload.

What are the safety ramifications of such a proposal? Louis Lasagna, chairman of the National Committee to Review Current Procedures for Approval of New Drugs for Cancer and AIDS, says that no human being was ever harmed in a Phase I study. The issue is the extent to which we need a federal regulatory structure to monitor the earliest phase of the drug development process. Could we do without it?

One other factor should be considered in terms of economic impact. The FDA has divergent requirements for investigational drugs and devices. Manufacturers cannot charge the patient for investigational drugs, but they can charge for investigational devices. It seems a clearcut rule. However, in cases involving drug-device combinations there is much confusion. Often, the FDA is unclear whether it will regulate such technologies as drugs or devices. The distinction is not trivial.

There are similar inconsistencies within the class of INDs. The recent treatment IND regulations stipulate that a manufacturer can charge for a product if it has been approved as a treatment IND but cannot charge if it was approved as a compassionate use IND. Nonpayment for certain INDs may be a barrier to entry for small pharmaceutical firms, particularly biotechnology firms, which need a cash flow to continue investigating potentially important new drugs.

The overall time required to do the clinical studies necessary to complete an NDA is highly variable, somewhere between 1 and 8 years. The large range is partly explained by the discretionary nature of the clinical development stage. For example, there are no uniform requirements on the number of Phase III trials, which are the largest, most expensive, and most time consuming.[4] If the FDA requires two or three Phase III studies, it is going to take a long time for your NDA. If only one Phase II study is required, as has been true in a few instances of expedited review,[5] it will take as little as 1 year.

Criteria for Phase III requirements are not mandated in the statute. The law is broad and nonspecific. It says there must be substantial evidence, supported by adequate and well-controlled clinical trials, sufficient to convince qualified experts that a drug is safe and effective. The statute also says safety must be proved by all tests reasonably applicable to show safety. This extraordinarily broad statutory requirement is nothing more than a slogan. It tells the FDA to approve good drugs and not to approve bad drugs.

## FDA Approval: The NDA Phase

When considering the FDA official assessment of new drugs, the first question is how to set priorities for regulatory review. Do you evaluate drugs in the chronological order in which you receive them—first in, first out—or do you set up some kind of priority system? The choice has serious economic implications. The FDA has established a priority system based upon its assessment of a drug's chemical novelty and potential treatment benefit over existing therapies.[6] Internal FDA review of pending NDAs results in an inventory that lists drugs from most important to least important.

The FDA priority system does not coincide with the economic needs of companies or the economic needs of the innovation process. The system currently give highest ranks to new chemical entities (NCEs) that are unusual and that will treat diseases that are otherwise untreatable. It might, for example, rate as the most important drugs compounds for treatment of orphan diseases, which might have as few as 100 or 200 patients in each category. Because the FDA criteria place emphasis on breakthrough drugs, second- and third-generation drugs for cancer and cardiovascular disease may be lower on the list.

If a manufacturer has two drugs, an orphan drug of no economic consequence and another of major economic importance, the orphan drug may well be reviewed first. The second could be held up 3 or 4 years while all the other orphan drugs go through. Do we as a society want that kind of priority system? This is a key issue that we must address explicitly. At present, the FDA has total discretion. It could easily reverse the system if it wanted to.

Another question is how much data are needed to show safety and effectiveness. How many adequate and well-controlled clinical trials should there be, with how many patients, under what protocols, and involving how many subpopulations (such as the elderly, children, or any other group)? The statute leaves these issues to FDA discretion. De facto criteria vary from drug category to drug category and among individual reviewers. Such variations can result in differences in regulatory approval time of 2 or 3 years for a drug.

Finally, there is the impact of social and political pressure on the process. The degree of public pressure on the National Institutes of Health (NIH) to develop new drugs to combat acquired immune deficiency syndrone (AIDS) and on the FDA to expeditiously approve such innovations is unprecedented. No group of heart patients or cancer patients ever marched on the FDA or even succeeded in getting a congressional hearing to object to the way that

FDA was doing its job. It is reasonable that the FDA concluded from the absence of public protest that it was doing its job correctly. Perhaps it has been. If that is true, we should not pay any attention to what the academic community, the economic community, the industry, and patient advocacy groups are complaining about.

It is important to understand that the regulatory process is most crucially driven by individuals and not by policies. Thus, it is the decision-making style of the people who review and approve NDAs that drives what happens. Every NDA for AIDS drugs has gone through in record time. Every biotechnology drug, whether or not it is a breakthrough, has gone through in record time. The reason is that some people in the agency wanted to prove that the FDA and the United States were going to be the leaders in biotechnology. They sought to show this by making biologic agents a high priority. This has not been true for cancer drugs, which have been slower to receive NDA approval. The same has been true for cardiovascular drugs. Surprisingly, there has been no vocal public constituency pushing for the development of cancer and cardiovascular drugs.

Overall, the FDA approval system is like a balloon. If you squeeze it in one place, it bulges out in another. A choice to approve one drug expeditiously means that another will wait longer. Grabowski has shown that the average time to NDA approval has not changed dramatically in 20 years. The example of AZT, which got approved in 6 months, only meant that some other drug that would have gotten through in 2 years is going to get through in 3.5 years.

Surprisingly, the work of Cook and colleagues has shown that it is not these global issues of safety and effectiveness that hold up most NDAs. A study done a decade ago showed 60 percent of issues delaying approval were related to manufacturing, chemistry, and quality control data, and only 20 percent were related to safety and effectiveness issues—the big issues that we all tend to associate with delays. Furthermore, almost all drugs that enter Phase III trials get approved. The only exceptions occur when manufacturers give up on a drug after years of testing because the market has changed or the compound is not worth marketing for some other reason. In fact, a new phenomenon has been emerging recently: drug companies receive FDA approval but decide not to market the compound because it has become obsolete while awaiting official clearance.

How could we change this system? There are two major strategies. We could approve all NDAs at the end of Phase II and eliminate Phase III entirely. We could get rare adverse reaction information in another way. This proposal would have a truly major impact. Richard Crout used to tell me, when he was Director of the FDA Bureau of Drugs, that he knew at the end of Phase II whether 90 percent of drugs were safe and effective. Approving drugs at the end of Phase II would cut out an average of 3 or 4 years from the approval process.

One other way of reforming the system is to shift the burden of balancing risk and benefit to the doctor-patient relationship. Advocates envision the pharmaceutical companies giving information about new drugs to physicians and having them openly discuss the risks and benefits of the new therapies with patients, rather than the current FDA approval process. I think this approach goes too far. Some form of FDA approval is necessary. It is clear from the history of Western drug development that the lack of regulatory standards means there will be more failures, more people hurt, and more drug tragedies, as well as more drug triumphs.

Other things that have been suggested I think are also unrealistic. For example, it has been argued for 15 years that if we had more Phase IV studies—post-marketing studies to monitor side effects—we could approve drugs earlier. Everyone I have talked to who has worked in the process believes that we would have the same drug approval time with additional Phase IV studies on top of that. It might be a more complete system, but it would not shorten approval times.

People have suggested making better use of FDA advisory committees and critics have called for institutional changes whereby FDA reviewers would have a chance to do research in a better working environment. These suggestions are good ones. My analysis, however, is that these improvements probably would not decrease the time to approval.

## Post-Marketing Requirements

Let me now consider the fourth phase of the drug approval process: post-marketing requirements. This phase is composed of Phase IV testing[7] and post-marketing surveillance. Many fewer formal post-marketing studies are done than might be expected. Most information on adverse drug reactions comes from the current system of informal post-marketing surveillance and adverse reaction reporting, and the FDA believes that it works quite well. As a result, expensive formal studies are not needed.

One area worth considering in terms of economic impact on the pharmaceutical innovation process is the use of supplemental NDAs to gain approval for new uses of approved drugs, changes in the drug label, changes in manufacturing procedures, or other changes in the original NDA. It is important to understand that the original NDA is a contract. Once an NDA is approved, no one can vary one iota from it.

It is a system that makes enforcement easy. From an innovation perspective, however, such a rigid system makes pharmaceutical manufacturing and development very difficult. Supplemental NDA are the lowest priorities for the FDA to review. Thousands of supplemental NDAs go to the bottom of the bottom of the reviewers' pile. They can sit there for months and years. This inefficiency in the system is significant because approving the new clinical indication often would allow the drug to be reimbursed for a previously unapproved use.[8] Here is something that is ripe for reform.

### Generic Drug Competition

The fifth and final phase of the process involves generic drugs and generic competition. The major impact of post-marketing approval of generic competition began in 1984 with the passage of the Drug Price Competition and Patent Term Restoration act. I think it is fair to say that this has had a bigger impact than any of us who worked on it at the time anticipated. Basically, the act is a trade-off of patent term extension for generic competition as soon as the patent runs out. Because of the way in which generic competition has shortened the effective commercial life of a drug there is a smaller window of time within which all the profit has to be made to recoup the investment on that drug and to set up a reserve for research for future drugs.

That window used to be much longer—10, 20, even 30 years. We are, therefore, seeing increased prices. Congress passed a statute that gave the pharmaceutical industry two alternatives: get rid of research or raise prices to finance research. Generic competition has caused drug companies to raise prices while they still have marketing exclusivity, and these higher prices are what finance drug research.

On the other hand, the American public and Congress are concerned about these price increases. The economic return on investment in research and development is a major public policy issue that needs to be addressed.

### The Overall Impact of Regulation on Innovation

It is clear that the total impact of the regulatory system on pharmaceutical innovation is very large. There are barriers and impediments at almost every stage in the process, many of which could be lower. The conglomeration of barriers has, among other things, resulted in an overall barrier to entry. How many new small pharmaceutical companies are there? There are a few in the biotechnology field, but how many are surviving the consolidation process, and how many are being swallowed up by mergers or outright acquisition? How many of those will survive another decade because of the enormous cost that we as a society have placed upon the drug development process?

## REIMBURSEMENT AND PHARMACEUTICAL INNOVATION

### The Big Players: Public and Private Payers

Two basic categories of major players affect the reimbursement of new medicines. One is the public sector—federal and state governments with

Medicare and Medicaid—and the other is the private insurance industry. There are even more rules for reimbursement than for getting new drugs approved. They vary widely from company to company and from city to city in the same company. There is no nationwide reimbursement rule for the Health Care Financing Administration (HCFA), Medicaid, the private insurance industry, or even individual insurers.

## Inconsistencies in Payment Policies

There is no consistency, no predictability, and very little fairness in the system. One explanation of these inconsistencies seems understandable. Insurance programs are based on insurance principles. They are not public health programs. The job of the insurance companies is to conserve funds, not to conserve or improve public health. Payers usually disagree vigorously with such a characterization, so let me give three scenarios: use of an unapproved drug in a clinical investigation, use of an unapproved drug for treatment outside a clinical investigation (i.e., compassionate use of an investigational drug), and use of an approved drug for an unapproved purpose. Let us see how the insurance system handles these cases.

### *Investigational Therapies*

Suppose we have an unapproved drug, an NCE, in a clinical investigation for a life-threatening disease. All physicians who participate in that investigation attest that the drug represents the best opportunity for the patient. In this case, the HCFA will not only deny reimbursement for the drug but will also deny all attendant hospital costs unless it can be proved the patient would have had to be in the hospital or would have needed the physician's services anyway.

There is one exception to this rule. Individuals suffering from cancer can be reimbursed for the use of investigational cancer drugs categorized as Group C drugs. However, although it is legitimate to pay for investigational therapies (treatment INDs) for patients suffering from malignancies, it is not for persons suffering from AIDS.

### *Compassionate Use*

A second scenario regards the use of an unapproved drug for treatment outside a clinical trial. Imagine a situation in which the clinical trials for an investigational drug are filled and there is a patient who cannot get in the clinical trial and will die without the drug. Assume that this takes place in an outpatient setting where the medicine has to be infused. If it were an approved drug, the HCFA would pay for the doctor visit and for the use of the drug, but the HCFA will not pay in this situation because an investigational drug is not covered (except if it is a drug for cancer).

*New Indications and Off-Label Use*

Finally, let us look at the use of an approved new drug for a new unapproved indication. The drug is approved for cancer A but not for cancer B. Use for cancer B is considered state-of-the art medicine. The NCI recommends it, but no supplemental NDA has yet been submitted for it or the NDA has not yet been approved by FDA. In this case there is no consistent payment policy. The decision to pay for off-label use is left to the discretion of local insurance carriers. Every group in the country decides the issue differently. If you happen to be in Cleveland, and they are in favor of this drug, then you get reimbursed. If you live in Buffalo, and they are against it, you do not get reimbursed. I doubt that we could invent a more inconsistent system.

## Assessing the Overall Impact of Payment Policies

Having said all of this, though, I believe the impact of payment policies on pharmaceutical innovation is relatively small. There is a potential impact in two places. One is on clinical trials. Lack of reimbursement for all the attendant hospital costs and other services certainly serves to discourage some clinical trials. I am told, however, that as a practical matter a practitioner usually can find a way to say that the patient would have been hospitalized anyway and thus guarantee payment. The second impact is in the area where there is, say, no diagnosis-related group that covers a very expensive new drug that will not be paid for. The lack of proper reimbursement may reduce the frequency of the use of drug and limit the companies' ability recoup their research investment.

In conclusion, I do not think that reimbursement policies retard the innovation process the way the FDA approval system does. However, the reimbursement system is likely to be reformed, so its impact may be changing.

## NOTES

1. The FDA is composed of different divisions, called centers, that evaluate different kinds of products. The Center for Drug Evaluation and Research is responsible for ensuring the safety and effectiveness of all drugs. The Center for Biologics Evaluation and Research regulates vaccines, blood products, and analogous biological products. The Center for Devices and Radiological Health regulates medical devices and radiological products. There is also a Center for Food Safety and Applied Nutrition that regulates foods and cosmetics and a Center for Veterinary Medicine that regulates animal food and drugs.

2. Phase I clinical testing studies a drug's safety profile with particular attention to the safe dosage range. The studies also determine how a drug is absorbed, distributed, metabolized, and excreted. They usually involve testing normal, healthy volunteers.
3. IRBs are nongovernmental organizations that review research plans and can approve, disapprove, or make changes to a proposed protocol before the drug, device, or procedure is tested in humans. They evaluate the scientific rigor of the research designs, as well as seek to minimize risk to subjects, ensure informed consent, and monitor data as they are collected to ensure continued safety.
4. Phase III trials usually involve 1,000 to 3,000 patients and are carried out at several different medical centers. The purpose of the trials is to verify the therapeutic effectiveness of the compound and to provide information about adverse side effects of long-term use by studying a larger clinical population. Phase III trials last an average of 1 to 4 years. Ninety-five percent of all the compounds that initiate Phase III trials are eventually approved.
5. Expedited review is a process whereby Phases II and III are combined to shorten the approval process for new drugs to treat serious and life-threatening diseases.
6. The priority categories for the degree of novelty of the chemical compound, in decreasing order of importance, are new molecular entity, new derivative, new formulation, new combination, already-marketed drug product, and already-marketed drug product by the same firm. The magnitude of treatment potential is graded as being important gain, modest gain, or little or no gain. Drugs also can be assigned orphan drug status, but this does not independently affect their priority.
7. The purpose of Phase IV studies is twofold. For the manufacturer, the FDA, and researchers, such studies provide information about long-term effectiveness and rare or delayed side effects, qualities that can only be assessed after use in everyday clinical practice. (Phase IV data may be used also to substantiate an application for a new clinical indication or to change the drug labeling.)
8. The official policy of most payers in the United States is to pay only for the use of the drug for the clinical indications for which it was approved by the FDA—"on-label use." While many routine and effective uses of drugs are acknowledged to be "off-label use," many payers are increasingly using the official FDA label contract language to deny their coverage and reimbursement.

## SELECTIVE BIBLIOGRAPHY

1. Grabowski H. Health Care Cost Containment and Pharmaceutical Innovation. Boston: Center for the Study of Drug Development, 1986, Reprint RS3707.
2. Cook J. et al. Approvals and non-approvals of new drug applications during the 1970's. Office of Planning and Evaluation, Study 57. Rockville, Md.: Food and Drug Administration, 1988.
3. Hutt PB. Regulation in the United States. International Journal of Technology Assessment in Health Care 1986;2:619-628.

# Appendix B

## The Economics of Pharmaceutical Research and Development: An Industry Perspective

Commentary by
FRANCIS H. SPIEGEL, JR.

The purpose of this commentary is not to provide a complete view of all the risks, rewards, decisions, and debates inherent in research investment and drug development in the pharmaceutical industry, but instead to provide a personal perspective based on 25 years of wrestling with investment decisions and the requirement to address the needs of various interest groups: physicians and patients, government law makers and regulators, employees, and stockholders. I want to begin from a slightly different economic perspective, because our nation today finds itself not only in economic transition but also in a very precarious position that threatens our way of life and our standard of living. I want to first look at the U.S. pharmaceutical industry and its value to our nation's economy and competitiveness. In light of America's competitive slippage in world markets, it is curious that we are so slow to learn lessons from the past, even though we have seen our world leadership and market share erode in one industry after another.

Thus far, one exception has been the U.S.-based pharmaceutical industry, which maintains its world leadership, principally because of the industry's willingness to invest huge sums of money in research and development (R&D). As a secondary source of our success, however, we must cite a favorable public policy environment; a spirit of cooperation; and a collaborative relationship among industry, government, and academia on research projects.

Now, unfortunately, the environment threatens to change—in part, at least, because of a sincere concern for rising health care costs but also because of a poor understanding and simplistic analyses of the economics of the drug development process. As a nation, we must reach a better understanding of the case for public policies that encourage medical research and innovation, which will result in dramatic improvements in health, quality of life, and the economic well-being of our country. This nation can ill afford policies that discourage innovation in the pharmaceutical industry.

Those of us in the pharmaceutical industry frequently find ourselves having to develop a primer on the industry, its economics, and the nature of the discovery process. There is very little recognition, for example, that the R&D risk is enormous in our industry. Few people realize that it takes an average of 12 years and $230 million to develop a new drug (1). Nor do people realize that 7 of every 10 products that do reach the marketplace never recover the average cost of development. Most discouraging is that the message must be repeated in so many different ways. In the light of much-needed academic analyses—now planned or under way—of such subjects as the pharmaceutical industry's risks versus returns, I am hopeful that the economics of innovation in medicine will some day be better understood.

In the meantime, several broad-based initiatives are essential for drug innovation: we need increased government collaboration and support of basic biomedical research; we need better and broader science education at all levels; we need more equitable treatment for U.S. industry in world trade; and we need stronger worldwide protection of intellectual property—patents, copyrights, and trademarks. These are the specific issues of this paper.

Progress on these issues rests first on public policy, and any policy actions that affect the research-based pharmaceutical industry should be grounded firmly on an understanding of the economics of innovation in medicine. Merck & Co., Inc., the world's largest prescription drug company, is well positioned to contribute to such understanding. Merck has first-hand knowledge of the realities of the global marketplace, the challenges of research, and the economic policy environment that is conducive to success in business competition and in fighting disease.

## THE COMPETITIVE, COSTLY SEARCH FOR NEW DRUGS

Let us approach public policy in the context of a global pharmaceutical industry. Merck, for example, does business in nearly 200 countries, and about half of its sales are made outside the United States. The company is part of an enormous industry: annual sales of ethical drugs for human use by all pharmaceutical companies worldwide are estimated at $120 billion (2). The industry is highly competitive, with no company holding as much as 5 percent of the world market (2). Even though Merck ranks number one worldwide, with 1989 sales of approximately $6.6 billion, its market share is only 4.7 percent.

This competition forces those who want to succeed to be aggressive in the search for new drugs—a search that is increasingly expensive. In 1989 U.S.-based pharmaceutical companies spent $7.3 billion on R&D (3), exceeding the $7.1 billion that the National Institutes of Health (NIH) spent on biomedical research (4).

## MEGAMERGERS

In addition to rising R&D costs and intensifying foreign and domestic competition, research-based drug companies face growing pressures on their pricing, profits, and patents. In this environment many pharmaceutical companies have found it necessary to merge in order to expand their research capacities and maintain their rate of growth. Such mergers are motivated by the need to make increasingly large R&D investments on the slim chance of bringing out new products that will have only a limited market life before their patents expire. Of course, in addition to the aim of building R&D mass and efficiency, companies merge to gain better market penetration.

Recently, Bristol-Myers merged with Squibb; Dow Chemical acquired Marion Laboratories; SmithKline merged with Beecham, the British firm; and Rhone-Poulenc acquired a majority interest in the Rorer Group. Other large foreign companies also are showing great interest in acquiring U.S. drug companies, no doubt because they are attracted by the huge size and free competition of the U.S. market.

Merck has chosen not to make a major merger or acquisition. Although it plans to obtain new products primarily from its own R&D efforts, the company will also continue to enter into strategic alliances to increase its access to new products and new research. Merck has determined that, in a global marketplace, it needs both internal and external strategies for growth.

Internally, Merck's total R&D spending for the 10 years 1980 to 1989 was nearly $4.5 billion, with a compound growth rate of 14.8 percent (5). The Pharmaceutical Manufacturers Association estimates that the U.S. pharmaceutical industry will have spent $8.2 billion on R&D in 1990. Thus, Merck's 1990 R&D budget of $850 million accounts for more than 10 percent of the total, and Merck accounts for an estimated 5 percent of the total worldwide spending for pharmaceutical R&D (6).

## IMPACT ON TAX RECEIPTS AND BALANCE OF TRADE

Public policies must take into account that, in addition to benefiting patients' health, the pharmaceutical industry's R&D productivity has a strong positive economic impact—on U.S. tax receipts, our economy, and the balance of trade. For example, Merck paid $788 million in worldwide income taxes for 1989—a sum quite close to the $751 million it spent on R&D (5).

Much of the money Merck pays in taxes comes from the return on its investment in research facilities and scientists in the United States. In 1989 Merck made a favorable contribution to the U.S. current account of approximately $1.1 billion. That amount, though relatively small, stood in dramatic contrast to the huge total trade deficit in other industries.

## ACADEMIC ANALYSES: ECONOMIC AND FINANCIAL

If the pharmaceutical industry is a national asset, we should enact public policies to protect and strengthen it. Therefore, those of us in industry, medicine, and universities need to demonstrate effectively the dynamics of drug discovery something we may not have been well equipped to do up to this point.

This effort will be helped by university scholars who are working to develop a model for analyzing pharmaceutical risk versus return, as well as other related subjects. In addition, studies are being conducted at Merck to complement university efforts. At a minimum, I would suggest that any economic model for the industry should consider four important issues:

1. We must reexamine the way research is treated. Should it be a profit and loss (P&L) expense or amortized as an asset? The answer is important because it will change a number of financial measurements, most notably return on assets.
2. Our analyses must consider pricing, including costs of research and launch prices fair to the patient and to the innovating company.
3. We need an adequate period of exclusivity for innovative products.
4. We need to factor in the impact of inflation on the cost of doing business and of future research.

Economic analyses are under way in four broad areas: industry dynamics, risk/return trade-offs, research productivity and innovation, and the regulatory environment.

## SHORTER PRODUCT LIFE CYCLES

Studies of industry dynamics will focus in part on product life cycles through development of economic models that accurately reflect the competitive environment, starting with R&D investments and going through all stages of the product cycle. This analysis is critical because of the rapid changes in the product life cycle, which has been getting shorter for two major reasons.

The first is the emergence of so-called fast-follower drugs. Today's rapid dissemination of scientific advances throughout the worldwide biomedical research community leads to simultaneous—often closely similar—research efforts by several companies. Even though the first company to succeed has the "breakthrough," runner-up companies may introduce improved therapies shortly thereafter.

Although these fast-follower products intensify competition, they also serve useful purposes for society. Some patients, for example, may tolerate a fast-follower better than the breakthrough product. Fast-followers also permit more companies to enter the field, and the income these companies make can fund research.

A second reason for shorter product life cycles is generic competition. Generics today are being introduced very rapidly after patents expire, and they are supported by intense marketing efforts. From a public policy standpoint, we must ask ourselves if generics should be controlled more tightly. Clearly, the answer is important in terms of product safety. But also, from an economic viewpoint, if generics are able to reap windfall profits without investing in research, we must ask ourselves if our public policies are discouraging research by the U.S. pharmaceutical industry and thereby putting its worldwide leadership and competitiveness at risk.

## ADVANCED MARKETING STRATEGIES

In addition to life cycles, promotion, sales, and marketing practices are important elements to be considered in the dynamics of the industry. In many ways they are just as essential as R&D for delivering medicines to people who need them. With regard to any recent innovation in drug therapy, the largest single repository of scientific and medical information is the company that invented and/or developed it.

## RISK-ADJUSTED ECONOMIC RETURNS

Perhaps the most valuable studies will be those of risk/return trade-offs, which will focus on the development of risk-adjusted economic returns. These studies will present a better view of the industry simply because economic returns are far more accurate than accounting returns as measures of profitability. They capture the asset value of patents and the time value of the very large investments necessary to conduct research, and they clarify the nature of the R&D enterprise.

An example will demonstrate how the accounting and economic models yield different results. In 1989, based on the accounting model, the average return on assets (ROA) for eight leading U.S.-based health care companies was approximately 16 percent.[1] Since the accounting methodology considers research an expense rather than an asset, the accounting model makes ROA appear high in comparison with other industries that are less committed to long-term R&D.

With the economic model R&D expenditures are capitalized and amortized on the theory that a firm's R&D investment is part of its economic asset base. Cash flow also is adjusted to reflect the capitalization of R&D. Consequently, use of the economic model lowers ROA for many industries. The effect is greatest for research-intensive industries.

Based on the economic model for the 1989 results of the eight leading health care companies, the average ROA is approximately 11 percent because of our substantial commitment to research.

## PROTECTING INTELLECTUAL PROPERTY

In addition to R&D investments, public policy must focus on patent protection of new pharmaceutical products—another critical economic asset. It is well known that patents are essential to the future of the pharmaceutical industry, but it is not well known that patent laws often give less protection to pharmaceutical companies than to other industries.

In other U.S. industries patents may be only months old when new products reach the market. For the pharmaceutical industry the average prescription medicine, because of the long period of development and regulatory approval, has lost an average of 6.5 years of its patent life before it reaches the market (7).

Thus, for pharmaceuticals the 17-year patent term mandated by Congress is shortened dramatically, further compounding the risks of drug development. Public policy, therefore, should take account of the unique nature and extraordinary risks of pharmaceutical R&D: shorter effective patents, the fact that many projects never succeed, and, indeed, the fact that the overwhelming majority of projects fail to result in a viable product (8).

The studies of research productivity and innovation now under way will explore the many interrelated factors that drive innovation and will seek to define an optimal industry structure for productivity. Pharmaceutical research requires the investment of vast sums of money over long periods of time under extremely uncertain conditions. According to Grabowski, 12 years is now the industry average for drug development (1).

## THE REGULATORY ENVIRONMENT

In addition to studies on risk, return, research productivity, and innovation, studies of the regulatory environment will assess the impact of government regulation—an impact that can determine a company's future. In many countries where the government is responsible for providing health care, government agencies intervene in virtually all aspects of research, marketing, and pricing of pharmaceuticals.

In response to concerns about rising health care costs, certain countries have pursued policies with the effect of limiting drug prices and profits. This is, I think, a very dangerous game in terms of discouraging the discovery process and threatening the battle against disease. I also think it more than coincidental that many of the countries that exercise the most control have failed to contribute significantly to the discovery of new chemical entities of therapeutic importance. In fact, only four nations have contributed to drug R&D in a meaningful way: the United States, the United Kingdom,

Switzerland, and Germany. In the last three decades these four countries have contributed more than 70 percent of all significant drug products introduced in the U.S. market, with the United States being responsible for half of these.[2] Not surprisingly, Japan is developing quickly and may join this group in the near future (9).

A salient characteristic of all five countries is government policies that encourage innovation and reward success. Not coincidentally, in these countries prices are commensurate with those in the United States.

## DRUG PRICES

Unfortunately, many of the complex issues I have just covered are not prominent in public policy debates. All too often the debate boils down to one issue: how much medicines cost. It is a critical issue to the public and to innovation for two major reasons:

1. Health care costs continue to increase faster than the rate of inflation and are causing budget problems for all who provide or pay for health care, including federal and state governments and corporations;
2. This situation sometimes causes payers, such as corporations, health maintenance organizations, and state governments, to make decisions aimed primarily at minimizing costs rather than helping patients. Whenever policy makers look for solutions to the problem of ever-increasing costs, pharmaceutical companies, with their rapid growth and relatively high levels of accounting profitability can easily be seen as constituting a large part of the problem.

The facts are very much at variance with this popular impression. Prescription drugs account for less than seven cents of every health care dollar (10). In addition, the percentage of health care costs attributable to drugs has been declining for many years (10). But the most important fact (and one that is hard to quantify) is that prescription drugs, by preventing, curing, or managing disease, often keep patients from entering higher-cost portions of a nation's healthcare system.

## GOVERNMENT SUPPORT OF BASIC RESEARCH

If we accept the fact that our nation's research-intensive industries hold the key to America's future, we have to conclude that the United States is not paying adequate attention to basic research—the foundation of new knowledge upon which technological innovation is built. The situation abroad is very different. Over the past decade West Germany has doubled spending on basic research—now 22 percent of its R&D budget and nearly twice the 12.2 percent that the United States invests (11). Japan's outlay has tripled, with approximately 13 percent of R&D going toward basic research (11).

One of the most important public policies that would significantly encourage pharmaceutical R&D in this country is increased government support of basic research through the NIH and the National Science Foundation. As a major source of basic biomedical research, training of scientists, and research funding for U.S. universities, the NIH has provided a tremendously fertile support structure for drug development by the industry.

Our nation's long term record of innovation notwithstanding, other countries are now rivaling traditional U.S. ascendancy in biomedical discovery. Since 1975, according to analyses by Merck, foreign firms have provided close to half of the new chemical entities that the U.S. Food and Drug Administration regards as therapeutic advances.

## INDUSTRY'S ROLE IN APPLIED RESEARCH

In addition to government-funded research, we must appreciate the vital role that universities play in the drug discovery process. That role is also one of basic research, not applied research. Industry—particularly in pharmaceuticals, still is the best source for applied research. The key to this industry's success is its ability to make optimal use of basic research findings flowing from the NIH and from universities. These findings serve as springboards for applied research by individual competing companies—research aimed at discovering new compounds and developing new drugs.

## U.S. SCIENCE EDUCATION

Other nations, realizing that a stronger base in science and technology will give them an edge in fiercely competitive international markets, are according research a high priority. As an integral part of this focus, they are allocating funding, establishing incentives, and training the talent pool needed to do research and commercialize technology. They are removing barriers to technological development and coordinating efforts to achieve economic growth. Unfortunately, the United States is not doing these things as well as other countries.

Even though U.S. universities and research institutions remain the envy of the world, this country clearly is failing to make its young people literate in science and mathematics. In the past decade we have witnessed a decline in the proportion of U.S. students majoring in science and engineering or receiving advanced degrees in those fields. Only 7 of every 1,000 U.S. students earn engineering degrees; in contrast, in Japan the figure is 40 of every 1,000 students (12). More than half of new U.S. doctoral degrees in engineering, mathematics, and physics are awarded to foreign nationals (13). Public policy must give science education a higher priority in our national agenda.

## THE WORLDWIDE ENVIRONMENT

In a global economy it is clear that policy confined to the United States will not ensure technological progress or U.S. competitiveness. All around the world efforts should be made to establish a business and political climate in which innovation will flourish. As Eastern Europe finally admits to the potential rewards of such an environment, we in America need to remind ourselves and others of the benefits of free trade and competition. Local economies benefit as industry is encouraged; nations benefit by adding new export products. In terms of pharmaceuticals, society benefits through victories in our fight against disease.

Among our own national needs, one of the most urgent is for the United States to adopt policies that will result in more equitable international trade arrangements. We must encourage Congress and the administration to take steps to equalize the flow of trade by measures that will enhance the competitiveness of U.S. industry, eliminate unfair trade practices, and open markets to U.S. goods.

In particular, there is a need for increased worldwide protection of rights to patents, copyrights, and trademarks. Such protection will contribute significantly to the ability of research-based companies to compete successfully in the global marketplace.

## A FINAL CHALLENGE

Whatever policy positions we develop regarding specific issues affecting innovation in medicine, all issues fall under the shadow of another serious concern: the enormous and increasing U.S. national debt, now totaling almost $3 trillion (14). This debt burden increases risks for all innovative industries, including pharmaceuticals, that require long-range planning. A balanced plan to lower the budget deficit by cutting spending and selectively increasing taxes is critically needed.

Academic, economic, and financial studies will no doubt be very helpful in framing public policy. But the national debt creates economic burdens that hurt everyone across the board; they drive up interest rates, limit the financial strategies available to business and government, cause fluctuations in the value of the dollar, make our economy unduly dependent on foreign investment, and lower the standard of living for us and future generations.

The importance of correcting this pattern of living beyond the nation's means cannot be overemphasized. Hard decisions on resource allocation are needed and will have direct relevance to the economics of technological innovation in medicine, simply because money applied to reducing the national debt is no longer available to meet healthcare needs.

## THE FUTURE

Since the pharmaceutical industry has been subject to a great deal of pressure and change in recent years, we must wonder where the industry is headed. Looking at its own future, Merck believes the company will continue to prosper only if it has an environment conducive to innovation. Merck can maximize its contribution to society by helping people remain healthy and productive. In this way Merck expects to continue to help contain health care costs and thereby demonstrate that the innovative drug industry is not part of the problem but is instead part of the solution.

As for the industry, we believe it will continue to thrive if it does the following:

1. It remains successful in discovering, developing, manufacturing, and selling innovative, cost-effective drugs;
2. it can be sure of a fair return on its R&D investment; and
3. in the arena of public policies, it can successfully convey the message of the costeffectiveness of its products and the reality of risk versus return in drug R&D.

The best way to reduce the cost of disease is to find cures. Makers of public policy should bear in mind that Alzheimer's disease costs the United States $88 billion a year because there is no effective treatment (15). Smallpox, in contrast, costs the world not one penny because it has been eliminated by medicine.

If Merck or any other drug company could discover an effective drug for Alzheimer's, it would reduce health care costs by billions of dollars and end untold suffering. Public policy should be aimed at encouraging this kind of outcome rather than primarily at cutting costs.

Studies of the kind mentioned above will be critical in enlightening legislators and the public about all facets of the economics of the pharmaceutical industry. In addition, such findings will help Merck and other companies move into the twenty-first century as members of a vital and viable industry, serving society by meeting the needs of patients everywhere.

## NOTES

1. Merck's financial analysts developed this figure from 1989 annual reports of the following top research-based U.S. companies: Abbott, Johnson & Johnson, Eli Lilly, Merck, Pfizer, Schering-Plough, Upjohn, and Warner Lambert. Four companies were excluded: Glaxo, because it had not been resolved which accounting method—U.S. or U.K.—would be used; Bristol-Myers Squibb and American Home, because they both experienced major acquisitions, making it difficult to obtain historical data; and SmithKline Beecham, which was excluded for both reasons.

2. According to the Pharmaceutical Manufacturers Association New Product Survey, of the 1,217 new single chemical entity drugs introduced to the U.S. market between 1940 and 1988, nearly 62 percent were discovered in the United States. Switzerland ranked second with 7 percent.

## REFERENCES


1. Grabowski H. The changing economics of pharmaceutical research and development. In this volume. Washington, D.C.: National Academy Press, 1991.
2. Teitelman R, Siwolop S, Baldo A. Global report on pharmaceuticals. Financial World 1989;158:53-80.
3. Pharmaceutical Manufacturers Association. PMA Statistical Fact Book. Washington, D.C.: Pharmaceutical Manufacturers Association, 1989.
4. Pharmaceutical Manufacturers Association. 1989 Annual Report. Washington, DC: Pharmaceutical Manufacturers Association, 1989.
5. Merck & Co., Inc. 1989 Annual Report. Rahway: Merck & Co., Inc., 1990.
6. Veverka MJ. Pharmaceuticals. New York, Booz Allen & Hamilton, 1989.
7. Patent Departments, Merck & Co., Inc., and Hoffman-La Roche. Unpublished study of 77 human and animal health products approved from September 1984 through 1989.
8. Worldwide pharma R&D trends. Scrip 1989;1471:25.
9. Narin F, Davidson FJ. The growth of Japanese science and technology. Science 1989;245:600-606.
10. Pharmaceutical Manufacturers Association. Industry Perspective: Drug Prices. Washington, D.C.: Pharmaceutical Manufacturers Association, 1989.
11. Gannes S. The good news about U.S. R&D. Fortune 1988;117:48-56.
12. National Science Foundation. NSF Fact Book. Washington, D.C.: National Science Foundation, 1988.
13. National Science Foundation, Science and Engineering Education Studies Group. Selected data on graduate science engineering students and postdoctorates by citizenship. Washington, D.C.: National Science Foundation, 1987.
14. U.S. Bureau of the Census. Statistical Abstract of the United States: 1989. Washington, D.C.: U.S Government Printing Office, 1989.
15. Truschke EF. Expand support for medical research and development. In: Alzheimer's Medicines. Washington, D.C.: Pharmaceutical Manufacturers Association, 1989.

# Appendix C

## Contributors

**MICHAEL L. BURSTALL** is a partner in REMIT Consultants Limited, London, an economic consulting group. He has been active in research in the pharmaceutical industry for many years, and has published a number of reports on its various aspects, including studies of the role of multinational companies, the European pharmaceutical industry, and American drug companies in Britain and Europe. He was the principal author of the part of the Cecchini report that dealt with the impact of the 1992 harmonization of the European common market on the sector. A chemist by training, Dr. Burstall has worked for Procter & Gamble in Newcastle, England, and Cincinnati, Ohio, and has taught at the University of Surrey, where he built up an interdisciplinary research team studying problems in the areas of technology, economics, and politics. He was educated at Oxford University, and his Ph.D. concerned the synthesis of tetracycline antibiotics.

**SOPHIA W. CHANG** is a National Center for Health Services Research fellow in health services research at the Institute for Health Policy Studies of the University of California, San Francisco (UCSF), and the School of Public Health at the University of California, Berkeley (UCB). Dr. Chang is also a clinical instructor of medicine at UCSF. Her primary research interest is in issues of health care access for the uninsured. She recently completed a study of the working uninsured using public hospital services in San Francisco. Her clinically oriented work deals with quality of life outcome measures, most recently in conjunction with trials testing the potential side effects of diuretic treatment for hypertension. She received her undergraduate degree in political science at Amherst College and her medical degree at the

College of Physicians and Surgeons at Columbia University. Prior to beginning her fellowship, Dr. Chang completed residency training in primary care general internal medicine at UCSF. She has completed an M.P.H. degree at UCB.

**SUSAN BARTLETT FOOTE** is an associate professor of business and public policy at the Walter A. Haas School of Business, University of California, Berkeley and a member of the faculty at the School of Public Health at Berkeley. Professor Foote has written widely in the field of safety regulation and business-government relations, with a special emphasis on medical devices. Her work has appeared in the *Journal of Health Policy, Politics and Law, Milbank Quarterly*, and numerous law and business journals. Her book on the influence of public policy on medical device innovation is forthcoming from California University Press. Professor Foote is a member of the Institute of Medicine (IOM) Committee on Technological Innovation in Medicine and the Forum on Drug Development. She served as a consumer representative for the Office of Device Evaluation at the Food and Drug Administration and contributed to reports of the Office of Technology Assessment of the U.S. Congress. She holds a J.D. degree from Boalt Hall, UCB. In 1990-1991, she is a Robert Wood Johnson Health Policy Fellow working on issues of medical technology in the U.S. Senate.

**ANNETINE C. GELIJNS** joined the Institute of Medicine (IOM) as an international fellow, and now is the study director for the IOM Committee on Technological Innovation in Medicine. Before joining the IOM, she was senior researcher for the Project on Future Health Care Technology, cosponsored by the European office of the World Health Organization (WHO) and the Dutch Government. From 1983 to 1985 Ms. Gelijns worked for the Steering Committee on Future Health Scenarios, where she helped develop models for long-term health planning in the areas of cancer, cardiovascular disease, and aging. At the time, she had a joint appointment with the Staff Bureau for Health Policy Development, the Department of Health, the Netherlands. Ms. Gelijns has been a consultant to various national and international organizations, including the WHO and the Organization for Economic Cooperation and Development. Her research interests are in the dynamics of the development process of drugs, devices and clinical procedures. In 1983 she received her LL.M. degree from the University of Leyden, and she will receive her Ph.D. degree from the medical faculty, the University of Amsterdam in August 1991. She is a member of the board of the International Society on Technology Assessment in Health Care.

**HENRY GRABOWSKI** has been at Duke University since 1972, where he is currently professor of economics. He is also director of the Program in Pharmaceuticals and Health Economics, which is part of the Center for

Business, Regulation, and Economic Policy. Dr. Grabowski's principal research interests involve the economics of the innovation process, business regulation, and industrial organization. He has published numerous studies on the pharmaceutical industry. Under a series of grants from the National Science Foundation, he has investigated the international diffusion of new drugs and the effects of various government policy decisions on drug innovation. He is the author of two books published by the American Enterprise Institute, *The Regulation of Pharmaceuticals: Balancing the Benefits and Risks* (1983) and *Drug Regulation and Innovation* (1976). He has also authored cost-benefit studies of government regulatory actions in various other industrial sectors. Dr. Grabowski has been an advisor and consultant to several organizations, including the National Academy of Engineering, the Federal Trade Commission, the General Accounting Office, and the Office of Technology Assessment. He has also served on the faculty of Yale University and held visiting appointments at the Health Care Financing Administration in Washington, D.C., and the International Institute of Management in Berlin, Germany. He received his undergraduate degree in engineering physics at Lehigh University and his doctorate in economics from Princeton University.

**ETHAN A. HALM** received his undergraduate education at Wesleyan University and will graduate from the Yale University School of Medicine in May 1991. During 1989-1990, he worked as a research associate for the Institute of Medicine (IOM) Committee on Technological Innovation in Medicine and the Council on Health Care Technology. In addition to his involvement with this book and its antecedent conference on Public Policy and the Economics of Innovation, he worked on the IOM report National Priorities for the Assessment of Clinical Conditions and Medical Technologies. He also helped run an IOM conference on Improving Methods of Consensus Development for Medical Practice and Technology Assessment. His research interest includes the impact of payment policies on innovation, medical decision making, and molecular neuroscience. At Yale, he has been actively involved in medical education reform and the teaching of medical ethics. He will begin residency training in internal medicine in July 1991.

**PETER BARTON HUTT** is a partner in the Washington, D.C., law firm of Covington & Burling, specializing in food and drug law and in the government regulation of health and safety. He began his practice of law with Covington & Burling in October 1960, and became a partner in 1968. From 1971 to 1975 he was chief counsel for the Food and Drug Administration (FDA). In September 1975 he returned to private law practice with Covington & Burling. During his service as chief counsel for FDA, Mr. Hutt was instrumental in establishing the over-the-counter drug review and the biological drugs review and in shaping the drug efficacy study implementation

(DESI) program for pre-1962 new drugs. He also participated in drafting the Drug Listing Act of 1972, the Consumer Product Safety Act of 1972, and the Medical Device Amendments of 1976. Mr. Hutt is a member of the Institute of Medicine (IOM) and, at the time of writing the paper contained in this volume, of the presidentially appointed National Committee to Review Current Procedures for Approval of New Drugs for Cancer and AIDS (a.k.a. the Lasagna Committee). Mr. Hutt has coauthored (with Professor Richard A. Merrill) a legal casebook, *Food and Drug Law: Cases and Materials* (Foundation Press, 1980) and serves on the editorial boards of several journals. He holds a B.A. from Yale University, an LL.B. from Harvard University, and an LL.M. from New York University, and he is a member of the New York, District of Columbia, and Supreme Court Bars.

**JOHN HUTTON** is senior research fellow at the Center for Health Economics at the University of York, United Kingdom. He is responsible for managing the Center's program of research and teaching in the field of medical technology. This ranges from studies of specific technologies, such as magnetic resonance imaging and computerized tomography, to the study of organizational structures and the organization of courses on the principles of economic evaluation. Current projects include evaluation of the use of information technology in health care, the economics of cancer treatment, and the effects of National Health Service reforms on the use of medical technologies in the United Kingdom. Mr. Hutton is responsible for organizing the U.K.-based Health Economists' Study Group, and he is an active member of the International Society for Technology Assessment in Health Care. Recent consultant work has included studies for the World Bank, World Health Organization, U.K. government, and medical equipment companies. Prior to joining the Center, he was a research fellow in the Institute of Social and Economic Research at the University of York, where his work focused on the U.K. medical equipment market. He has also worked for the Transport Planning Department of Strathclyde Regional Council in Glasgow and taught economics at the University of Aberdeen. He received a B.Sc. Econ. degree from the London School of Economics and a master degree in the economics of public finance at the University of York.

**ALAN KAHN** is president of Human Dimensions, Inc., and a research professor of electrical and computer engineering at the University of Cincinnati. Dr. Kahn is a physician and private consultant with extensive experience in biomedical engineering applications and in the development of new products for clinical use. His research interests include the application of new research in brain physiology, artificial intelligence, human behavior, and communications. From 1982 to 1985 he served in a panel assessing federal policies and the medical device industry for the Office of Technological Assessment of the U.S. Congress. He also helped organize the Alliance of Engineering in

Biology and Medicine and served as its third president in 1973. From 1970 to 1977 Dr. Kahn was senior vice president for research and development at Medtronic, Inc., in Minneapolis, Minnesota. Dr. Kahn is a fellow of the Institute of Electrical and Electronics Engineers, the American College of Cardiology, and the American College of Chest Physicians.

**HAROLD S. LUFT** is professor of health economics and associate director of the Institute for Health Policy Studies at the University of California, San Francisco. His research has covered a wide range of health policy areas, including applications of benefit cost analysis, studies of medical care utilization, the relationship between volume of selected medical and surgical patients in hospitals and hospital mortality, regionalization of hospital services, duplication of health insurance coverage, adverse selection in multiple-option health insurance settings, competition in the medical care market, and health maintenance organizations. In addition to numerous articles in scientific journals, he has authored *Poverty and Health: Economic Causes and Consequences of Health Problems* (Ballinger, 1978) and *Health Maintenance Organizations: Dimensions of Performance* (Wiley-Interscience, 1981/Transaction Books, 1988). Prior to coming to the University of California, San Francisco, in 1978, Dr. Luft was an assistant professor in the Health Services Research Program at Stanford University. Professor Luft is a member of the Institute of Medicine (IOM) and serves on the IOM governing council. He has also participated in study sections and review panels of the Agency for Health Care Policy and Research, Health Care Financing Administration, and numerous private foundations. He is on the editorial board of the *Journal of Health Politics, Policy and Law, Medical Care Review, Inquiry*, and *Health Services Research.* He received his undergraduate and graduate training at Harvard University, majoring in economics with a specialization in health economics.

**LEE MORTENSON** has served as the executive director of the Association of Community Cancer Centers since 1978, overseeing the daily management of the association and acting as liaison with a number of national cancer organizations, including the National Cancer Institute and American Cancer Society. Dr. Mortenson is also the chief executive officer of ELM Services, Inc., which provides consulting and data management services to the health care community and markets tumor registry software. He has served as project manager and special consultant to a number of organizations, institutions, and government agencies on health care issues relating to organizational design and development. He has also been involved in the development and evaluation of institutional plans; certificates of need; patient load projections of university-based, interdisciplinary cancer centers and multicenter consortia of community hospitals; and single institution programs. Dr. Mortenson has authored over 100 books, monographs, articles, abstracts, and limited circulation reports, and he has spoken widely on health policy issues. He completed his doctorate in public administration through the University of Southern California, Washington Public Affairs Center.

**ROBERT NEIMETH** is a vice president of Pfizer, Inc., and president of Pfizer International, Inc., with responsibility for the pharmaceutical business in Europe, Africa, the Middle East, Eastern Europe, the USSR, China, Japan, and Korea. He joined Pfizer in 1962, and prior to his current position served as president of Pfizer Europe, vice president and director of operations, Pfizer Laboratories in the United States, and president of Pfizer Asia. Twenty of his twenty-seven years with the company have been spent abroad, with assignments in West Africa, Europe, and the Far East. He is a graduate of Cornell University, with a degree in anthropology and sociology granted in 1957.

**PETER J. NEUMANN** is Special Assistant to Administrator Gail R. Wilensky at the Health Care Financing Administration. He is currently on leave of absence from the doctoral program at the Harvard University School of Public Health where he is studying health economics and health decision sciences in the Department of Health Policy and Management. He has co-authored a number of papers and reports regarding payment policies for new technologies. Previously, he worked as a health policy analyst at the Project HOPE Center for Health Affairs. At the time the paper contained in this volume was written, he was a student at Harvard.

**MILTON C. WEINSTEIN** is the Henry J. Kaiser Professor of Health Policy and Management at the Harvard School of Public Health, where his major activities include research and teaching on the cost-effectiveness of health care and medical technologies. He joined the faculty of the Harvard School of Public Health as a full professor in 1980 and became the Henry J. Kaiser Professor of Health Policy and Management in 1986. Dr. Weinstein's research concerns the use of quantitative models to guide health care resource allocation. He has contributed to the development of the methods of decision analysis and cost-effectiveness analysis in health care and has applied them to assess technologies for coronary heart disease, postmenopausal hormone replacement, childhood immunization, and numerous other problems. He is the principal author of two books, *Clinical Decision Analysis* (with Harvey V. Fineberg) and *Hypertension: A Policy Perspective* (with William B. Stason), and of more than 60 publications in peer-reviewed journals, ranging from the *New England Journal of Medicine* and *Science* to *Operations Research* and the *Quarterly Journal of Economics*. Dr Weinstein, a member of the Institute of Medicine, is a past president of the Society for Medical Decision Making, and a current member of the editorial board of its journal, *Medical Decision Making*. During 1986 and 1987, while on sabbatical leave from

Harvard, he served as special assistant to the chief administrative officer of the New England Medical Center Hospital. Dr. Weinstein earned his A.B. and A.M. in applied mathematics at Harvard University in 1970, an M.P.P. from the John F. Kennedy School of Government in 1972, and a Ph.D. in public policy at Harvard in 1973.

# Index


**A**

Abbott Laboratories, 190n.1
Abbreviated new drug application (ANDA), 6, 40–41
Abdominal aortic aneurysm repair, 116
Access
  to health care, 22, 86, 144
  to new drugs, 53–67
ACE inhibitors, 37, 50n.10
Adrenal medulla tissue transplantation, 100
Adriamycin, 60
AIDS (acquired immune deficiency syndrome), 5, 55, 83, 144
  drug therapies, 145, 172, 174–175, 178
Alcon Laboratories, Inc., 81
Allergan Medical Optics, 81
Allergy treatment, 89
Alzheimer's disease, 190
American Home Products Corporation, 190n.1
American Medical Association, 7, 107–108
  *Drug Evaluations*, 7, 61
Ancillary services, 24
Anesthesia, 76, 94
Angina pectoris, 4, 99
Angioplasty equipment, 77
Animal research, 5, 99, 128, 170–171
Annual update factor, 28
Antibacterials, 160
Antibiotics, 37
Antihistamines, 89
Antihypertensive drugs, 25–26
Antitrust legislation, 2
Appendectomies, 97
Applied research, 188
Arterial switch surgery, 98
Arthroscopy, 96, 107, 108
Artificial heart, 85, 92
Artificial Heart Program (NIH), 74, 75
Assessment of technology, 31, 84, 100, 111, 141, 144–145
"Assignment," 117, 120n.6
Association of Community Cancer Centers (ACCC), 55, 58
Austenal Dental, Inc., 73
Austria, 129
Autologous bone marrow transplantation, 56
Axid, 50n.10
Azidothymidine (AZT), 175

**B**

Baby boom, 22
Banyu Pharmaceutical Company, Ltd., 164
Baxter Healthcare Corporation, 149
Beckman, Arnold, 91
Beckman Instruments, Inc., 91
Beecham Group P.L.C., 160, 183
Belgium, 138n.3, 147

medical device industry, 81
pharmaceutical industry, 126–127, 130, 133, 134
Beta blockers, 4, 25
Biliary lithotripsy, 79–80, 98
"Bioequivalence," 17n.4
Biologics Evaluation and Research Center (FDA), 179–180n.1
Biotechnology, 8
drug regulation, 129, 173, 175, 177
drug research, 36, 49–50n.8
Japanese industry, 161, 165
Blood cardioplegia, 98
Blue Cross and Blue Shield Association, 61–62, 105
Medical Advisory Panel, 106
Blue Shield of California, 108, 113, 116, 117, 120n.5
Breast cancer, 56
Breast reconstruction, 116
Bristol-Myers Squibb, 158, 183, 190n.1

C

Calcium channel blockers, 37
California, 29–30
Medicaid coverage, 47–48, 107, 113
Office of Statewide Health Planning and Development, 112
Canada, 28, 29
Cancer
chemotherapy innovations, 53–56, 64
chemotherapy reimbursement, 7, 56–65
drugs, 5, 17n.5, 40, 55, 59–62, 64, 83, 172, 174, 175, 178
patients, 56, 61, 66
screening, 144, 171
Capitated plans, 11–12, 29
Capoten, 50n.10
Carcinogenicity bioassay, 171
Cardiac arrhythmias, 4
Cardiac catheterization, 28, 116
Cardiac Pacemaker Registry, 85
Cardiac pacemakers, 76, 85, 91
Cardiac surgery, 28, 96–97, 98, 112, 113, 116
Cardiac transplantation, 99, 112, 113–114, 120n.5, 151
Cardiovascular disease
drug therapies, 37, 40, 174, 175
mortality, 37
Carte Sanitaire, 151
Case management, 13
Case studies, 23, 24, 73
Cataracts, 80, 81
Catastrophic Care Act (1988), 61, 62
Catheter ablation of abnormal cardiac conduction foci, 116
Cefazolin, 160
"Centers of excellence," 115
Cephalosporins, 25
Certificate-of-need regulations, 1, 113
Chemonucleolysis, 108
Chemotherapy
innovations, 53–56, 64
reimbursement policies, 7, 56–65, 66
Chest radiographs, 30
Chiron Corporation, 81
Chiron Ophthalmics, Inc., 81
Cholecystectomy, 14, 97, 108
Cholesterol-reducing drugs, 26, 37, 162
Chronic disease drugs, 40
Ciba-Geigy Corporation, 158, 161
Cimetidine, 25
Class action suits, 136
Class I devices, 17n.8, 76
Class II devices, 17n.8, 76
Class III devices, 17n.8, 76, 79, 80–81
Clinical practice, 37, 55, 141
Clinical trials
cancer therapies, 54, 55, 61, 62, 63, 64, 65, 66, 67
pharmaceutical, 7, 40, 128, 136, 158–159, 171–174, 178–179, 180n.2
Phases of, 5, 170–176, 180nn.2, 4, 5, and 7
surgical procedures, 13, 99, 102, 103
Cochlear implants, 11, 28, 109–110
Coding
medical devices, 94–95
surgical procedures, 13, 97, 102, 105, 107–111, 118
Compassionate use, 7, 17n.5, 173, 178–179
Computerized tomography, 24, 29–30, 103, 146, 148–149, 151
Concurrent review, 13
Consensus NCEs, 37, 38
Consumer groups, 130
Contact lenses, 18n.12
Contingency fees, 136
Contraception, 10, 76
Coopervision G.m.b.H., 81
Copyrights, 182, 189
Coronary artery bypass grafting (CABG), 24, 26, 98, 99, 112–113
reimbursement policy, 108, 111
selective contracting, 14, 115, 116
Coronary artery disease, 26

Cost containment, 1–2, 6–7, 31, 77
  Europe, 130–131, 133
  and medical device innovation, 10–12, 77–79, 82, 83, 86
  private insurers, 57
  and surgical procedure innovation, 13–14, 96, 108, 111, 113, 116, 118, 119
Cost-effectiveness, 119
  cardiac transplantation, 113–114
  of drug formularies, 50n.20
  HMOs and, 11–12, 29, 30
  lithotripsy, 149–150
  and medical device innovation, 10–12, 91, 142, 146, 152
  model of diffusion and, 22, 24–26, 27, 30–31
  MRI utilization, 29
  pharmaceutical studies, 8, 25–26, 190
  public policy and, 144, 145, 190
Costs
  of disease, 190
  health care, 1, 4, 15–16, 21–22, 25, 26–27, 50n.20, 77, 85, 151, 181, 186, 187, 190
  hospital, 7, 75, 77, 111, 147–148
  induced costs, 23, 24, 31
  lithotripsy, 78
  medical device innovation, 10, 18n.12, 91–92
  pharmaceutical research and development, 6, 37–40, 41, 42–43, 44, 45, 46, 100, 127, 182–183, 187
  physicians and, 27
  surgery, 14, 79, 81, 97, 98, 99–100, 105, 110–111, 112, 114, 115, 116, 118, 119
  of technology, vii, 63, 145–146
  *See also* Prices, pharmaceutical
Coverage, 1, 13, 16n.1, 25
  interim, 12, 14
  *See also* Reimbursement
Crippled Children's Services, 113
Crout, Richard, 175
Current Procedural Terminology (CPT), 13, 57, 107–108, 119n.1
Cyclosporine, 96
Cytoxan, 60

**D**

Demand
  for health services, 142
  for medical devices, 75
  for pharmaceuticals, 139n.8, 157
  for technology, 1, 3, 4–5, 22
Denial of payment, 56, 58, 61, 63, 65
Denmark
  health care system, 147, 148, 150, 151
  pharmaceutical industry, 126–127, 131–132, 134
Development of technology. *See* Research and development
"Device lag," 10, 83
Devices. *See* Medical devices
Devices and Radiological Health Center (FDA), 179–180n.1
Diagnosis-related groups (DRG), 1–2
  hospitals and, 13, 27, 28, 56–57, 63, 77, 109, 110, 117, 119n.2
  medical devices, 10, 11, 77
  pharmaceutical therapies, 56–57, 179
  surgical procedures, 11, 109–110, 117
Diagnostic technologies, 26, 75, 144
Dialysis machines, 151
Diasonics, Inc., 79
Diffusion of technology, 16, 27, 29, 66
  control of, 1, 2, 10, 21, 56, 73
  and health care costs, 21–22, 24–26, 30–31
  medical devices, 10, 70, 71, 72, 73, 85, 91, 141, 144, 146, 149–150
  payment policies and, 14, 28, 53, 77, 109, 119, 144, 150–151
  surgical procedures, 13, 96, 97, 101–102, 112–113, 114, 119
DiMasi, Joe, 39
Diuretics, 37, 50n.10
Dornier Medical Systems, 9, 79, 149–150
Dow Chemical Company, 183
Doxazosin, 156
Drug Amendments (1962, Food, Drug, and Cosmetic Act), 169
Drug Evaluation and Research Center (FDA), 179–180n.1
*Drug Evaluations* (American Medical Association), 7, 61
*Drug Information* (U.S. Pharmacopeia), 7, 61
Drug Price Competition and Patent Term Restoration Act (Waxman-Hatch Act, 1984), 6, 40–41, 42, 129–130, 135, 139n.9, 177
Drugs. *See* Pharmaceuticals
Duke University, 42
Dutch Organization for Applied Scientific Research, 149

**E**

Education, 182, 188
Effectiveness evaluation, 21

pharmaceuticals, 174, 175, 179–180n.1, 180n.4
Efficacy evaluation
medical devices, 4, 12, 15, 18n.10
pharmaceuticals, 4, 5, 63
surgical procedures, 99, 101–102
Elderly, 80, 81, 85
Electrocardiograms, 30
Electronic fetal monitoring, 24
Electron microscopy, 36
Electrophysiologic mapping (EPS), 116
EMI Medical, Inc., 148–149
Endoscopic papillotomies, 103
End-stage renal disease, 25, 26, 98
Europe, 2, 139n.10, 189
health care systems, 14, 123, 124, 147–148, 152
medical device innovation, 15, 141–146, 148–153
patent laws, 14, 15, 17n.2, 123, 129–130, 133, 137, 138n.5, 139n.9
pharmaceutical innovation, 14–15, 37, 123–138, 157–158, 163, 165
European Commission, 124, 128, 129, 134, 135, 137, 152
European Court of Justice, 134, 138n.1, 139n.12
European Economic Community (EEC), 137, 163, 164
medical device policies, 141–146, 149–153
pharmaceutical regulation, 15, 128, 130, 131, 132, 133, 135, 136, 138n.1, 139n.11, 161
European Parliament, 130
European Patent Convention, 129, 138n.5
Evaluation
medical device, 76, 93
pharmaceutical, 4, 5, 61, 63, 174, 175, 179–180n.1, 180nn.2 and 4, 185
surgical procedures, 12–13, 99, 101–102, 104–105, 111
Exercise tolerance testing, 26
Experimental therapies, 7, 17n.5, 64, 99, 102
Extracorporeal shock wave lithotripsy (ESWL), 78–80
Extracranial/intracranial arterial bypass surgery, 99
Eye diseases, 80, 81

F

"Fast-follower" drugs, 184–185
Federalism, 85
Fee-for-service systems, 1, 26, 30, 108
Fiberoptic endoscopes, 96
Fluorouracil, 60
Food, Drug, and Cosmetic Act (1938), 5, 169
Drug Amendments (1962), 169
510(k) provision, 9–10, 11, 18n.10, 93
Medical Device Amendments (1976), 9, 10, 76
Food and Drug Administration (FDA)
cancer drug approval and labeling, 55, 58, 59–61, 64, 65, 66–67, 83, 175
Cardiac Pacemaker Registry, 85
evaluation centers, 179–180n.1
510(k) applications, 9–10, 11, 18n.10, 93
generic drug regulations, 6, 139n.9, 170
medical device regulation, 4, 9–10, 11, 12, 18nn.10 and 11, 28, 76, 79–81, 82, 83, 85, 93, 100, 108
pharmaceutical regulation, 4, 5–6, 7, 8, 17n.3 and 6, 39, 47, 50n.19, 70, 76, 83, 92–93, 97, 100, 101, 102, 108, 128, 136, 169–176, 177, 179, 180nn.7 and 8, 188
Food Safety and Applied Nutrition Center (FDA), 179–180n.1
Formularies, 7–8, 17n.7, 30, 47–48, 50n.20, 61, 102
Fox, Renee, 4
France
health care system, 138nn.3 and 6, 147–148, 151
medical device industry, 81, 149, 150
pharmaceutical industry, 126, 127, 130, 134, 137–138
pharmaceutical regulation, 128, 132, 133
Fujisawa Pharmaceutical Company, Ltd., 160, 162

G

Gallstone lithotripsy, 79–80, 98
Gastric balloon placement, 99
General Accounting Office (GAO), 10, 18n.11, 76
General Electric Company, 73
Generic drugs, 7, 43, 46, 47, 61, 65
in Europe, 15, 123–124, 131, 133
HMOs and, 30
regulation of, 6, 17n.4, 40–41, 42, 139n.9, 170, 177, 185
Generic substitution laws, 7
Genetic engineering, 145
Germany, 138n.3, 147, 148
medical device industry, 81, 149–150

medical device regulation, 151
pharmaceutical industry, 126, 127, 133, 138, 162, 163, 166, 186–187
pharmaceutical regulation, 128, 130, 132, 134
Gibbon, John H., Jr., 96–97
Glaxo Holdings P.L.C., 161, 190n.1
Global budgeting, 28–29, 31
Good Licensing Practices, 161
Good Manufacturing Practices, 150, 161
Greece, 127, 138n.6, 147
Gross National Product price deflator, 43, 50n.14
Group C drugs, 5, 17n.5, 55, 62, 63, 178
*See also* Cancer: drugs

## H

Hairy cell leukemia, 64
Hansen, Ron, 39, 44
Hatch, Orrin G., 85
Health care, 56
access to, 22, 86, 144
costs, 1, 4, 15–16, 21–22, 25, 26–27, 50n.20, 75, 77, 85, 151, 181, 186, 187, 190
Europe, 14, 123, 124, 147–148, 152
Japan, 163
liability, 94
technology and, 22–24, 53, 82, 142
Health Care Financing Administration (HCFA), 8, 24
Bureau of Eligibility, Reimbursement and Coverage (BERC), 106
Cardiac Pacemaker Registry, 85
Common Procedure Coding System, 119n.1
experimental therapy coverage, 62–63, 67, 179
medical device coverage, 10–11, 12, 80, 81–82, 85
Office of Coverage Policy, 10–11
pharmaceutical coverage, 17n.5, 178
surgical procedures coverage, 105, 106, 109–110, 113, 114, 115
Health care market, 3–4
Health insurance, 4, 22, 26, 138n.7, 148, 178
Health Insurance Association of America, 7, 62
Health maintenance organizations (HMO), 57
cost containment, 1–2, 11–12, 58, 187
drug formularies, 17n.7
selective contracting, 105, 115
technology utilization, 29–30, 31
Health outcomes
surgical, 14, 99, 100, 112–113, 114, 115, 116
technology and, 21, 22, 24–26, 28
Heart valves, 76
Hemodialysis, 25, 98
Herniorrhaphy, 14, 104, 106
Hewlett-Packard Company, 73, 149
High Technology Directive (1987), 130
Hip fracture patients, 116
Hoechst-Roussel Pharmaceuticals, Inc., 158
Hoffman-LaRoche, Inc., 90, 161
Home health care, 12
Honeywell, Inc., 115
Hospital Provisions Act (Netherlands), 151
Hospitals, 144
cancer care, 54–55, 66
clinical research, 63, 66, 128, 179
coding practices, 13, 105, 109–110, 118, 119n.2
competition for patients and surgeons, 29, 55, 104, 112–113, 114
cost shifting, 57
costs of technology utilization, 24, 26
drug formularies, 17n.7, 61
Europe, 147–148, 150, 151
liability, 94
payment systems and cost containment, 1, 7, 26, 75, 77, 79, 91, 105, 111, 118, 119
Prospective Payment System and, 11, 14, 27–29, 56, 63, 77, 117, 118, 119
Howmedica, Inc., 73
Humana Hospital Audubon, 104
Human immunodeficiency virus (HIV), 5
Hydroxyzine, 156
Hypertension, 30

## I

Imaging devices, 23, 26, 75, 91
Immunostimulants, 162
Immunosuppressive drugs, 96
Income tax law, 90, 183
Induced costs, 23, 24, 31
Inflation, 43, 50n.14, 184, 187
Innovation, 1–2
dynamic model of, 2–5
medical devices, 4, 8–12, 89–95, 97
medical devices, Europe, 15, 141–153
medical devices, public policy and, 69–86, 89, 92, 95
pharmaceutical, 4, 5–8, 66, 166, 184, 186, 188, 189, 190

pharmaceutical, Europe, 14–15, 37, 123–138, 157–158, 163, 165
pharmaceutical, public policy and, 5, 47–49, 123–124, 135–138, 181–182, 183, 184, 185, 186, 188, 189, 190
pharmaceutical, regulation and, 169–177, 181–182, 186–187
pharmaceutical, reimbursement and, 63–65, 178–179
public policy and, 2, 16, 56
surgical procedures, 4, 12–14, 96–119
Inpatient treatment, 57
Institutional Review Boards (IRB), 13, 99, 171, 173, 180n.3
Insurance
claims systems, 6–7, 13
Europe, 147
health, 4, 22, 26, 138n.7, 148, 178
Japan, 157
liability, 10
Insurers, 178
denial of payment, 56, 58, 64
and drug labeling, 59, 61, 62, 64, 65–66
and surgical procedures, 14, 105, 106, 115, 120n.4
Intensive care units, 24, 75
Interferon, 64–65
Interim coverage, 12, 14
Internal Revenue Service, 90
International Classification of Diseases, 109
Intraocular lenses, 18n.12, 73, 80–82, 111, 117
Intrauterine devices, 76
Investigational device exemption (IDE), 81, 82
Investigational drugs, 17n.5, 62–63, 173, 178–179
Investigational New Drug (IND), 37–38, 55, 170, 171–174
treatment IND, 5–6, 55, 62, 178
IOLAB Corporation, 81
IOPTEX Research, Inc., 73, 81
Ireland, 129, 133–134, 138nn.3 and 5, 147
Israel, 81
Italy, 130
health care system, 138n.3, 147, 149
pharmaceutical industry and regulation, 130, 133, 134, 137–138, 162

J

Japan, 81, 188
National Health Insurance, 157, 159, 161, 163–164
pharmaceutical industry and regulation, 2, 14, 15–16, 126, 127, 129–130, 139n.11, 155–166, 187
Johnson & Johnson Products, Inc., 81, 190n.1
*Journal of the American Medical Association*, 104

K

Kaiser Permanente, 29–30
Kentucky, 47–48
Kidney stone lithotripsy, 78, 79, 80, 149–150
Kyowa Chemical Industry Company, Ltd., 157

L

Laparoscopic gynecological surgery, 14
Lasagna, Louis, 39, 173
Lasagna Committee. *See* National Committee to Review Current Procedures for Approval of New Drugs for Cancer and AIDS
Laser atherectomies, 96
Lasers, 18n.12, 75, 77
Lawyers, 137
Lederle Laboratories, 158
Liability law
and diffusion of technology, 2, 10, 71, 72, 75–76, 84, 94
Europe, 15, 136
Lilly, Eli, & Company, 160, 164, 190n.1
Linear accelerators, 151
Lithotripsy, 9, 28, 73, 78–80, 98, 149–150, 151
Liver transplantation, 98, 112, 151
Louisville, Ky., 104
Lung cancer, 56

M

Magnetic resonance imaging, 26, 29, 146, 149, 151
Managed care plans, 13, 29–30, 48, 57, 58
Marion Laboratories, Inc., 183
Marketing, 185
Massachusetts General Hospital, 112
Mastectomy, 116
Medicaid, 1
and medical devices, 75, 77
pharmaceutical reimbursement, 8, 17n.7, 47–48, 50n.19, 178
surgical procedures coverage, 106–107
Medical care. *See* Health care

Medical compendia, 7, 17n.6, 61, 67
Medical Device Amendments (1976, Food, Drug, and Cosmetic Act), 9, 10, 76
Medical devices
Classes of regulation, 17n.8, 76, 79, 80–81
diffusion of, 10, 70, 71, 72, 73, 85, 91, 102, 141, 144, 146, 149–150
and health care costs, 22, 23
patent protection, 9, 70–71, 89–90, 100–101
regulation of, 4, 9–10, 11, 12, 17nn.8 and 9, 18n.10 and 11, 28, 76, 79–81, 82, 83, 84, 85–86, 97, 100, 108, 173
and surgical innovation, 96, 108
Medical devices industry, 8–9, 12, 95, 152
patents and, 9, 89–90
regulation and, 9–10, 69–73, 74, 76, 79, 86, 86n.1
research spending, 18n.12, 75, 90, 91–92, 145–146
Medical devices innovation, 4, 8–12, 89–95, 97
Europe, 15, 141–153
public policy and, 69–86, 89, 92, 95, 141–142, 144–145
Medical oncology, 54
Medical practice. *See* Clinical practice
Medicare, 77
and demand for technology, 1, 75
medical device reimbursement, 12, 25, 28, 79, 80, 81, 82, 85
pharmaceutical reimbursement, 6, 57, 62–63, 178
surgical procedure reimbursement, 105, 106, 107, 109, 113, 114, 115, 116–117, 120n.6
*See also* Prospective Payment System
Medstone International, 79
Medtronic, Inc., 91
Meiji Seika Pharmaceutical International, Ltd., 157
Merck & Company, Inc., 158, 161, 164, 182, 183–184, 188, 190, 190n.1
Mergers, 183
Meta-analysis, 101
Methotrexate, 60
Methylmethacrylate, 96
Metropolitan Life Insurance Company, 115
Microprocessors, 93
Modifiable selective reimbursement, 14
Monitoring technologies, 94
Morbid obesity, 99
Mortality and morbidity, 14, 37, 99, 100, 111, 115
Mutamycin, 60
Myocardial infarction, 25

## N

National Aeronautics and Space Administration, 74–75
National Cancer Act (1971), 54
National Cancer Institute (NCI), 55, 62, 64, 172, 179
National Center for Health Statistics, 109
National Committee to Review Current Procedures for Approval of New Drugs for Cancer and AIDS (Lasagna Committee), 62, 172, 173
National Health Insurance (Japan), 157, 159, 161, 163–164
National Health Service (United Kingdom), 132, 150, 153n.2
National Hospital Formulary, 61
National Institutes of Health (NIH), 63
and AIDS drugs, 174
Artificial Heart Program, 74, 85
cancer therapy media campaign, 55
research spending, 49, 54, 67, 72, 74, 75, 85, 102, 103, 182–183, 188
Small Business Innovation Research grants, 92
National Science Foundation, 188
Netherlands, 126–127, 130, 131–132, 134, 138n.3, 147–148, 151
New chemical entities (NCE), 37, 126, 129, 186–187, 188, 191n.2
consensus, 37, 38
discoveries, Japan, 159, 160, 162, 164–165
regulation of, 159, 174
reimbursement policy, 178
research costs, 39, 49n.5
New Drug Application (NDA), 170
abbreviated, 6, 40–41
approval time, 37–38, 42, 172, 173, 174–176
available to generic competition, 139n.9
data requirements, 6, 50n.9, 171
supplemental, 7, 61, 64, 176–177, 179
New York (state), 113
Nixon, Richard M., 54
Non-steroidal anti-inflammatory drugs (NSAID), 37
Northgate Research Corporation, 79
Nursing home care, 11–12, 29, 116

## O

Office of Health Technology Assessment (OHTA), 10–11, 28
Off-label use, 7, 58–62, 64–65, 179, 180n.8
Omnibus Budget Reconciliation Act (1980), 117
Oncology, 54, 55, 57, 66
Oncovin, 60, 61
Open-heart surgery, 28, 98, 112, 113, 116
Ophthalmology, 80
Opportunity costs, 7, 49n.6, 50n.16
Oral H2 blockers, 103
Oregon, 107
Organ transplants, 28, 96, 107, 114
  bone marrow, 56
  cardiac, 99, 112, 113–114, 120n.5, 151
  liver, 98, 112, 151
  renal, 98, 107
Orphan disease drugs, 174
Outcomes. *See* Health outcomes
Outpatient services, 11, 12, 27, 57, 77, 116–117

## P

Parallel importing, 132
"Parallel track system," 6
Parkinsonism, 100
Patent protection, 100–101, 182, 189
  effective patent life, 6, 14, 15, 17nn.2 and 3, 41–43, 47, 53, 64–65, 123
  Europe, 14, 15, 17n.2, 123, 129–130, 133, 137, 138n.5, 139n.9
  Japan, 15, 16, 156, 160, 163, 165
  medical devices, 9, 70–71, 89–90, 100–101
  pharmaceuticals, 5, 6, 40, 41–43, 46, 47, 50n.11, 64–65, 66, 139n.9, 163, 165, 177, 185, 186
Patient outcomes. *See* Health outcomes
Patients, 3, 185, 187
  cancer, 5, 54, 55, 56, 61, 66
  in clinical research, 50n.9, 62, 63
  and payment policies, 56, 62, 63, 66, 120n.6, 131, 147
  surgical, 99, 115, 116
Payers, 4
  and health care costs, 27, 119
  and medical devices, 94
  and pharmaceuticals, 17n.5, 62, 102, 178, 180n.8, 187
Payment, 67, 96
  denial of, 56, 58, 61, 63, 65
  hospital, 75, 77, 105, 118
  for investigational therapies, 62–63, 178–179
  Medicare, 62–63, 77, 81–82, 85, 116–117, 120n.6
  physician, 1–2, 18n.13, 30, 105, 110, 118
  public policy, 1–2, 5, 6–7, 12, 13–14, 15–16, 16n.1, 75, 178–179
  surgical procedure, 97, 104–117
  *See also* Coverage; Prospective Payment System; Reimbursement
Peer review, 13, 105, 111, 117
Penicillin, 156
Pepcid, 50n.10
Peptic ulcer disease, 25, 98, 99, 103
Percutaneous biopsy, 103
Percutaneous catheter ablation, 116
Percutaneous endoscopic techniques, 78
Percutaneous transluminal coronary angioplasty (PTCA), 11, 108, 112
Peter Principle, 26
Pfizer, Inc., 73, 156, 158, 163, 190n.1
Pfizer Laser Systems, 73
Pharmaceutical Affairs Law (Japan), 161
Pharmaceutical Manufacturers Association, 49n.5, 183, 191n.2
Pharmaceutical producer price index (PPPI), 43, 50nn.13 and 14
Pharmaceuticals, 22
  AIDS drugs, 144, 145, 172, 174–175, 178
  approval time, 17n.3, 37–38, 42, 172, 173, 174–176, 180nn.5 and 6
  cancer drugs, 5, 17n.5, 40, 54, 55, 59–62, 64, 83, 172, 174, 175, 178
  cardiovascular disease drugs, 37, 40, 174, 175
  cholesterol-reducing drugs, 26, 37, 162
  clinical trials, 7, 40, 128, 136, 158–159, 171–174, 178–179, 180n.2, 4, 5 and 7
  cost-effectiveness analysis, 8, 25–26, 190
  denial of payment, 58, 61, 65
  diffusion of technology, 102
  drug formularies, 7–8, 17n.7, 30, 47–48, 50n.20, 102
  drug utilization, 15–16, 30, 125, 138n.3
  labeling, 17n.6, 59, 64
  new drugs, 8, 23, 36, 40, 45, 46–47, 48, 53–67
  new indications, 58–62, 179
  off-label use, 7, 58–62, 64–65, 179, 180n.8
  patent protection, 5, 6, 40, 41–43, 46, 47, 50n.11, 64–65, 66, 89, 100–101, 139n.9, 163, 165, 177, 185, 186

Phases of clinical trials, 5, 170–176, 180nn.2, 4, 5 and 7
polypharmacy, 69
product life cycle, 40–41, 43, 46, 47, 50n.18, 93, 184–185
regulation, Europe, 15, 123, 128–129, 131–132, 133, 135, 136, 137, 138n.1, 139n.11, 161
regulation, FDA, 4, 5–6, 7, 8, 17nn.3 and 6, 39, 47, 50n.19, 70, 76, 83, 92–93, 97, 100, 101, 102, 108, 128, 136, 169–176, 177, 179, 180nn.5, 6, 7 and 8, 188
regulation, Japan, 156, 158–159, 160–161, 164
research and development, 6, 35–49, 126–127, 128–129, 135, 138n.4, 181–190
side effects, 6, 176, 180n.7
and surgical innovation, 96, 108
used in lithotripsy, 80
*See also* Prices, pharmaceutical
Pharmaceuticals industry, 37, 65, 73, 89, 90, 95
and cancer drugs, 54, 55, 66
and clinical trials, 61, 64, 172, 176
Europe, 15, 126–127, 129, 132, 133–134, 135–136, 137, 138n.1, 139n.10
Japan, 15, 16, 155–166
patent protection and, 129–130, 177, 186
pricing behavior, 8, 43, 177, 187
research and development, 8, 35, 36, 38, 40, 46–47, 49, 127, 181–188, 190
return on investment, 8, 43–46, 47, 49n 6, 50n.16, 53, 64, 65, 123, 129, 177, 183, 185–186, 190
Pharmaceuticals innovation, 4, 5–8, 66, 166, 184, 186, 188, 189, 190
Europe, 14–15, 37, 123–138, 157–158, 163, 165
public policy and, 5, 47–49, 123–124, 135–138, 181–182, 183, 184, 185, 186, 188, 189, 190
regulation and, 169–177, 181–182, 186–187
reimbursement and, 63–65, 178–179
Phase I trials, 171, 173, 180n.2
Phase II trials, 5, 172, 175–176, 180n.5
Phase III trials, 173–174, 175–176, 180nn.4 and 5
Phase IV studies, 5, 176, 180n.7
Philips Medical Systems International, 149
pH meter, 91
Physician Payment Review Commission (PPRC), 109
Physicians, 31, 117
and coding systems, 13, 107–109, 118
and health care costs, 27–28, 119
in Japan, 15, 157, 159
liability and, 94
payment systems, 1–2, 18n.13, 30, 105, 110, 118
prescription practices, 59, 64–65, 69, 176
reimbursement policies and, 1, 30, 53, 58, 85
and technological innovation, 4, 17n.6, 53, 65–66
*Physician's Desk Reference*, 59
Platelet activating factor antagonists, 162
Platinol, 60
Pneumonia, 25
"Polyintervention," 69–70, 73–74, 78, 83–85, 86, 86n.1
Polypharmacy, 69
Portugal, 127, 129, 133, 138n.5, 147
Post-marketing surveillance
medical devices, 10, 76, 83, 101–102
pharmaceuticals, 5, 6, 136, 170, 176–177
Pre-certification, 13
Preclinical testing, 170–171
Preferred provider organizations (PPO), 1–2, 11
Pre-marketing application (PMA), 10, 79, 81, 82
Pre-marketing approval, 2, 15, 16, 136
medical devices, 9–10, 76, 79, 82, 83
pharmaceuticals, 5–6, 169
Prices, pharmaceutical, 8, 43, 44, 45, 50nn.13, 14, and 16, 139n.8, 186, 187
Europe, 123, 130–133, 134, 135, 136, 137, 138nn.6 and 7
generics and, 65, 133, 177
Japan, 157, 161, 166
Private foundations, 103
Private sector
European health care systems, 148
insurance industry, 178
public policy and, 78
research, 48–49, 70, 75, 149
Professional Review Organizations, 117
Prospective Payment Assessment Commission (ProPAC), 28, 110
Prospective Payment System (PPS)
and clinical research, 63
and diffusion of technology, 1–2, 27, 28, 31, 56–57
and medical devices, 10, 11, 77
and surgical procedures, 13, 28, 110, 116, 118, 119

Prudential Insurance Company of America, 115
Public Health Service, 10–11
Public policy, 16, 25, 31, 56
  Europe, 14–15, 123–138, 141–153
  Japan, 15–16, 165
  medical device innovation, 69–86, 89, 92, 95, 141–142, 144–145
  payment, 1–2, 5, 6–7, 12, 13–14, 75, 178–179
  pharmaceutical innovation, 5, 47–49, 123–124, 135–138, 181–182, 183, 184, 185, 186, 188, 189, 190
Pulse oximetry, 89–90

## Q

Quality-adjusted life years, 25, 31n.1
Quality of life, 25–26, 142–143
Quinolones, 162

## R

Regulation, 2, 13
  approval time, 17n.3, 37–38, 42, 172, 173, 174–176, 180nn.5 and 6
  certificate-of-need, 1, 113
  Classes of medical devices, 17n.8, 76, 79, 80–81
  generic drugs, 6, 17n.4, 40–41, 42, 139n.9, 170, 177, 185
  medical devices, 4, 9–10, 11, 12, 17nn.8 and 9, 18nn.10 and 11, 28, 71, 72, 75–76, 78–81, 82, 83, 84, 85, 89, 92–93, 100, 108
  medical devices, Europe, 15, 143–144, 150, 152
  pharmaceuticals, 4, 5–6, 7, 8, 17nn.3 and 6, 39, 47, 50n.19, 70, 76, 83, 92–93, 97, 100–102, 108, 169–177, 186–187
  pharmaceuticals, Europe, 15, 123, 128–129, 131–132, 136, 137, 138n.1, 139n.11, 161
  pharmaceuticals, Japan, 156, 158–159, 160–161, 164
  Phases of clinical trials, 5, 170–176, 180nn.2, 4, 5 and 7
  "polyintervention," 69–70, 73–74, 78, 83–85, 86, 86n.1
  surgical procedures, 97, 100, 113
  *See also* Food and Drug Administration
Reimbursement, 16n.1, 21, 96
  and diffusion of technology, 26–30, 31, 53
  Europe, 131, 144, 145–146, 147, 148, 150–151
  HMOs and managed care plans, 13, 29–30, 57, 58
  hospital, 1, 27–29
  Japan, 161, 164
  Medicaid, 8, 17n.7, 47–48, 50n.19, 106–107, 178
  and medical devices, 71, 72, 77, 80, 83, 85, 94–95
  Medicare, 6, 11, 12, 25, 27, 28, 31, 56–57, 62–63, 77, 79, 80, 81, 82, 85, 105, 106, 107, 109, 113, 114, 115, 116–117, 120n.6, 178
  pharmaceutical, 6–8, 47–48, 56–65, 66, 177, 178–179, 180n.8
  physician, 1, 30, 53, 58, 85
  surgical procedures, 13, 96, 105, 106, 107, 109, 113, 114, 115, 116–117, 118, 120n.6
  *See also* Coverage; Payment
Reischauer, Edwin O., 155
Renal dialysis, 24, 151
Renal lithotripsy, 98, 110
Renal transplantation, 98, 107
Renin inhibitors, 162
Research, 16, 23–24, 74, 102, 103, 127, 142
  animal studies, 5, 99, 128, 170–171
  biomedical, 2–3, 48–49, 72, 75, 82, 138n.2, 182–183, 184, 188
  cost-effectiveness, 8, 22, 24–26, 27
  translation of, 70, 141
  university, 13, 14, 54, 55, 92, 103, 149, 173, 184, 188
Research Councils (United Kingdom), 149
Research and development
  cancer and AIDS drugs, 40, 54–55, 64, 144, 145
  contraceptives, 10
  demand for technology and, 3, 4–5
  medical devices, 9, 11, 12, 70, 74–75, 85, 89, 90–91, 92, 95
  medical devices, Europe, 144, 145, 149–150, 152
  patent protection and, 6, 9, 41–43, 47, 64–65, 185, 186
  payment policies and, 11, 47–48, 64, 187
  pharmaceutical, 6, 35–49, 64–65, 66, 181–190
  pharmaceutical, costs of, 8, 37–40, 41, 42–43, 44, 45, 46–47, 49, 49nn.4, 5 and 6, 50n.17, 162, 182–183
  pharmaceutical, Europe, 15, 123, 127, 131, 133–134, 135–136, 137, 186–187

pharmaceutical, Japan, 159–160, 162, 164, 165, 166, 186–187
pharmaceutical, return on investment, 8, 43–46, 47, 50n.16, 53, 64, 65, 123, 177, 183, 185–186, 190
public policy and, 2, 47–48, 66–67, 85, 181–182, 183–184, 188
surgical procedures, 12, 103
Resource-based relative value scale (RBRVS), 1–2, 13, 18n.13, 30, 118–119
Return on assets (ROA), 185–186, 190n.1
Rhône-Poulenc, Inc., 183
Risk-adjusted economic returns, 185
Rorer Group, Inc., 183
Roussel Uclaf, 158

## S

Safety
medical devices, 12, 15, 18n.10, 79, 82, 83, 84, 85, 86
pharmaceuticals, 4, 5, 174, 175, 179–180n.1, 180n.2, 185
Sandoz, Inc., 158
Schering AG, 158
Schering-Plough Corporation, 190n.1
Science, 2–3, 70, 102
education, 182, 188
research spending, 74, 75, 103, 127, 135
Selective contracting, 13–14, 113–118, 119, 120n.4
Self-insured employers, 67, 115
Shionogi & Company, Ltd., 164
Shumway, Norman Edward, 99
Sick Funds Council (Netherlands), 151
Side effects, 6, 176, 180n.7
Siemens Corporation, 149
Small Business Innovation Research program, 92
Smallpox, 190
SmithKline Beecham P.L.C., 81, 183, 190n.1
Social security health care systems, 147–148
Spain
health care system, 138n.3, 147, 148
pharmaceuticals in, 127, 129, 132, 133, 134, 138nn.5 and 6
Squibb Corporation, 183
Stanford University, 99, 112, 113, 120n.5
States, 1, 8, 47–48, 50n.19, 76, 85, 187
"Substantial equivalence," 17n.9
Supplemental NDA, 7, 61, 64, 176–177, 179
Supratentorial craniotomy, 107
Surgeons, 14, 115
Surgical procedures, 2, 22
cardiac, 28, 96–97, 98, 112, 113, 116
case loads, 112
cataract, 81
coding, 13, 97, 102, 105, 107–111, 118
innovation, 4, 12–14, 96–119
kidney stone, 78, 79
selective contracting, 13–14, 113–118, 119, 120n.4
Swan-Ganz catheter monitoring, 108
Sweden, 129, 136, 147, 150, 153n.2
Switzerland, 138n.3
pharmaceutical development, 126, 129, 132, 138, 166, 186–187, 191n.2

## T

Tagamet, 50n.10
Taito Corporation, 157
Taxation, 90, 183
Tax Equity and Fiscal Responsibility Act (1982), 56
Technology, 82, 104, 112, 188
assessment of, 31, 84, 100, 111, 141, 144–145
cost-effectiveness of, 12, 91, 152
demand for, 1, 3, 4–5, 22
dynamic model of innovation, 2–5
and health care costs, 1, 6, 21, 22–24, 114
policy incentives and, 1–2, 16, 53, 75, 77, 141, 142
translation of, vii, 70, 141
use of, reimbursement and, 26–30, 56–63
*See also* Diffusion of technology; Research and development
Technomed International, Inc., 79
Texas Heart Institute, 115
Thalidomide, 5, 158, 171
Thatcher, Margaret, 127
Tissue plasminogen activator, 110
Total hip joint replacement, 96
Toyo Jozo Company, Ltd., 157
Trade, 2, 148, 182, 189
import restrictions, 138n.1, 139nn.11 and 12, 156
parallel importing, 132
Trademarks, 182, 189
Translation of technology, 70, 141
Transparency Directive (1990), 134
Transurethral resection of the prostate (TURP), 109
Treatment IND, 5–6, 55, 62, 178

Treaty of Rome, 124, 131, 132, 134, 138n.1, 139nn.11 and 12
Tufts University, 39

U

Ulcer treatment, 103
Ultrasound, 75
"Unbundling," 108, 120n.3
Uninsured persons, 22
United Kingdom
health care system, 138n.3, 147, 148
medical device industry, 146, 148–149
medical device regulation, 150, 151
National Health Service, 132, 150, 153n.2
pharmaceutical industry, 126, 127, 132, 134, 138, 138n.2 and 4, 139n.14, 166, 186–187
pharmaceutical regulation, 128, 130, 132–133, 134, 136
United States, 2, 14, 15–16, 29, 31, 123
Defense Department, 75, 92
generic drug policy, 15, 40–41, 133
and medical device industry, 69–70, 73–78, 85–86, 152
medical device market, 148, 150, 153
national debt, 189
Occupation Administration (Japan), 155, 156
patent law, 17n.2, 129–130, 165
pharmaceutical industry in, 36–40, 126, 127, 135–136, 157–158, 162, 163, 166, 183, 186–187, 188, 189, 191n.2
U.S. Congress, 25, 61, 62, 67
and cost containment, 8, 30, 77, 81, 85, 110
medical device regulation, 10, 76, 81, 83
pharmaceutical regulation, 170, 171, 177, 186, 189
U.S. Pharmacopeia, 7, 17n.6, 61
Universities, 13, 14, 54, 55, 92, 103, 149, 173, 184, 188
University of California at San Francisco, 111
"Upcoding," 108
Upjohn Company, 190n.1
Uruguay Round trade talks, 164, 165
Utilization review, 6–7, 29, 30, 62, 117

V

Vagotomy techniques, 98
VAMP Ltd., 139n.14
Vasotec, 50n.10
Vepesid, 60
Vernon, John, 40, 41, 43
Veterinary Medicine Center (FDA), 179–180n.1

W

Warner Lambert Company, 190n.1
Washington (state), 47–48
Waxman-Hatch Act. *See* Drug Price Competition and Patent Term Restoration Act
West Germany. *See* Germany
World War II, 15, 139n.10, 155

X

X-ray crystallography, 36

Y

YAG laser, 18n.12
Yarbro, John W., 63

Z

Zantac, 50n.10